Plato's Apology and Crito

PLATO'S

APOLOGY AND CRITO

WITH NOTES

BY

W. S. TYLER

WILLISTON PROFESSOR OF GREEK IN AMHERST COLLEGE

WITH THE ASSISTANCE OF

H. M. TYLER

PROFESSOR OF GREEK IN SMITH COLLEGE

Nae ego haud paullo hunc animum malim, quam eorum omnium fortunas, qui de hoc judicaverunt. *Cic. Tusc. Disp.* i. 42

REVISED EDITION

NEW YORK

D. APPLETON AND COMPANY

1887

TO

PROFESSOR FELTON,

OF HARVARD UNIVERSITY,

THIS EDITION OF THE APOLOGY AND CRITO

Is Dedicated,

AS A MEMORIAL OF PERSONAL FRIENDSHIP,

AND AS A TOKEN OF HIGH REGARD

FOR HIS DISTINGUISHED SERVICES TO CLASSICAL SCHOLARSHIP,

AND HIS PHIL-HELLENIC SPIRIT.

PREFACE TO THE FIRST EDITION.

THE "Græca Majora," which was all the Greek read in college by many successive generations of American students, contained Plato's Crito and the narrative part of the Phædo; and, among all the extracts in that admirable collection, none are cherished in fresher remembrance or with a more reverential love than these inimitable productions of the great spiritual philosopher of ancient Greece. The simple beauty of the style and the almost inspired truth and grandeur of the sentiments have graven these immortal compositions, as with the point of a diamond, on thousands of hearts, and entitle them to the high place which they have held among the select educational instruments of former generations. Many a scholar saw with regret *Plato* dropped for a time entirely out of the *academic* course, and accessible to American students only in the obsolete Græca Majora, or in the imported editions of foreign scholars. And, though their favorite classic author is now brought again within the reach of American students, and restored in some measure to his proper place in college education, in President Woolsey's scholarly edition of the Gorgias, and Professor Lewis' profound Annotations on portions of the Laws, still many an older and many a younger scholar cannot but sigh to see the simpler and more Socratic Dialogues of Plato *superseded*, even by the more finished dramatic imitations of his middle life, or the more profound moral and political speculations of his riper years. It is to meet expressed regrets and felt wants of this kind that the present edition of the Apology and Crito is given to the public.

While these pieces breathe in every part the moral purity, the poetic beauty, and the almost prophetic sublimity, which pervade all Plato's writings, and which have won for him the epithet "*divine*," they exhibit Socrates more adequately than he appears in any of the works of Xenophon, more truly and purely, just as he was, than he is seen in any of the other writings of Plato. They are therefore the connecting link between the two beloved disciples, and the clue to the interpretation of both. The Apology, especially, written shortly after the death of the Moral Philosopher, and under the full inspiration of his last words and last hours, gives us the very soul of Socrates speaking, as it were, with the very lips of Plato. Mr. Grote has seen this and, with characteristic wisdom, has made the Apology the corner-stone of his admirable chapter on Socrates. How superior to the cold and barren defence which bears the name of Xenophon on the one hand, and on the other, how free from the unpractical and impracticable speculations which Plato has interwoven in some of his later dialogues! It is doubtless a faithful representation of the defence, or rather justification, we might almost say, glorification, of his own life, character, and mission, which Socrates actually pronounced before his judges. At the same time, perhaps, it may be regarded as an exemplification of Plato's beau ideal of the true Orator, whose aim and office it is, not to save the life of the accused by whatever means of falsehood, bribery, and seduction he can invent, but to set forth the claims of truth and justice in all their native right to command universal obedience. In this view the Apology may, perhaps, be considered as the counterpart of the exposure of rhetoric falsely so called in the Gorgias, and so take its place among the consecutive labors of Plato to realize the idea of all the arts and sciences; though it must be confessed that the want of the introduction and the dialectic structure, which are so characteristic of the scientific dialogues, seems rather (not to set it aside, as Ast would set it aside, as un-Platonic, for it has all the palpable and marked peculiarities of Plato's style), but to set it apart to the more specific and no less sacred purpose of a defence by a gifted and beloved disciple of his honored and revered master.

The exordium opens, if we may be allowed to go before the reader with a brief analysis of the piece, with an expression of the astonishment of Socrates at the misrepresentations of his accusers, who have represented nothing as it is, and a declaration of his purpose to speak the plain and simple truth, in the same plain and simple language which he has been accustomed to use in his every day conversations; and as this is his whole office as an orator speaking in his own defence, so it is their sole duty, as judges, to consider whether or not he speaks the truth. (17, 18, A.) This exordium, if it does not set forth Plato's ideal of true oratory, in contrast with the studied and false rhetoric of the forum and the schools, yet no doubt exhibits the author's idea of the style and manner in which Socrates actually defended himself when on trial for his life. Accordingly, we shall find the Socrates of the Apology excluding all artificial rhetoric, all appeals to prejudice or passion, and declaring the truth, the whole truth, and nothing but the truth, with the simplicity and directness, the frankness and fearlessness of a philosopher who values truth and justice far more than life.*

After this brief and plain exordium, Socrates asks leave to reply first to his first accusers, those less formal but more powerful and formidable accusers, to wit, who had been insinuating their slanders into the public mind during his life, and who had all the advantage of numbers and time, of a tribunal numerous and credulous, and of not being confronted with the accused; nay, of being personally unknown, except some one of them might chance to be a comic poet (18, B. C.), alluding especially to Aristophanes, whose name is mentioned further on, and his comedy of The Clouds distinctly pointed out. (19, C.) The charges thus informally brought against him were, that, "with a wicked and mischievous curiosity, he inquired into things in heaven above and things under the earth; that he made the worse appear the better reason; and that he taught others to do the same; in short, that he was a natural philosopher and a sophist." (19, B. cf. 18, B.) Socrates utterly denies the truth of these charges; declares his entire ignorance of natural philosophy as then taught, as well as of the sophist's art; offers to present witnesses in proof

* Cf. Valer. Max. VI., 4: Maluitque Socrates extingui, quam Lysias superesse—in allusion to the Oration which Lysias prepared for the use of Socrates, but which Socrates refused to deliver.

that he taught no such things to his disciples, and calls upon all present to testify against him, if they had ever heard from him any conversation, great or small, on such subjects. (19, C. D.) Moreover, he did not profess to be a teacher, like Gorgias the Leontine, Prodicus the Cean, Hippias the Elean, and Evenus the Parian, who drew away the young from the society of the wisest and best citizens (which they might enjoy gratuitously), to receive their instructions at a great price. He congratulated the possessors of such wisdom and power, and would doubtless be very proud if he possessed it himself. But truth obliges him to confess, that he has no part nor lot, great or small, in such knowledge. (19, E.; 20 C.) The modesty and irony which mark this passage, the short dialogue, into which he runs unconsciously, and which is given in the form and the words of the original conversation, and the unfavorable view which he takes of the vague and unprofitable speculations of the physical philosophers who preceded him, are all highly characteristic of Socrates, as he appears in the Memorabilia of Xenophon. (Cf. Mem. I., 1, 11, seqq.; I., 2, 3, seqq. et passim.)

"But what then is your business or profession? What have you said or done to raise all this hue and cry about you?" In answer to this question, Socrates admits that he bore the name of philosopher, or wise man. But he pretended to merely human wisdom, such as man may properly aspire to, and such as pertains to the proper regulation of human life. (20, D. E.) This wisdom he did indeed possess. And in proof that he did, he would refer them to no less authority than the God at Delphi. (21, A.) He never supposed himself to be wise in any sense, till, in response to a question of his friend and the friend of the people (Chærephon), the Delphic Oracle declared, that there was none wiser than he. Not daring to discredit the Oracle, he then set himself to discover in what possible sense, if indeed in any sense, he was wiser than others. (21, B. C.) Accordingly he visited successively various classes of men in high repute for wisdom — politicians, poets, orators, philosophers, artisans, &c.; and he discovered to his surprise, that while they really understood pretty well their respective departments, they fancied they understood every thing else (22, D.), though, in fact, with a partial exception in favor of the artisans, they did not understand the fundamental principles even of their own profession. (22, C.) And they all, without exception, thought they knew a great deal more than they did know, while he was conscious that he knew almost nothing. (21, D.) And when he came to inquire whether he would choose to be as he was, or to have their wisdom with their want of self-knowledge, he was constrained to answer, that he would rather be as he was, and so to assent to the truth of the Oracle (22, E.); though he modestly adds, that the chief intent of the Oracle was doubtless to teach this general truth, that *he* was the wisest of men, who preferred that kind of wisdom which Socrates cultivated, viz., the moral and practical, and who, *like* Socrates, was conscious of the poverty of his acquirements in knowledge, and the comparative worthlessness of all the wisdom of men. (23, A. B.)

In the course of the investigation which he thus prosecuted, he offended all whom he visited, by showing them that they knew far less than they supposed. At the same time, his pupils (or rather his young friends and followers, for, as in Xenophon, so in Plato, Socrates never speaks of his disciples) delighted themselves in exposing, after his example, the ignorance of the many pretenders to superior knowledge. (23, C.) And they were angry, not with themselves, but with the innocent occasion of their humiliation. Accordingly they began to call him a most impious fellow, a corrupter of youth, and the like. When asked how; what he did; what he taught; having nothing else to say, they took up and turned against him the prejudice and calumny which the multitude were so ready to entertain against philosophers in general. (23, D.)

They confounded him with the very naturalists and sophists whom he had ever labored to confute, and thus sought to concentrate upon him the suspicion and indignation which they had incurred.

So much for the informal charges. And these prepared the way for the formal indictment for corrupting the youth and endeavoring to subvert the religion of his country. Of his three accusers, Socrates informs the judges that Meletus was angry with him for exposing, as above described, the poets, Anytus for the artisans and politicians, and Lycon for the orators. (23, E.) They were all actuated by selfish and revengeful feelings. Anytus, it should be added, was a rich leather-seller, and a man of influence in the democracy; and when Socrates, seeing signs of intellectual capacity in his son, endeavored to dissuade the father from bringing up his son to his own trade, Anytus was personally offended (Apol. Xen. 29), and was able easily to turn the passions of the populace against the reputed master of the tyrant Critias and the now hated Alcibiades. (Cf. Xen. Mem. I., 2, 12.)

In defence of himself against the charge of corrupting the youth, Socrates enters into a very characteristic dialogue with Meletus, asking, who it is that corrupts the youth, and who makes them wiser and better; whether the judges, senators, and members of the Assembly also corrupt them, or whether he is their only corrupter, and whether it is likely to be the single individual that corrupts, and the multitude that instruct and reform, or quite the contrary, just as it is in the training of horses and the lower animals; and if he is such a corrupter of the young, whether he does it voluntarily or involuntarily, of which alternatives the former is quite incredible, since he must know that he could not corrupt them without injuring himself, and in the latter alternative, he ought not to be impeached and punished, but to be instructed and made wiser. (24, B.; 26, A.) The conclusion of this very Socratic piece of extemporized dialectics is, that Socrates, if not too wise and good to corrupt the youth, must be too ignorant to deserve punishment for it; and that Meletus, with all his assumed superiority in wisdom and virtue, neither knows nor cares how young men can be made either better or worse. The argument, by which Socrates exculpates himself, will probably strike most modern readers as more subtle than conclusive in its reasoning, and somewhat dangerous withal in its practical tendency, since, carried out to its legitimate result, it would seem to prove that all crimes must be involuntary, and all criminals proper objects of commiseration and instruction, rather than of punishment. And we see not how the objection can be answered. It lies, however, not only against the argument here, but against the doctrine of Socrates, which, everywhere, in Xenophon and Plato alike, resolves all the virtues into knowledge, and, by consequence, all the vices into sins of ignorance.

Taking up the other point in the indictment, Socrates now asks, whether his accuser means to charge him only with denying the gods of the state, or with downright atheism; and on being distinctly charged with the latter, he shows that this is utterly inconsistent with the language of the indictment itself, which charges him with recognizing and teaching "other divine things," and if there are "divine things," then surely there must be divinities. Just as he who speaks of human affairs, must needs recognize the existence of human beings, so in teaching *δαιμόνια*, he must needs recognize *δαίμονες*; and if *δαίμονες*, then, according to the prevailing Greek idea, either gods or sons of gods; and if sons of gods, then of course gods. (26, B.; 27, E.)

Having thus disposed of his principal accuser, Socrates boldly tells the Athenians, that he has to fear, not the indictment of Meletus, but the envy and jealousy of the multitude, which have destroyed many other good men, and will probably destroy him. "Why then persist in a course of conduct which you expect will occasion your death?" "Because," such is the substance of the answer, "the great question for a man to ask is not whether life or death will be the result of his conduct, but whether he is doing right or wrong, and acting the part of a good or bad man; as the heroes of the Trojan war, and all true heroes, have ever despised danger and death in the path of duty and glory." (28, B. C. D.) "I should behave strangely," he continues, "if when your commanders, Athenians, stationed me at Potidæa, at Amphipolis, and at Delium, I kept my post at the peril of my life, but when the God sets me down in Athens to spend my life in the pursuit of philosophy and in the examination of myself and others, then I should leave my post through fear of death. In that case, I might well and truly be charged with not believing in the gods, since I disobeyed the Oracle and feared death, and thought myself wise when I was not. For to fear death is to think one's self wise, when he is not; for it is to think one knows what he does not know. None know death. They do not know but it is the greatest good; yet they fear it, as if they knew it was the greatest of evils. I will never flee from what may be the greatest good, viz., death, into such base and criminal acts as must be the greatest evils." (28, E.; 29, A. B.)

"If you were to assure me of my acquittal in case I would pledge myself to abandon this philosophizing and questioning manner of life, my reply would be, I respect and love you, but I will obey the God rather than you. While I live and breathe, I will never cease to proclaim the superiority of wisdom and virtue and the well-being of the soul, to riches and honor and the welfare of the body, to young and old, to citizens and foreigners, but especially to you, my fellow-citizens, as you are most nearly related to me, and because it especially becomes the honored name of Athenians. For this is the divine command, and this is for your highest interest. (29, C.; 30, C.) And if you put me to death, be assured you will not injure me so much as yourselves. Me none of my accusers could injure in the least; for I do not think it lawful, or possible, in the nature of things, for a better man to be injured by a worse man. I am therefore now defending, not so much myself as you; that you may not put me to death and so reject the gift of God to you, for you will not soon find another such. (30, D. E.) That I am the gift of God to the city, you will see from this. Does it seem merely human that I have neglected my own affairs so many years and attended to your interests, persuading you like a father or an elder brother, to cultivate virtue? And all this without any pecuniary compensation; for, among all their false accusations, they have not dared to accuse me of receiving pay for my instruction; and if they had, my poverty would have been a sufficient witness against them." (30, E.; 31, C.)

If any were disposed to ask why he went about and persuaded them privately and personally, instead of coming before the people and counselling them as a body, he had been kept back from the latter course by a certain divine monitor * which had attended him from his childhood—a sort of voice which always deterred him from doing what he should not do, and which had usually forbidden his participation in public affairs. And well it might, for, if he had undertaken to act his part in public, he would have been put to death long ago, and that without having rendered any real service to them or to himself; for no man could be safe in publicly opposing the inclinations of the Athenian or any other popular assembly, and forbidding them to do wrong. (31.) In proof of this, he adverts to the imminent peril to which he was exposed in the only instance in which he had held an office, when, as senator and presiding officer in the popular assembly, he resisted the will of the *demus*, and defended the lives of the ten generals when they were intent on putting them to death by one sweeping and extra-judicial decree. (32, A. B.) He had also incurred a similar peril, and exhibited the

* Touching the nature of this divine voice and monitor, see the discussion in the notes.

same disregard for danger and death, in refusing to obey an unrighteous command of the oligarchy, when they possessed the government. (32, C. D.)

These were well-known facts, which might be proved by any number of witnesses. And such facts showed that he, or any one else who would contend strenuously for the right, must do it privately rather than politically, if he would preserve his life even for a short period. They proved also that his influence over the young, by precept and especially by example, so far from corrupting, was suited to inspire them with an inflexible regard for justice. And if further proof was required, since his accusers had failed to bring forward the proper witnesses at the proper time, he would gladly yield the stand and let them bring forward now the fathers and elder brothers of the very young men who had been his most constant hearers and companions; for, though the young men themselves might have some reason for withholding the truth, if he had corrupted them, certainly their fathers and elder brothers could have no such motive, and the judges ought to be put in possession of their testimony. (33, D.; 34, B.)

Having thus finished his defence, Socrates proceeds to excuse himself from any attempt to enlist the sympathies and excite the compassion of the judges in his behalf. This practice had indeed become very common in the courts of justice—so common, that it might seem strange and even arrogant for him not to do likewise. He had a wife and children, and friends whom he tenderly loved, and whose grief at his death would doubtless be very great. But such weakness, worthy only of women, was especially unworthy of Athenian men; and if seen in their great men, particularly in one who, like himself, was reputed, whether justly or unjustly, to be a man of extraordinary virtue, it was not only dishonorable to him, but it would reflect dishonor on the whole people. (35, A. B. C.) Besides, it was doing a great wrong to the judges, who needed not entreaties, but instruction and persuasion, and whose duty it was, not to sacrifice justice to personal feelings and interests, but simply to execute the laws. And not only justice but piety forbade the offering of any inducements to them to violate their oath of office; and if he should hold out any such inducements, he would thereby teach them that there were no gods, and so convict himself of atheism in the very act of defending himself against the charge. They must therefore excuse him from resorting to such methods of securing his acquittal, which he could not but regard as at once dishonorable, unholy, and unjust. (35, D.)

With these noble sentiments, asking no favor of his judges, he submits himself to their sense of justice. They condemn him by a small majority of votes. Resuming his address, he declares that he is neither grieved nor surprised by the result. He is only surprised by the smallness of the majority by which he was condemned. (36, A.) Pronounced guilty by his judges, the next question was, what should be the penalty. His accusers said, Death. In naming a counter-proposition, as the laws allowed him to do, if he looked simply at the justice and fitness of the thing, he should propose that he be supported in the Prytaneum (State-House) at the public expense, that he might devote himself without interruption to the instruction of the people. This was a suitable return for his disinterested devotion to their highest good in time past, and this would be for their highest welfare in time to come. If this honor was justly conferred on the victor at the Olympic Games, who did not need it and who ministered only to their seeming happiness, much more was it due to him, who needed it, and who had spent his life in promoting their real good. (36, B. C. D.) And with longer time, he might perhaps be able to persuade them of his innocence. (37, A.) He deserved only good at their hands. If he should suffer death, that would perhaps prove a good. Why then should he propose an alternative penalty, which would be a certain evil? Should he propose imprisonment? That were to subject himself to the power and caprice of the Eleven, whoever they might chance to be. (37, B. C.) Exile? His countrymen could not endure his instruction and reproof, much less would strangers. (37, D.) And for him to keep silence, though they would not believe it, were to disobey the God, and for that reason it were quite impossible. (37, E.) To live without examining himself and others were no life to him—were a life not worthy to be lived by any human being. (38, A.) Should he then propose a fine? If he had property he would part with it cheerfully, for loss of property was no evil. But he had not property enough. If indeed a mina (about $17) would suffice, perhaps he could pay a mina. He would therefore propose a fine of one mina. And since his friends, Plato, Crito, Critobulus, and Apollodorus bade him propose thirty minæ, he would adjudge himself to pay a fine of thirty minæ, and give these friends as his security. (38, B.)

This high-toned vindication of his character and deserts, together with his virtual refusal to name any alternative punishment, sealed his death. He doubtless expected it would, and intended it should. The last chapter of Xenophon's Memorabilia is devoted to a statement of the reasons, and those for the most part assigned in a conversation by Socrates himself, why it was better, in his own view—better for his happiness and usefulness as well as for his fame—that he should die now, rather than live to a more advanced age. With this deliberate preference, and in full view of the consequences, he made his defence so as almost to necessitate the desired result. By an increased majority he was now condemned to death. And, in resuming the thread of his discourse, he tells those who condemned him that he did not regret the result—that death would have come soon in the course of nature, and he would much rather die uttering such a defence, than live by such ignoble means as many use. (38, C. D. E.) It is not difficult to escape death—he could readily have escaped it *—but the difficulty is to escape sin, which is a swifter runner than even death, and has already overtaken his accusers, younger and swifter though they be than himself. (39, A. B.) And, as men are sometimes inspired with something like prophetic vision in their last hours, he warns his judges, who voted for his condemnation, that speedy vengeance will overtake them in the reproofs of their own conscience and of the numerous friends of virtue who would come

* Cf. Xen. Mem. iv. 4, 4: ῥᾳδίως ἂν ἀφεθείς, κ.τ.λ.

after him; and the only escape was not by cutting off their reprovers, but by reforming their own character and life. (39, C. D.)

Then turning to the judges who had voted for his acquittal, and who alone deserved the sacred name of judges, he labors to console them touching the issue, which they so much deplore, by giving them the true interpretation of it. (39, E.) He could not but argue that it was meant for good. For the prophetic voice—the voice of the divinity—which had often and always warned him heretofore when he was going to do wrong even in the smallest matters, now when life was at stake, and he was exposed to what are commonly regarded as the extremest of evils, had given him no warning in the whole course of his trial. Hence he inferred that death was not, as it was commonly supposed to be, an evil, but a good. (40, A. B.)

The presumption thus suggested by the divine Providence towards himself might be justified and confirmed by the following considerations: Death is either annihilation, or, which is essentially the same thing, a state of entire unconsciousness; or else it is a departure of the soul from this world to another. On the former supposition, death would be a wonderful gain; for how few of our days and nights are so happy as the hours we pass in sound sleep, undisturbed by so much as a dream; and in that case, all time would seem no more than one such dreamless night. (40, C. D. E.) But if, on the other hand, death is a departure from this world to another, where dwell all the dead, what greater good could there be than this? There, freed from the power of judges falsely so called, he would find judges that deserved the name, such as Minos and Rhadamanthus; there he would associate with Orpheus, Musæus, Hesiod, and Homer; there he should meet with Palamedes, Ajax, and all who in past ages had fallen victims to perverted justice; and, what was better than all the rest, there he should examine and put to the test Agamemnon, Ulysses, and a multitude of other men and other women, as he examined men here, to see if they were truly wise, or only supposed themselves to be so; and this would be immense happiness: nor would he be put to death there for the exercise of this prerogative, since, besides their superior blessedness in other respects, the dwellers in that world are immortal. (41, A. B. C.) In conclusion, he assures his judges once more that no evil can befall a good man in life or death, since the gods take care of his interests, and these events have not befallen him by chance, but have been ordered by a wise and kind Providence; tells them that he harbors no resentment against them, since, though they meant it for evil, they had done him good; entreats them to take vengeance on his sons, by inflicting on them the same pains he had inflicted on his pleasure-loving countrymen, if they are ever seen caring more for riches or any thing else than for virtue, or thinking more highly of themselves than they ought to think, for this, and this only, will be a just recompense for what he has done for the Athenian people; and then he takes leave of them, saying, Now it is time that we depart—I to die, you to live; and which of us is going to the better destiny is known only to the Deity.

Such, in substance, is the Defence of Socrates. So far from believing that we are indebted to the imagination of Plato for the lofty character of Socrates, as he appears in this Apology, we cannot but feel that we owe the elevation and eloquence of the Apology to the real greatness and heroism of its subject. The form and the words may be Plato's; but the substance and the spirit must be Socrates'; and we need only to have heard it from his lips to perfect the moral sublime. Profane literature has nowhere furnished a better delineation of the spiritual hero, rising superior to the fear and the favor of man in the strength of his own conscious integrity and of a serene trust in God. Faith in God, which had been the controlling principle of his life, was the power that sustained him in view of approaching death, inspired him with more than human fortitude in his last days, and invested his dying words with a moral grandeur that "has less of earth in it than heaven." The consciousness of a divine mission was the leading trait in his character and the main secret of his power.* This directed his conversations, shaped his philosophy, imbued his very person, and controlled his life. This determined the time and manner of his death. And this abiding conviction, this "ruling passion strong in death," is the very life and breath and all-pervading atmosphere of the Apology.

Nor is the religious element less pervading and controlling in the Crito, though there social duty and political principle are also made prominent. This piece presents Socrates to us in prison awaiting the execution of his unjust sentence. There Crito—the friend and benefactor of his youth, the companion of his middle-life, and the stay and staff of his advanced years—calls upon him at break of day, and, finding him in sound sleep, sits down by his side in silent admiration of his calmness on the very eve of death. Socrates awakes, and a dialogue ensues, beginning in the natural and easy manner so characteristic of Plato, leading on easily to the

* Cf. Grote, Hist. of Greece, Part II., chap. lxviii.

discussion of the topic which lies nearest Crito's heart, viz., the release of his friend, and ending, like the Apology, in a strain of rapt and inspired eloquence, before which Crito himself stands convinced, silenced, and overawed, as in the presence of some superior being.

After inquiring the hour, how Crito gained admission so early, and why he had not awaked him sooner, which leads him to remark upon the absurdity of shrinking from death, especially at his advanced age, Socrates asks the errand of his friend at that early hour. Crito replies, that the sacred ship (during whose voyage no one could be put to death at Athens) was drawing near on its return from Delos—that it would probably arrive that day, and on the day following, Socrates must die. (43, A. B. C. D.) Socrates expresses his readiness to die whenever it pleases the gods, but adds his belief that the ship would not arrive till the next day, and his execution would take place on the third day, assigning as the reason for that opinion a dream and vision, which he had just seen in sleep, and which it was well that Crito had not disturbed. A beautiful woman, dressed in white, had appeared to him, calling him and repeating the words of Homer touching the return of Achilles to his native land: "On the third day, Socrates, you will arrive at the fertile Phthia," which he interpreted as a divine intimation, and therefore infallible proof, that on the third day he would reach his *home* in a better world. (44, A. B.) Beautiful fiction, if the dream was the offspring of Plato's imagination! More beautiful fact, if the dream was real! And we know not why we should doubt it. What more natural than that such a notorious dreamer, so familiar with all the poetry of his country, especially that of Homer, and meditating of his speedy departure with lively and joyful imaginings by day, should dream of it under so poetical and attractive a form by night!

Crito now proceeds to press him with various and urgent motives—justice to himself, duty to his wife and children, regard to the affection and reputation of his friends, and the like—to bribe his keepers, forfeit his bail, and make his escape, declaring that it can be done at a very small expense, and he and the other friends would gladly meet any losses or dangers which might befall them in such a course, rather than lose such a friend, and, moreover, incur the disgrace with the multitude of sacrificing him to the love of money. (44, C.; 46.) "But why, my dear Crito, why should we so much regard the opinion of the multitude? For the best men, whose opinion is most worthy of consideration, will *believe* that these things are, as they are in *reality*, and that not you, but myself, am responsible for my death." "Nevertheless, you see, Socrates, that it is *necessary* to pay attention to the opinion of the multitude, for the present circumstances show that the multitude can effect, not the smallest of evils only, but nearly the greatest, if one is calumniated among them." "I could wish, Crito, the multitude were able to effect the greatest evils, that they might also accomplish the greatest good; for then it would be well. But now they can do neither of these. For they can neither make a man wise nor unwise." The same simple but sublime sentiment with which we have become familiar in the Apology: Character is the only thing pertaining to man that is of any account; and this his bitterest enemies cannot touch. "But they do just what they happen to do." (44, D.) That is, the conduct of the multitude, instead of being regulated by intelligent principle, is governed by blind chance; and such labors, however strenuous, are always fruitless. Accordingly, next to his great moral and religious mission, it was the perpetual study of Socrates' life to bring his countrymen, especially the young men of Athens, to a right understanding of themselves, their duties, and their pursuits, and thereby to an intelligent discharge of all the functions of proper manhood in the light of established rules and fixed principles.

The opinions of the multitude, he goes on to

argue, are sometimes right and sometimes wrong; while the standard of rectitude is unchangeable and eternal. Our duty depends, not on the opinions of the multitude, nor does it change with the change of our circumstances and interests. It has nothing to do with the consequences of our actions. Imprisonment, exile, death itself—these are bugbears to frighten children with, but they will not deter the true man from the performance of his duty, or swerve him in the least from adherence to principle. As to his escape from the prison without the consent of the rulers of the state, the great question, and the only question he can entertain is, whether it is right, since right reason is the only friend to whose solicitation he ever allowed himself to yield. The alacrity of his friends was very commendable, if rightly directed, but if not, the greater it was, by so much it was the more blameworthy. Against the dictates of reason and conscience, he could not be influenced in the least by a regard to the reputation of his friends or his own life. (46, B.; 47, A.)

A discussion ensues, in which Socrates proves to the conviction of Crito himself, that, in such a question, regard must be had, not to the opinions of the ignorant multitude, but of the truly wise, just as, in gymnastic exercises, the gymnast gives heed to the approbation or censure only of the physician or the master of the gymnasium (47, B. C. D.), that by acting unwisely and unjustly the *soul* is corrupted and destroyed, which is a far greater evil than the disease or destruction of the body (47, E.; 48, B.); that it is not right to injure or retaliate an injury in any case, least of all against one's country (49, A. seqq.); that the well-being of our country depends on the sacredness of the laws and the obedience of the citizens (50, B.), and our country should be obeyed and reverenced as a more sacred thing than father, or mother, or the dearest friends (51, A. B.); that a citizen by no means stands on an equal footing with his country, so as to have a right to treat her as she treats him, or to pronounce judgment on her acts as she does on his (50, E.); that every citizen who remains in a free country, which allows the inhabitants full liberty to emigrate when and where they please (especially if, like Socrates, he has remained during a long life, and never gone abroad at all, and never complained of the laws), has virtually assented to the justice of the laws, and has entered into a tacit compact to obey them, as interpreted and executed by their appointed guardians, unless he can persuade them to alter their decisions (52, A.; 53, A.); and that by escaping the penalty imposed upon him by the laws, he would convict himself of being a law-breaker, and make himself an object of suspicion as an enemy of law and justice, wherever he might go on earth, and even in Hades (53, B.; 54, B.). As the discussion proceeds, the laws seem to rise in dignity and sacredness, till they are seen embodied in a form more than human and enthroned in unearthly majesty; and they are heard, in meek yet authoritative tones, expostulating with Socrates on the injustice, folly, and pernicious tendency of the course which his friends are recommending. Socrates, too, catches the spirit of the laws, becomes instinct, as it were, with their life, and, like the Pythian priestess or an inspired corybant, deaf to every other voice, can do only as the voice of law (which is the voice of God) commands him: "The voice of these expostulations rings in my ears, and I am unable to hear other arguments. Be assured, if you urge any thing of a contrary tenor, you will labor in vain. This way God leads; and in this way let us follow."

The Crito, like the Apology and the other dialogues that were written soon after the death of Socrates, has a twofold object—the one practical and personal, the vindication of Socrates from the charge of impiety, and corrupting the youth—the other ideal and universal, to exhibit the true idea of the good citizen, or the good man in his relation to the state. And, it is not too much to say, it accomplishes both these objects perfectly. It is a triumphant vindication of the character of Socrates, setting his patriotism in the strongest light, and showing that he sacrificed his life to what most men would deem an overscrupulous regard for the constituted authorities, even in an unjust and unrighteous exercise of the power intrusted to them. At the same time, it sets forth a perfect pattern of the patriotic and loyal citizen, submitting to an unrighteous sentence (so long as it was according to the form of law, and since it concerned only himself, while no usurped authority of oligarchy or democracy could force him to do wrong to others), and with heroic, nay, religious devotion, laying himself a willing victim before the laws and on the altar of his country.

As a work of art, the Crito ranks very high—higher than the Apology; though, we think, the latter is capable of full vindication in this light, and stands on higher ground, simply as a work of art, than is commonly supposed. But the Crito, though the plot is exceedingly simple, and the *moral* of the dialogue is every where conspicuous, is conformed to the most rigid rules of the drama. The unities of time, place and impression, are perfectly preserved. The scene is laid wholly in the prison—perhaps the same cell hewn out of the solid rock, near the Pnyx and the Agora, which now bears the name of "The Prison of Socrates." The hour is the morn of his anticipated execution, when he is awaked out of sound sleep by a visit of his most intimate personal friend, who comes, if possible, to persuade him to escape, as he easily may, the execution of his unjust sentence. The characters are of the highest dignity and interest in themselves, and most intimately related to each other — Athens' wisest and best philosopher, and one of her wealthiest and most deserving citizens. The subject of discussion, as stated in the traditionary caption of the dialogue, and in the dialogue itself, is *περὶ πρακτέου*, or, WHAT OUGHT TO BE DONE, involving the whole duty of the citizen to the laws of his country, and, more remotely, the fundamental theory of government and society. On the result hang the life of the philosopher, the reputation and happiness of his numerous friends, and the interests of good order and good government, not only in Athens, but wherever Athenian influence shall be felt to the end of time. The persons, the principles, the interests involved, all awaken the liveliest sympathy. The affectionate solicitations, the persuasive arguments, the pathetic appeals, the generous friendship and self-sacrificing devotion of Crito, go to our hearts. While he speaks, we are more than half inclined to think that not the desirable and the expedient only, but the true and the right, are on his side. But Socrates, forgetting himself, overlooking his family and friends, and looking beyond the mere reputation of Athens, and even the right and wrong of the present case in itself considered, holds us sternly to the consideration of the great principles of law and order which it involves, and compels the assent of our reason and conscience, though against all our inclinations, and against the first dictates of our understanding. The conflict enters the breast of the reader. His judgment is perplexed with doubts and difficulties. His heart alternately hopes and fears the success of either party in the argument. As he feels constrained to assent more and more to the reasoning of Socrates, he wishes he could have decided otherwise. In the felicitous language of Stallbaum: "Etenim generosa Critonis amicitia æque afficiat et commoveat legentium animos necesse est, atque Socratis in virtute, constantia et pia adversus leges publicas reverentia, ut velis idem et cum Socrate noluisse et cum Critone voluisse." And when, at the conclusion, Socrates, transported with veneration for the purity and dignity of the law, not of men only but of God also, and rapt with the vision of what awaited him beyond the grave, rises into something more than human, we sit looking on, by the side of his friend Crito and in the same state of mind, silenced, convinced against our will, no longer pitying, still less censuring, but admiring, envying, almost worshipping him, as he looks upward and longs to take his flight.

The Apology and the Crito bear unequivocal evidence of proceeding from the same author; and that author, Ast to the contrary notwithstanding, Plato, and Plato under the same hallowing and inspiring influence, and in the same happy state of mind. The language, the style, the constructions, the idioms, are all Platonic. The sentiments and the spirit are those of Plato under the immediate inspiration of the life and death of Socrates. They are both dramatic, and this marks them both as of Platonic origin. True, the one is a monologue, and the other is a dialogue. But thus only could he act his proper part in the different circumstances in which he is placed. In the one, he pleads his cause in open court before his judges; in the other, he argues his case in prison with his friend. But in both, we *see* him, we hear him, we sit at his feet, we drink in his words, we catch his spirit. In the one, he stands before us the impersonation of the true orator; in the other, the model of the good citizen. But in both, the man rises far above his relations; the spirit overmasters the body and triumphs over all its outward circumstances. In both, we feel a spontaneous and irresistible conviction, that we see and hear the real Socrates uttering essentially his own sentiments, in essentially his own language, in two of the most real and most critical emergencies of his life. But in both we see him dramatized and idealized, at the same time that he is made real and represented as he is, with that inimitable skill and grace, which, together with his high spirituality, are the undisputed prerogatives of the divine Plato.

The present edition is, in the main, an exact reprint of Stallbaum's third edition, 1846. The few exceptions are specified in the notes, and the reasons given for the choice of a different reading. The notes of Stallbaum are so felicitous, especially in the illustration of Plato's peculiar idioms and constructions, that any one who has read them bears the results almost unconsciously with him in all his subsequent reading of the same author. Wherever I have consciously borrowed from him, I have given him credit in the notes. I have also had before me the editions of Bekker, Fischer, Forster, Heindorf, Ast, Schleiermacher, Buttmann, Nüsslin, Elberling, etc., together with versions in German, French, and English, too numerous to mention; and have used them whenever they could be of use, though most of them have been of very little service. In conclusion, I can hardly leave a better wish for the student of these pages than that, with far less labor than they have cost me, he may receive some small portion of the pleasure and profit which I have derived from them. He must be more or less than human, who can rise from the study of these immortal works of Plato, without higher ideas of the authority of law, the sacredness of duty, the power of faith, and the dignity of man's rational, moral, and immortal nature.

PREFACE TO THE REVISED EDITION.

This edition has been carefully revised, the Notes have been largely rewritten, the text has been changed, and the whole has been reprinted and stereotyped anew. The text is that of Cron, in his eighth edition, which is the result of a more extended and careful recension of manuscripts, and which not only differs much, in orthographical particulars, from Stallbaum and other early standard texts, but shows greater irregularity than we were formerly wont to expect in Greek orthography, especially in regard to *ν ἐφελκυστικόν*, moveable ς, elision, hiatus, and the like details. The work of revision, begun by myself, but by necessity discontinued, has been mostly done by my son, Professor H. M. Tyler, of Smith College, under my own supervision and review however, and with valuable assistance from Mr. L. H. Elwell, instructor of Greek in Amherst College, who has made most of the grammatical references, and to whom we are also indebted for not a few useful suggestions, the result of many years' use of the book in the class-room.

The preface of the first edition is retained entire, partly because it is largely in the nature of an introduction, which a whole generation of teachers and students have found to be useful, and have assured me that they would not willingly dispense with, and partly as a sort of educational landmark, or historic monument, which incidentally marks and records the progress of classical studies since the time when the "Græca Majora" contained in a single volume all, and more than all, of the Greek that was read in our colleges and universities. The chief object of the preface or introduction was not to instruct students in the philosophy of Socrates or Plato—the Apology and Crito are so entirely practical that they do not seem to be a suitable medium of such instruction—but to help them understand the life and character of the great moral philosopher, catch the sentiments and style and spirit of the author, and come under the educating and inspiring influence of these sublime productions. The chief end of the Notes, in the first edition and also in the revision, is the same; they are educational rather than critical or philosophical; they have respect not so much to the grammar as to the ethics and the politics, not so much to the language as to the literature and the life. At the same time, it is hoped that the peculiarities of Plato's language, and the characteristic features of the Socratic philosophy, so far as they are contained or implied in the Apology and Crito, will be found to be sufficiently explained in the Notes. The grammatical references in this edition are chiefly to Goodwin and to Allen's edition of Hadley, occasionally to Jelf, and Goodwin's Moods and Tenses.

It is now almost thirty years since the appearance of the first edition. Meanwhile the book has gone through many editions, and borne some humble part in the education of no one knows how many thousands of noble youth in every section of our country. Thankful for the privilege of thus contributing to the discipline of young minds, the formation of right characters, and the inculcation of just and lofty sentiments in past years, we send it out again revised, we trust, improved, and we hope to meet with no less favor and do a still better work in time to come.

W. S. TYLER.

AMHERST, *January, 1887.*

ΑΠΟΛΟΓΙΑ ΣΩΚΡΑΤΟΥΣ.

I. Ὅτι μὲν ὑμεῖς, ὦ ἄνδρες Ἀθηναῖοι, πεπόνθατε
ὑπὸ τῶν ἐμῶν κατηγόρων, οὐκ οἶδα· ἐγὼ δ' οὖν καὶ
αὐτὸς ὑπ' αὐτῶν ὀλίγου ἐμαυτοῦ ἐπελαθόμην· οὕτω
πιθανῶς ἔλεγον. καίτοι ἀληθές γε ὡς ἔπος εἰπεῖν
οὐδὲν εἰρήκασι. μάλιστα δὲ αὐτῶν ἓν ἐθαύμασα τῶν
πολλῶν ὧν ἐψεύσαντο, τοῦτο ἐν ᾧ ἔλεγον ὡς χρὴ
ὑμᾶς εὐλαβεῖσθαι μὴ ὑπ' ἐμοῦ ἐξαπατηθῆτε ὡς δεινοῦ
ὄντος λέγειν. τὸ γὰρ μὴ αἰσχυνθῆναι ὅτι αὐτίκα ὑπ' B
ἐμοῦ ἐξελεγχθήσονται ἔργῳ, ἐπειδὰν μηδ' ὁπωστιοῦν
φαίνωμαι δεινὸς λέγειν, τοῦτό μοι ἔδοξεν αὐτῶν ἀναι-
σχυντότατον εἶναι, εἰ μὴ ἄρα δεινὸν καλοῦσιν οὗτοι
λέγειν τὸν τἀληθῆ λέγοντα· εἰ μὲν γὰρ τοῦτο λέγου-
σιν, ὁμολογοίην ἂν ἔγωγε οὐ κατὰ τούτους εἶναι ῥήτωρ.
οὗτοι μὲν οὖν, ὥσπερ ἐγὼ λέγω, ἤ τι ἢ οὐδὲν ἀληθὲς
εἰρήκασιν· ὑμεῖς δέ μου ἀκούσεσθε πᾶσαν τὴν ἀλή-
θειαν. οὐ μέντοι μὰ Δία, ὦ ἄνδρες Ἀθηναῖοι, κεκαλ-
λιεπημένους γε λόγους, ὥσπερ οἱ τούτων, ῥήμασί τε
καὶ ὀνόμασιν οὐδὲ κεκοσμημένους, ἀλλὰ ἀκούσεσθε C
εἰκῇ λεγόμενα τοῖς ἐπιτυχοῦσιν ὀνόμασιν· πιστεύω
γὰρ δίκαια εἶναι ἃ λέγω, καὶ μηδεὶς ὑμῶν προσδοκη-

σάτω ἄλλως· οὐδὲ γὰρ ἂν δήπου πρέποι, ὦ ἄνδρες, τῇδε τῇ ἡλικίᾳ ὥσπερ μειρακίῳ πλάττοντι λόγους εἰς ὑμᾶς εἰσιέναι. καὶ μέντοι καὶ πάνυ, ὦ ἄνδρες Ἀθηναῖοι, τοῦτο ὑμῶν δέομαι καὶ παρίεμαι· ἐὰν διὰ τῶν αὐτῶν λόγων ἀκούητέ μου ἀπολογουμένου, δι' ὧνπερ εἴωθα λέγειν καὶ ἐν ἀγορᾷ ἐπὶ τῶν τραπεζῶν, ἵνα ὑμῶν πολλοὶ ἀκηκόασι, καὶ ἄλλοθι, μήτε θαυμάζειν
D μήτε θορυβεῖν τούτου ἕνεκα. ἔχει γὰρ οὑτωσί. νῦν ἐγὼ πρῶτον ἐπὶ δικαστήριον ἀναβέβηκα, ἔτη γεγονὼς ἑβδομήκοντα· ἀτεχνῶς οὖν ξένως ἔχω τῆς ἐνθάδε λέξεως. ὥσπερ οὖν ἄν, εἰ τῷ ὄντι ξένος ἐτύγχανον
18 ὤν, ξυνεγιγνώσκετε δήπου ἄν μοι, εἰ ἐν ἐκείνῃ τῇ φωνῇ τε καὶ τῷ τρόπῳ ἔλεγον, ἐν οἷσπερ ἐτεθράμμην, καὶ δὴ καὶ νῦν τοῦτο ὑμῶν δέομαι δίκαιον ὥς γέ μοι δοκῶ, τὸν μὲν τρόπον τῆς λέξεως ἐᾶν — ἴσως μὲν γὰρ χείρων, ἴσως δὲ βελτίων ἂν εἴη — αὐτὸ δὲ τοῦτο σκοπεῖν καὶ τούτῳ τὸν νοῦν προσέχειν, εἰ δίκαια λέγω ἢ μή· δικαστοῦ μὲν γὰρ αὕτη ἀρετή, ῥήτορος δὲ τἀληθῆ λέγειν.

II. Πρῶτον μὲν οὖν δίκαιός εἰμι ἀπολογήσασθαι, ὦ ἄνδρες Ἀθηναῖοι, πρὸς τὰ πρῶτά μου ψευδῆ κατηγορημένα καὶ τοὺς πρώτους κατηγόρους, ἔπειτα δὲ
B πρὸς τὰ ὕστερα καὶ τοὺς ὑστέρους. ἐμοῦ γὰρ πολλοὶ κατήγοροι γεγόνασιν πρὸς ὑμᾶς καὶ πάλαι πολλὰ ἤδη ἔτη καὶ οὐδὲν ἀληθὲς λέγοντες, οὓς ἐγὼ μᾶλλον φοβοῦμαι ἢ τοὺς ἀμφὶ Ἄνυτον, καίπερ ὄντας καὶ τούτους δεινούς· ἀλλ' ἐκεῖνοι δεινότεροι, ὦ ἄνδρες, οἳ ὑμῶν τοὺς πολλοὺς ἐκ παίδων παραλαμβάνοντες ἔπειθόν τε

καὶ κατηγόρουν ἐμοῦ, ὡς ἔστι τις Σωκράτης, σοφὸς
ἀνήρ, τά τε μετέωρα φροντιστὴς καὶ τὰ ὑπὸ γῆς
ἅπαντα ἀνεζητηκὼς καὶ τὸν ἥττω λόγον κρείττω ποιῶν.
οὗτοι, ὦ ἄνδρες Ἀθηναῖοι, οἱ ταύτην τὴν φήμην κατα- C
σκεδάσαντες οἱ δεινοί εἰσί μου κατήγοροι. οἱ γὰρ
ἀκούοντες ἡγοῦνται τοὺς ταῦτα ζητοῦντας οὐδὲ θεοὺς
νομίζειν. ἔπειτά εἰσιν οὗτοι οἱ κατήγοροι πολλοὶ καὶ
πολὺν χρόνον ἤδη κατηγορηκότες, ἔτι δὲ καὶ ἐν ταύτῃ
τῇ ἡλικίᾳ λέγοντες πρὸς ὑμᾶς, ἐν ᾗ ἂν μάλιστα ἐπι-
στεύσατε, παῖδες ὄντες, ἔνιοι δ' ὑμῶν καὶ μειράκια,
ἀτεχνῶς ἐρήμην κατηγοροῦντες ἀπολογουμένου οὐδε-
νός. ὃ δὲ πάντων ἀλογώτατον, ὅτι οὐδὲ τὰ ὀνόματα
οἷόν τε αὐτῶν εἰδέναι καὶ εἰπεῖν, πλὴν εἴ τις κωμῳδιο- D
ποιὸς τυγχάνει ὤν. ὅσοι δὲ φθόνῳ καὶ διαβολῇ χρώ-
μενοι ὑμᾶς ἀνέπειθον, οἱ δὲ καὶ αὐτοὶ πεπεισμένοι
ἄλλους πείθοντες, οὗτοι πάντες ἀπορώτατοί εἰσιν·
οὐδὲ γὰρ ἀναβιβάσασθαι οἷόν τ' ἐστὶν αὐτῶν ἐνταυθοῖ
οὐδ' ἐλέγξαι οὐδένα, ἀλλ' ἀνάγκη ἀτεχνῶς ὥσπερ
σκιαμαχεῖν ἀπολογούμενόν τε καὶ ἐλέγχειν μηδενὸς
ἀποκρινομένου. ἀξιώσατε οὖν καὶ ὑμεῖς ὥσπερ ἐγὼ
λέγω διττούς μου τοὺς κατηγόρους γεγονέναι, ἑτέρους
μὲν τοὺς ἄρτι κατηγορήσαντας, ἑτέρους δὲ τοὺς πάλαι E
οὓς ἐγὼ λέγω, καὶ οἰήθητε δεῖν πρὸς ἐκείνους πρῶτόν
με ἀπολογήσασθαι· καὶ γὰρ ὑμεῖς ἐκείνων πρότερον
ἠκούσατε κατηγορούντων, καὶ πολὺ μᾶλλον ἢ τῶνδε
τῶν ὕστερον. εἶεν· ἀπολογητέον δή, ὦ ἄνδρες Ἀθη-
ναῖοι, καὶ ἐπιχειρητέον ὑμῶν ἐξελέσθαι τὴν διαβολήν,
ἣν ὑμεῖς ἐν πολλῷ χρόνῳ ἔσχετε, ταύτην ἐν οὕτως

ὀλίγῳ χρόνῳ. βουλοίμην μὲν οὖν ἂν τοῦτο οὕτως γενέσθαι, εἴ τι ἄμεινον καὶ ὑμῖν καὶ ἐμοί, καὶ πλέον τί με ποιῆσαι ἀπολογούμενον· οἶμαι δὲ αὐτὸ χαλεπὸν εἶναι, καὶ οὐ πάνυ με λανθάνει οἷόν ἐστιν. ὅμως δὲ τοῦτο μὲν ἴτω ὅπῃ τῷ θεῷ φίλον, τῷ δὲ νόμῳ πειστέον καὶ ἀπολογητέον.

B III. Ἀναλάβωμεν οὖν ἐξ ἀρχῆς, τίς ἡ κατηγορία ἐστὶν ἐξ ἧς ἡ ἐμὴ διαβολὴ γέγονεν, ᾗ δὴ καὶ πιστεύων Μέλητός με ἐγράψατο τὴν γραφὴν ταύτην. εἶεν· τί δὴ λέγοντες διέβαλλον οἱ διαβάλλοντες; ὥσπερ οὖν κατηγόρων τὴν ἀντωμοσίαν δεῖ ἀναγνῶναι αὐτῶν· Σωκράτης ἀδικεῖ καὶ περιεργάζεται ζητῶν τά τε ὑπὸ γῆς καὶ οὐράνια καὶ τὸν ἥττω λόγον κρείττω ποιῶν C καὶ ἄλλους τὰ αὐτὰ ταῦτα διδάσκων. τοιαύτη τίς ἐστι· ταῦτα γὰρ ἑωρᾶτε καὶ αὐτοὶ ἐν τῇ Ἀριστοφάνους κωμῳδίᾳ, Σωκράτη τινὰ ἐκεῖ περιφερόμενον, φάσκοντά τε ἀεροβατεῖν καὶ ἄλλην πολλὴν φλυαρίαν φλυαροῦντα, ὧν ἐγὼ οὐδὲν οὔτε μέγα οὔτε μικρὸν πέρι ἐπαΐω. καὶ οὐχ ὡς ἀτιμάζων λέγω τὴν τοιαύτην ἐπιστήμην, εἴ τις περὶ τῶν τοιούτων σοφός D ἐστιν, μή πως ἐγὼ ὑπὸ Μελήτου τοσαύτας δίκας φύγοιμι· ἀλλὰ γὰρ ἐμοὶ τούτων, ὦ ἄνδρες Ἀθηναῖοι, οὐδὲν μέτεστι. μάρτυρας δὲ αὐτοὺς ὑμῶν τοὺς πολλοὺς παρέχομαι, καὶ ἀξιῶ ὑμᾶς ἀλλήλους διδάσκειν τε καὶ φράζειν, ὅσοι ἐμοῦ πώποτε ἀκηκόατε διαλεγομένου. πολλοὶ δὲ ὑμῶν οἱ τοιοῦτοί εἰσι· φράζετε οὖν ἀλλήλοις, εἰ πώποτε ἢ μικρὸν ἢ μέγα ἤκουσέ τις ὑμῶν ἐμοῦ περὶ τῶν τοιούτων διαλεγομένου· καὶ ἐκ τούτων γνώσεσθε ὅτι τοιαῦτ᾽ ἐστὶ καὶ τἆλλα περὶ ἐμοῦ ἃ οἱ πολλοὶ λέγουσιν.

IV. Ἀλλὰ γὰρ οὔτε τούτων οὐδέν [ἐστιν], οὐδέ γ᾽ εἴ τινος ἀκηκόατε ὡς ἐγὼ παιδεύειν ἐπιχειρῶ ἀνθρώπους καὶ χρήματα πράττομαι, οὐδὲ τοῦτο ἀληθές. ἐπεὶ E
καὶ τοῦτό γέ μοι δοκεῖ καλὸν εἶναι, εἴ τις οἷός τ᾽ εἴη παιδεύειν ἀνθρώπους ὥσπερ Γοργίας τε ὁ Λεοντῖνος καὶ Πρόδικος ὁ Κεῖος καὶ Ἱππίας ὁ Ἠλεῖος. τούτων γὰρ ἕκαστος, ὦ ἄνδρες, οἷός τ᾽ ἐστὶν ἰὼν εἰς ἑκάστην τῶν πόλεων τοὺς νέους, οἷς ἔξεστι τῶν ἑαυτῶν πολιτῶν προῖκα ξυνεῖναι ᾧ ἂν βούλωνται, τούτους πείθουσι τὰς ἐκείνων ξυνουσίας ἀπολιπόντας σφίσιν ξυνεῖναι 20
χρήματα διδόντας καὶ χάριν προσειδέναι. ἐπεὶ καὶ ἄλλος ἀνήρ ἐστι Πάριος ἐνθάδε σοφός, ὃν ἐγὼ ᾐσθόμην ἐπιδημοῦντα· ἔτυχον γὰρ προσελθὼν ἀνδρὶ ὃς τετέλεκε χρήματα σοφισταῖς πλείω ἢ ξύμπαντες οἱ ἄλλοι, Καλλίᾳ τῷ Ἱππονίκου· τοῦτον οὖν ἀνηρόμην—ἐστὸν γὰρ αὐτῷ δύο υἱέε—ὦ Καλλία, ἦν δ᾽ ἐγώ, εἰ μέν σου τὼ υἱέε πώλω ἢ μόσχω ἐγενέσθην, εἴχομεν ἂν αὐτοῖν ἐπιστάτην λαβεῖν καὶ μισθώσασθαι, ὃς ἔμελλεν αὐτὼ καλώ τε καὶ ἀγαθὼ ποιήσειν τὴν προσήκουσαν ἀρετήν· B
ἦν δ᾽ ἂν οὗτος ἢ τῶν ἱππικῶν τις ἢ τῶν γεωργικῶν· νῦν δ᾽ ἐπειδὴ ἀνθρώπω ἐστόν, τίνα αὐτοῖν ἐν νῷ ἔχεις ἐπιστάτην λαβεῖν; τίς τῆς τοιαύτης ἀρετῆς, τῆς ἀνθρωπίνης τε καὶ πολιτικῆς, ἐπιστήμων ἐστίν; οἶμαι γάρ σε ἐσκέφθαι διὰ τὴν τῶν υἱέων κτῆσιν. ἔστι τις, ἔφην ἐγώ, ἢ οὔ; Πάνυ γε, ἦ δ᾽ ὅς. Τίς, ἦν δ᾽ ἐγώ, καὶ ποδαπός, καὶ πόσου διδάσκει; Εὔηνος, ἔφη, ὦ

Σώκρατες, Πάριος, πέντε μνῶν· καὶ ἐγὼ τὸν Εὔηνον
C ἐμακάρισα, εἰ ὡς ἀληθῶς ἔχοι ταύτην τὴν τέχνην καὶ οὕτως ἐμμελῶς διδάσκει. ἐγὼ οὖν καὶ αὐτὸς ἐκαλλυνόμην τε καὶ ἡβρυνόμην ἄν, εἰ ἠπιστάμην ταῦτα· ἀλλ' οὐ γὰρ ἐπίσταμαι, ὦ ἄνδρες Ἀθηναῖοι.

V. Ὑπολάβοι ἂν οὖν τις ὑμῶν ἴσως· ἀλλ', ὦ Σώκρατες, τὸ σὸν τί ἐστι πρᾶγμα; πόθεν αἱ διαβολαί σοι αὗται γεγόνασιν; οὐ γὰρ δήπου σοῦ γε οὐδὲν τῶν ἄλλων περιττότερον πραγματευομένου ἔπειτα τοσαύτη φήμη τε καὶ λόγος γέγονεν, εἰ μή τι ἔπραττες ἀλλοῖον ἢ οἱ πολλοί· λέγε οὖν ἡμῖν τί ἐστιν, ἵνα μὴ ἡμεῖς
D περὶ σοῦ αὐτοσχεδιάζωμεν. ταυτί μοι δοκεῖ δίκαια λέγειν ὁ λέγων, κἀγὼ ὑμῖν πειράσομαι ἀποδεῖξαι τί ποτ' ἐστὶν τοῦτο ὃ ἐμοὶ πεποίηκε τό τε ὄνομα καὶ τὴν διαβολήν. ἀκούετε δή. καὶ ἴσως μὲν δόξω τισὶν ὑμῶν παίζειν, εὖ μέντοι ἴστε, πᾶσαν ὑμῖν τὴν ἀλήθειαν ἐρῶ. ἐγὼ γάρ, ὦ ἄνδρες Ἀθηναῖοι, δι' οὐδὲν ἀλλ' ἢ διὰ σοφίαν τινὰ τοῦτο τὸ ὄνομα ἔσχηκα. ποίαν δὴ σοφίαν ταύτην; ἥπερ ἐστὶν ἴσως ἀνθρωπίνη σοφία. τῷ ὄντι γὰρ κινδυνεύω ταύτην εἶναι σοφός· οὗτοι δὲ
E τάχ' ἂν οὓς ἄρτι ἔλεγον μείζω τινὰ ἢ κατ' ἄνθρωπον σοφίαν σοφοὶ εἶεν, ἢ οὐκ ἔχω τί λέγω· οὐ γὰρ δὴ ἔγωγε αὐτὴν ἐπίσταμαι, ἀλλ' ὅστις φησὶ ψεύδεταί τε καὶ ἐπὶ διαβολῇ τῇ ἐμῇ λέγει. καί μοι, ὦ ἄνδρες Ἀθηναῖοι, μὴ θορυβήσητε, μηδὲ ἂν δόξω τι ὑμῖν μέγα λέγειν· οὐ γὰρ ἐμὸν ἐρῶ τὸν λόγον ὃν ἂν λέγω, ἀλλ' εἰς ἀξιόχρεων ὑμῖν τὸν λέγοντα ἀνοίσω. τῆς γὰρ ἐμῆς εἰ δή τίς ἐστι σοφία καὶ οἵα μάρτυρα ὑμῖν παρέ-

ξομαι τὸν θεὸν τὸν ἐν Δελφοῖς. Χαιρεφῶντα γὰρ ἴστε
που. οὗτος ἐμός τε ἑταῖρος ἦν ἐκ νέου καὶ ὑμῶν τῷ 21
πλήθει ἑταῖρός τε καὶ ξυνέφυγε τὴν φυγὴν ταύτην καὶ
μεθ' ὑμῶν κατῆλθε. καὶ ἴστε δὴ οἷος ἦν Χαιρεφῶν,
ὡς σφοδρὸς ἐφ' ὅτι ὁρμήσειε. καὶ δή ποτε καὶ εἰς
Δελφοὺς ἐλθὼν ἐτόλμησε τοῦτο μαντεύσασθαι· καὶ
ὅπερ λέγω μὴ θορυβεῖτε, ὦ ἄνδρες· ἤρετο γὰρ δὴ εἴ
τις ἐμοῦ εἴη σοφώτερος. ἀνεῖλεν οὖν ἡ Πυθία μηδένα
σοφώτερον εἶναι. καὶ τούτων πέρι ὁ ἀδελφὸς ὑμῖν
αὐτοῦ οὑτοσὶ μαρτυρήσει, ἐπειδὴ ἐκεῖνος τετελεύτηκεν.

VI. Σκέψασθε δὲ ὧν ἕνεκα ταῦτα λέγω· μέλλω B
γὰρ ὑμᾶς διδάξειν ὅθεν μοι ἡ διαβολὴ γέγονε. ταῦτα
γὰρ ἐγὼ ἀκούσας ἐνεθυμούμην οὑτωσί· τί ποτε λέγει
ὁ θεός, καὶ τί ποτε αἰνίττεται; ἐγὼ γὰρ δὴ οὔτε μέγα
οὔτε σμικρὸν ξύνοιδα ἐμαυτῷ σοφὸς ὤν· τί οὖν ποτε
λέγει φάσκων ἐμὲ σοφώτατον εἶναι; οὐ γὰρ δήπου
ψεύδεταί γε· οὐ γὰρ θέμις αὐτῷ. καὶ πολὺν μὲν
χρόνον ἠπόρουν τί ποτε λέγει, ἔπειτα μόγις πάνυ ἐπὶ
ζήτησιν αὐτοῦ τοιαύτην τινὰ ἐτραπόμην. ἦλθον ἐπί
τινα τῶν δοκούντων σοφῶν εἶναι, ὡς ἐνταῦθα, εἴπερ
πού, ἐλέγξων τὸ μαντεῖον καὶ ἀποφανῶν τῷ χρησμῷ C
ὅτι οὑτοσὶ ἐμοῦ σοφώτερός ἐστι, σὺ δ' ἐμὲ ἔφησθα.
διασκοπῶν οὖν τοῦτον — ὀνόματι γὰρ οὐδὲν δέομαι
λέγειν, ἦν δέ τις τῶν πολιτικῶν πρὸς ὃν ἐγὼ σκοπῶν
τοιοῦτόν τι ἔπαθον, ὦ ἄνδρες Ἀθηναῖοι—καὶ διαλεγό-
μενος αὐτῷ, ἔδοξέ μοι οὗτος ὁ ἀνὴρ δοκεῖν μὲν εἶναι
σοφὸς ἄλλοις τε πολλοῖς ἀνθρώποις καὶ μάλιστα
ἑαυτῷ, εἶναι δ' οὔ· κἄπειτα ἐπειρώμην αὐτῷ δεικνύναι

D ὅτι οἴοιτο μὲν εἶναι σοφός, εἴη δ' οὔ. ἐντεῦθεν οὖν τούτῳ τε ἀπηχθόμην καὶ πολλοῖς τῶν παρόντων· πρὸς ἐμαυτὸν δ' οὖν ἀπιὼν ἐλογιζόμην ὅτι τούτου μὲν τοῦ ἀνθρώπου ἐγὼ σοφώτερός εἰμι· κινδυνεύει μὲν γὰρ ἡμῶν οὐδέτερος οὐδὲν καλὸν κἀγαθὸν εἰδέναι, ἀλλ' οὗτος μὲν οἴεταί τι εἰδέναι οὐκ εἰδώς, ἐγὼ δὲ ὥσπερ οὖν οὐκ οἶδα οὐδὲ οἴομαι. ἔοικά γ' οὖν τούτου γε σμικρῷ τινι αὐτῷ τούτῳ σοφώτερος εἶναι, ὅτι ἃ μὴ οἶδα οὐδὲ οἴομαι εἰδέναι. ἐντεῦθεν ἐπ' ἄλλον ᾖα τῶν
E ἐκείνου δοκούντων σοφωτέρων εἶναι, καί μοι ταὐτὰ ταῦτα ἔδοξε· καὶ ἐνταῦθα κἀκείνῳ καὶ ἄλλοις πολλοῖς ἀπηχθόμην.

VII. Μετὰ ταῦτ' οὖν ἤδη ἐφεξῆς ᾖα αἰσθανόμενος μὲν καὶ λυπούμενος καὶ δεδιὼς ὅτι ἀπηχθανόμην, ὅμως δὲ ἀναγκαῖον ἐδόκει εἶναι τὸ τοῦ θεοῦ περὶ πλείστου ποιεῖσθαι· ἰτέον οὖν σκοποῦντι τὸν χρησμὸν τί λέγει ἐπὶ ἅπαντας τούς τι δοκοῦντας εἰδέναι.
22 καὶ νὴ τὸν κύνα, ὦ ἄνδρες Ἀθηναῖοι—δεῖ γὰρ πρὸς ὑμᾶς τἀληθῆ λέγειν—ἦ μὴν ἐγὼ ἔπαθόν τι τοιοῦτον· οἱ μὲν μάλιστα εὐδοκιμοῦντες ἔδοξάν μοι ὀλίγου δεῖν τοῦ πλείστου ἐνδεεῖς εἶναι ζητοῦντι κατὰ τὸν θεόν, ἄλλοι δὲ δοκοῦντες φαυλότεροι ἐπιεικέστεροι εἶναι ἄνδρες πρὸς τὸ φρονίμως ἔχειν. δεῖ δὴ ὑμῖν τὴν ἐμὴν πλάνην ἐπιδεῖξαι ὥσπερ πόνους τινὰς πονοῦντος, ἵνα μοι καὶ ἀνέλεγκτος ἡ μαντεία γένοιτο. μετὰ γὰρ τοὺς πολιτικοὺς ᾖα ἐπὶ τοὺς ποιητὰς τούς τε τῶν
B τραγῳδιῶν καὶ τοὺς τῶν διθυράμβων καὶ τοὺς ἄλλους, ὡς ἐνταῦθα ἐπ' αὐτοφώρῳ καταληψόμενος ἐμαυτὸν

ἀμαθέστερον ἐκείνων ὄντα. ἀναλαμβάνων οὖν αὐτῶν τὰ ποιήματα, ἅ μοι ἐδόκει μάλιστα πεπραγματεῦσθαι αὐτοῖς, διηρώτων ἂν αὐτοὺς τί λέγοιεν, ἵν' ἅμα τι καὶ μανθάνοιμι παρ' αὐτῶν. αἰσχύνομαι οὖν ὑμῖν εἰπεῖν, ὦ ἄνδρες, τἀληθῆ· ὅμως δὲ ῥητέον. ὡς ἔπος γὰρ εἰπεῖν ὀλίγου αὐτῶν ἅπαντες οἱ παρόντες ἂν βέλτιον ἔλεγον περὶ ὧν αὐτοὶ ἐπεποιήκεσαν. ἔγνων οὖν καὶ περὶ τῶν ποιητῶν ἐν ὀλίγῳ τοῦτο, ὅτι οὐ σοφίᾳ ποιοῖεν C *ἃ ποιοῖεν, ἀλλὰ φύσει τινὶ καὶ ἐνθουσιάζοντες ὥσπερ οἱ θεομάντεις καὶ οἱ χρησμῳδοί· καὶ γὰρ οὗτοι λέγουσι μὲν πολλὰ καὶ καλά, ἴσασι δὲ οὐδὲν ὧν λέγουσι. τοιοῦτόν τί μοι ἐφάνησαν πάθος καὶ οἱ ποιηταὶ πεπονθότες· καὶ ἅμα ᾐσθόμην αὐτῶν διὰ τὴν ποίησιν οἰομένων καὶ τἆλλα σοφωτάτων εἶναι ἀνθρώπων ἃ οὐκ ἦσαν. ἀπῄα οὖν καὶ ἐντεῦθεν τῷ αὐτῷ οἰόμενος περιγεγονέναι ᾧπερ καὶ τῶν πολιτικῶν.*

VIII. Τελευτῶν *οὖν ἐπὶ τοὺς χειροτέχνας ᾖα. ἐμαυτῷ γὰρ ξυνῄδειν οὐδὲν ἐπισταμένῳ ὡς ἔπος εἰπεῖν,* D *τούτους δέ γ' ᾔδειν ὅτι εὑρήσοιμι πολλὰ καὶ καλὰ ἐπισταμένους. καὶ τούτου μὲν οὐκ ἐψεύσθην, ἀλλ' ἠπίσταντο ἃ ἐγὼ οὐκ ἠπιστάμην, καί μου ταύτῃ σοφώτεροι ἦσαν. ἀλλ', ὦ ἄνδρες* Ἀθηναῖοι, *ταὐτόν μοι ἔδοξαν ἔχειν ἁμάρτημα, ὅπερ καὶ οἱ ποιηταί, καὶ οἱ ἀγαθοὶ δημιουργοί· διὰ τὸ τὴν τέχνην καλῶς ἐξεργάζεσθαι ἕκαστος ἠξίου καὶ τἆλλα τὰ μέγιστα σοφώτατος εἶναι, καὶ αὐτῶν αὕτη ἡ πλημμέλεια ἐκείνην τὴν σοφίαν ἀπέκρυπτεν, ὥστε με ἐμαυτὸν ἀνερωτᾶν ὑπὲρ τοῦ χρησμοῦ,* E *πότερα δεξαίμην ἂν οὕτω ὥσπερ ἔχω ἔχειν μήτε* τι σοφὸς ὢν τὴν ἐκείνων σοφίαν μήτε ἀμαθὴς τὴν ἀμαθίαν, ἢ ἀμφότερα ἃ ἐκεῖνοι ἔχουσιν ἔχειν. ἀπεκρινάμην οὖν ἐμαυτῷ καὶ τῷ χρησμῷ ὅτι μοι λυσιτελοῖ ὥσπερ ἔχω ἔχειν.

IX. Ἐκ ταυτησὶ δὴ τῆς ἐξετάσεως, ὦ ἄνδρες Ἀθη- 23 ναῖοι, πολλαὶ μὲν ἀπέχθειαί μοι γεγόνασι καὶ οἷαι χαλεπώταται καὶ βαρύταται, ὥστε πολλὰς διαβολὰς ἀπ᾽ αὐτῶν γεγονέναι, ὄνομα δὲ τοῦτο λέγεσθαι, σοφὸς εἶναι. οἴονται γάρ με ἑκάστοτε οἱ παρόντες ταῦτα αὐτὸν εἶναι σοφόν, ἃ ἂν ἄλλον ἐξελέγξω· τὸ δὲ κινδυνεύει, ὦ ἄνδρες, τῷ ὄντι ὁ θεὸς σοφὸς εἶναι, καὶ ἐν τῷ χρησμῷ τούτῳ τοῦτο λέγειν, ὅτι ἡ ἀνθρωπίνη σοφία ὀλίγου τινὸς ἀξία ἐστὶ καὶ οὐδενός, καὶ φαίνεται τοῦτο λέγειν τὸν Σωκράτη, προσκεχρῆσθαι δὲ τῷ ἐμῷ ὀνόματι ἐμὲ παράδειγμα ποιούμενος, ὥσπερ ἂν εἰ εἴποι B ὅτι οὗτος ὑμῶν, ὦ ἄνθρωποι, σοφώτατός ἐστιν, ὅστις ὥσπερ Σωκράτης ἔγνωκεν ὅτι οὐδενός ἄξιός ἐστι τῇ ἀληθείᾳ πρὸς σοφίαν. ταῦτ᾽ οὖν ἐγὼ μὲν ἔτι καὶ νῦν περιιὼν ζητῶ καὶ ἐρευνῶ κατὰ τὸν θεόν, καὶ τῶν ἀστῶν καὶ ξένων ἄν τινα οἴωμαι σοφὸν εἶναι· καὶ ἐπειδάν μοι μὴ δοκῇ, τῷ θεῷ βοηθῶν ἐνδείκνυμαι ὅτι οὐκ ἔστι C σοφός. καὶ ὑπὸ ταύτης τῆς ἀσχολίας οὔτε τι τῶν τῆς πόλεως πρᾶξαί μοι σχολὴ γέγονεν ἄξιον λόγου οὔτε τῶν οἰκείων, ἀλλ᾽ ἐν πενίᾳ μυρίᾳ εἰμὶ διὰ τὴν τοῦ θεοῦ λατρείαν.

X. Πρὸς δὲ τούτοις οἱ νέοι μοι ἐπακολουθοῦντες οἷς μάλιστα σχολή ἐστιν, οἱ τῶν πλουσιωτάτων, αὐτόματοι χαίρουσιν ἀκούοντες ἐξεταζομένων τῶν ἀνθρώπων, καὶ αὐτοὶ πολλάκις ἐμὲ μιμοῦνται, εἶτ' ἐπιχειροῦσιν ἄλλους ἐξετάζειν· κἄπειτα, οἶμαι, εὑρίσκουσι πολλὴν ἀφθονίαν οἰομένων μὲν εἰδέναι τι ἀνθρώπων, εἰδότων δὲ ὀλίγα ἢ οὐδέν. ἐντεῦθεν οὖν οἱ ὑπ' αὐτῶν ἐξεταζόμενοι ἐμοὶ ὀργίζονται, ἀλλ' οὐχ αὑτοῖς, καὶ λέγουσιν ὡς Σωκράτης τίς ἐστι μιαρώτατος καὶ διαφθείρει D τοὺς νέους· καὶ ἐπειδάν τις αὐτοὺς ἐρωτᾷ ὅτι ποιῶν καὶ ὅτι διδάσκων, ἔχουσι μὲν οὐδὲν εἰπεῖν, ἀλλ' ἀγνοοῦσιν, ἵνα δὲ μὴ δοκῶσιν ἀπορεῖν, τὰ κατὰ πάντων τῶν φιλοσοφούντων πρόχειρα ταῦτα λέγουσιν, ὅτι τὰ μετέωρα καὶ τὰ ὑπὸ γῆς καὶ θεοὺς μὴ νομίζειν καὶ τὸν ἥττω λόγον κρείττω ποιεῖν. τὰ γὰρ ἀληθῆ, οἴομαι, οὐκ ἂν ἐθέλοιεν λέγειν, ὅτι κατάδηλοι γίγνονται προσποιούμενοι μὲν εἰδέναι, εἰδότες δὲ οὐδέν. ἅτε οὖν, οἶμαι, φιλότιμοι ὄντες καὶ σφοδροὶ καὶ πολλοὶ καὶ ξυντεταγμένως E καὶ πιθανῶς λέγοντες περὶ ἐμοῦ, ἐμπεπλήκασιν ὑμῶν τὰ ὦτα καὶ πάλαι καὶ νῦν σφοδρῶς διαβάλλοντες. ἐκ τούτων καὶ Μέλητός μοι ἐπέθετο καὶ Ἄνυτος καὶ Λύκων, Μέλητος μὲν ὑπὲρ τῶν ποιητῶν ἀχθόμενος, Ἄνυτος δὲ ὑπὲρ τῶν δημιουργῶν καὶ τῶν πολιτικῶν, Λύκων δὲ ὑπὲρ τῶν ῥητόρων· ὥστε, ὅπερ ἀρχόμενος 24 ἐγὼ ἔλεγον, θαυμάζοιμ' ἂν εἰ οἷός τ' εἴην ἐγὼ ὑμῶν ταύτην τὴν διαβολὴν ἐξελέσθαι ἐν οὕτως ὀλίγῳ χρόνῳ οὕτω πολλὴν γεγονυῖαν. ταῦτ' ἔστιν ὑμῖν, ὦ ἄνδρες Ἀθηναῖοι, τἀληθῆ, καὶ ὑμᾶς οὔτε μέγα οὔτε μικρὸν ἀποκρυψάμενος ἐγὼ λέγω οὐδ' ὑποστειλάμενος. καίτοι οἶδα σχεδὸν ὅτι τοῖς αὐτοῖς ἀπεχθάνομαι· ὃ καὶ τεκμήριον ὅτι ἀληθῆ λέγω καὶ ὅτι αὕτη ἐστὶν ἡ δια-

βολὴ ἡ ἐμὴ καὶ τὰ αἴτια ταῦτά ἐστιν. καὶ ἐάν τε νῦν
B ἐάν τε αὖθις ζητήσητε ταῦτα, οὕτως εὑρήσετε.

XI. Περὶ μὲν οὖν ὧν οἱ πρῶτοί μου κατήγοροι κατηγόρουν αὕτη ἐστὶν ἱκανὴ ἀπολογία πρὸς ὑμᾶς· πρὸς δὲ Μέλητον τὸν ἀγαθόν τε καὶ φιλόπολιν, ὥς φησι, καὶ τοὺς ὑστέρους μετὰ ταῦτα πειράσομαι ἀπολογεῖσθαι. αὖθις γὰρ δὴ ὥσπερ ἑτέρων τούτων ὄντων κατηγόρων λάβωμεν αὖ τὴν τούτων ἀντωμοσίαν. ἔχει δέ πως ὧδε· Σωκράτη φησὶν ἀδικεῖν τούς τε νέους διαφθείροντα καὶ θεοὺς οὓς ἡ πόλις νομίζει οὐ νομί-
C ζοντα, ἕτερα δὲ δαιμόνια καινά. τὸ μὲν δὴ ἔγκλημα τοιοῦτόν ἐστιν· τούτου δὲ τοῦ ἐγκλήματος ἓν ἕκαστον ἐξετάσωμεν. φησὶ γὰρ δὴ τοὺς νέους ἀδικεῖν με διαφθείροντα. ἐγὼ δέ γε, ὦ ἄνδρες Ἀθηναῖοι, ἀδικεῖν φημι Μέλητον, ὅτι σπουδῇ χαριεντίζεται ῥᾳδίως εἰς ἀγῶνα καθιστὰς ἀνθρώπους, περὶ πραγμάτων προσποιούμενος σπουδάζειν καὶ κήδεσθαι ὧν οὐδὲν τούτῳ πώποτε ἐμέλησεν. ὡς δὲ τοῦτο οὕτως ἔχει πειράσομαι καὶ ὑμῖν ἐπιδεῖξαι.

XII. Καί μοι δεῦρο, ὦ Μέλητε, εἰπέ· ἄλλο τι ἢ
D περὶ πολλοῦ ποιεῖ ὅπως ὡς βέλτιστοι οἱ νεώτεροι ἔσονται; Ἔγωγε. Ἴθι δὴ νῦν εἰπὲ τούτοις τίς αὐτοὺς βελτίους ποιεῖ; δῆλον γὰρ ὅτι οἶσθα, μέλον γέ σοι. τὸν μὲν γὰρ διαφθείροντα ἐξευρών, ὡς φῄς, ἐμὲ εἰσάγεις τουτοισὶ καὶ κατηγορεῖς· τὸν δὲ δὴ βελτίους ποιοῦντα ἴθι εἰπὲ καὶ μήνυσον αὐτοῖς τίς ἐστιν. ὁρᾷς, ὦ Μέλητε, ὅτι σιγᾷς καὶ οὐκ ἔχεις εἰπεῖν; καίτοι οὐκ αἰσχρόν σοι δοκεῖ εἶναι καὶ ἱκανὸν τεκμήριον οὗ δὴ

ἐγὼ λέγω, ὅτι σοι οὐδὲν μεμέληκεν; ἀλλ' εἰπέ, ὠγαθέ,
τίς αὐτοὺς ἀμείνους ποιεῖ; Οἱ νόμοι. Ἀλλ' οὐ τοῦτο E
ἐρωτῶ, ὦ βέλτιστε, ἀλλὰ τίς ἄνθρωπος, ὅστις πρῶτον
καὶ αὐτὸ τοῦτο οἶδε, τοὺς νόμους. Οὗτοι, ὦ Σώκρατες,
οἱ δικασταί. Πῶς λέγεις, ὦ Μέλητε; οἵδε τοὺς νέους
παιδεύειν οἷοί τέ εἰσι καὶ βελτίους ποιοῦσιν; Μάλιστα.
Πότερον ἅπαντες, ἢ οἱ μὲν αὐτῶν, οἱ δ' οὔ; Ἅπαντες.
Εὖ γε νὴ τὴν Ἥραν λέγεις καὶ πολλὴν ἀφθονίαν τῶν
ὠφελούντων. τί δὲ δή; οἵδε οἱ ἀκροαταὶ βελτίους
ποιοῦσιν ἢ οὔ; Καὶ οὗτοι. Τί δὲ οἱ βουλευταί; Καὶ 25
οἱ βουλευταί. Ἀλλ' ἄρα, ὦ Μέλητε, μὴ οἱ ἐν τῇ
ἐκκλησίᾳ, οἱ ἐκκλησιασταί, διαφθείρουσι τοὺς νεωτέ-
ρους; ἢ κἀκεῖνοι βελτίους ποιοῦσιν ἅπαντες; Κἀκεῖ-
νοι. Πάντες ἄρα, ὡς ἔοικεν, Ἀθηναῖοι καλοὺς κἀγα-
θοὺς ποιοῦσι πλὴν ἐμοῦ, ἐγὼ δὲ μόνος διαφθείρω.
οὕτω λέγεις; Πάνυ σφόδρα ταῦτα λέγω. Πολλήν γ'
ἐμοῦ κατέγνωκας δυστυχίαν. καί μοι ἀπόκριναι· ἦ
καὶ περὶ ἵππους οὕτω σοι δοκεῖ ἔχειν· οἱ μὲν βελτίους
ποιοῦντες αὐτοὺς πάντες ἄνθρωποι εἶναι, εἷς δέ τις ὁ B
διαφθείρων; ἢ τοὐναντίον τούτου πᾶν εἷς μέν τις ὁ
βελτίους οἷός τε ὢν ποιεῖν ἢ πάνυ ὀλίγοι, οἱ ἱππικοί·
οἱ δὲ πολλοί, ἐάνπερ ξυνῶσι καὶ χρῶνται ἵπποις, δια-
φθείρουσιν; οὐχ οὕτως ἔχει, ὦ Μέλητε, καὶ περὶ
ἵππων καὶ τῶν ἄλλων ἁπάντων ζῴων; πάντως δήπου,
ἐάν τε σὺ καὶ Ἄνυτος οὐ φῆτε ἐάν τε φῆτε· πολλὴ
γὰρ ἄν τις εὐδαιμονία εἴη περὶ τοὺς νέους, εἰ εἷς μὲν
μόνος αὐτοὺς διαφθείρει, οἱ δ' ἄλλοι ὠφελοῦσιν. ἀλλὰ C
γάρ, ὦ Μέλητε, ἱκανῶς ἐπιδείκνυσαι ὅτι οὐδεπώποτε

ἐφρόντισας τῶν νέων, καὶ σαφῶς ἀποφαίνεις τὴν σαυ-
τοῦ ἀμέλειαν, ὅτι οὐδέν σοι μεμέληκε περὶ ὧν ἐμὲ
εἰσάγεις.

XIII. Ἔτι δὲ ἡμῖν εἰπέ, ὦ πρὸς Διὸς Μέλητε,
πότερόν ἐστιν οἰκεῖν ἄμεινον ἐν πολίταις χρηστοῖς ἢ
πονηροῖς; ὦταν, ἀπόκριναι· οὐδὲν γάρ τοι χαλεπὸν
ἐρωτῶ. οὐχ οἱ μὲν πονηροὶ κακόν τι ἐργάζονται τοὺς
ἀεὶ ἐγγυτάτω ἑαυτῶν ὄντας, οἱ δ' ἀγαθοὶ ἀγαθόν τι;
Πάνυ γε. Ἔστιν οὖν ὅστις βούλεται ὑπὸ τῶν ξυνόν-
D των βλάπτεσθαι μᾶλλον ἢ ὠφελεῖσθαι; ἀποκρίνου,
ὦ ἀγαθέ· καὶ γὰρ ὁ νόμος κελεύει ἀποκρίνεσθαι. ἔσθ'
ὅστις βούλεται βλάπτεσθαι; Οὐ δῆτα. Φέρε δή,
πότερον ἐμὲ εἰσάγεις δεῦρο ὡς διαφθείροντα τοὺς νεω-
τέρους καὶ πονηροτέρους ποιοῦντα ἑκόντα ἢ ἄκοντα;
Ἑκόντα ἔγωγε. Τί δῆτα, ὦ Μέλητε; τοσοῦτον σὺ
ἐμοῦ σοφώτερος εἶ τηλικούτου ὄντος τηλικόσδε ὤν,
ὥστε σὺ μὲν ἔγνωκας ὅτι οἱ μὲν κακοὶ κακόν τι ἐργά-
ζονται ἀεὶ τοὺς μάλιστα πλησίον ἑαυτῶν, οἱ δὲ ἀγαθοὶ
E ἀγαθόν· ἐγὼ δὲ δὴ εἰς τοσοῦτον ἀμαθίας ἥκω, ὥστε
καὶ τοῦτο ἀγνοῶ, ὅτι, ἐάν τινα μοχθηρὸν ποιήσω τῶν
ξυνόντων, κινδυνεύσω κακόν τι λαβεῖν ἀπ' αὐτοῦ, ὥστε
τοῦτο τὸ τοσοῦτον κακὸν ἑκὼν ποιῶ, ὡς φῂς σύ; ταῦτα
ἐγώ σοι οὐ πείθομαι, ὦ Μέλητε, οἶμαι δὲ οὐδὲ ἄλλον
ἀνθρώπων οὐδένα· ἀλλ' ἢ οὐ διαφθείρω, ἤ, εἰ διαφθεί-
26 ρω, ἄκων, ὥστε σύ γε κατ' ἀμφότερα ψεύδει. εἰ δὲ
ἄκων διαφθείρω, τῶν τοιούτων καὶ ἀκουσίων ἁμαρτη-
μάτων οὐ δεῦρο νόμος εἰσάγειν ἐστίν, ἀλλ' ἰδίᾳ λαβόντα
διδάσκειν καὶ νουθετεῖν· δῆλον γὰρ ὅτι, ἐὰν μάθω,

παύσομαι ὅ γε ἄκων ποιῶ. σὺ δὲ ξυγγενέσθαι μέν μοι καὶ διδάξαι ἔφυγες καὶ οὐκ ἠθέλησας, δεῦρο δὲ εἰσάγεις, οἷ νόμος ἐστὶν εἰσάγειν τοὺς κολάσεως δεομένους, ἀλλ' οὐ μαθήσεως.

XIV. Ἀλλὰ γάρ, ὦ ἄνδρες Ἀθηναῖοι, τοῦτο μὲν δῆλον ἤδη ἐστίν, ὃ ἐγὼ ἔλεγον, ὅτι Μελήτῳ τούτων οὔτε μέγα οὔτε μικρὸν πώποτε ἐμέλησεν· ὅμως δὲ δὴ B λέγε ἡμῖν πῶς με φῂς διαφθείρειν, ὦ Μέλητε, τοὺς νεωτέρους; ἢ δῆλον δὴ ὅτι κατὰ τὴν γραφὴν ἣν ἐγράψω θεοὺς διδάσκοντα μὴ νομίζειν οὓς ἡ πόλις νομίζει, ἕτερα δὲ δαιμόνια καινά; · οὐ ταῦτα λέγεις ὅτι διδάσκων διαφθείρω; Πάνυ μὲν οὖν σφόδρα ταῦτα λέγω. Πρὸς αὐτῶν τοίνυν, ὦ Μέλητε, τούτων τῶν θεῶν ὧν νῦν ὁ λόγος ἐστίν, εἰπὲ ἔτι σαφέστερον καὶ ἐμοὶ καὶ τοῖς ἀνδράσι τούτοις. ἐγὼ γὰρ οὐ δύναμαι μαθεῖν πότερον C λέγεις διδάσκειν με νομίζειν εἶναί τινας θεούς, καὶ αὐτὸς ἄρα νομίζω εἶναι θεούς, καὶ οὐκ εἰμὶ τὸ παράπαν ἄθεος οὐδὲ ταύτῃ ἀδικῶ, οὐ μέντοι οὕσπερ γε ἡ πόλις, ἀλλὰ ἑτέρους, καὶ τοῦτ' ἔστιν ὅ μοι ἐγκαλεῖς, ὅτι ἑτέρους· ἢ παντάπασί με φῂς οὔτε αὐτὸν νομίζειν θεοὺς τούς τε ἄλλους ταῦτα διδάσκειν. Ταῦτα λέγω, ὡς τὸ παράπαν οὐ νομίζεις θεούς. Ὦ θαυμάσιε Μέλητε, ἵνα τί ταῦτα λέγεις; οὐδὲ ἥλιον οὐδὲ σελήνην ἄρα νομίζω D θεοὺς εἶναι ὥσπερ οἱ ἄλλοι ἄνθρωποι; Μὰ Δί', ὦ ἄνδρες δικασταί, ἐπεὶ τὸν μὲν ἥλιον λίθον φησὶν εἶναι, τὴν δὲ σελήνην γῆν. Ἀναξαγόρου οἴει κατηγορεῖν, ὦ φίλε Μέλητε, καὶ οὕτω καταφρονεῖς τῶνδε καὶ οἴει αὐτοὺς ἀπείρους γραμμάτων εἶναι, ὥστε οὐκ εἰδέναι

ὅτι τὰ Ἀναξαγόρου βιβλία τοῦ Κλαζομενίου γέμει τούτων τῶν λόγων; καὶ δὴ καὶ οἱ νέοι ταῦτα παρ' ἐμοῦ μανθάνουσιν, ἃ ἔξεστιν ἐνίοτε, εἰ πάνυ πολλοῦ,
E δραχμῆς ἐκ τῆς ὀρχήστρας πριαμένοις Σωκράτους καταγελᾶν, ἐὰν προσποιῆται ἑαυτοῦ εἶναι, ἄλλως τε καὶ οὕτως ἄτοπα ὄντα. ἀλλ' ὦ πρὸς Διός, οὑτωσί σοι δοκῶ οὐδένα νομίζειν θεὸν εἶναι; Οὐ μέντοι μὰ Δί' οὐδ' ὁπωστιοῦν. Ἄπιστός γ' εἶ, ὦ Μέλητε, καὶ ταῦτα μέντοι, ὡς ἐμοὶ δοκεῖς, σαυτῷ. ἐμοὶ γὰρ δοκεῖ οὑτοσί, ὦ ἄνδρες Ἀθηναῖοι, πάνυ εἶναι ὑβριστὴς καὶ ἀκόλαστος, καὶ ἀτεχνῶς τὴν γραφὴν ταύτην ὕβρει τινὶ καὶ ἀκολασίᾳ καὶ νεότητι γράψασθαι. ἔοικε γὰρ ὥσπερ
27 αἴνιγμα ξυντιθέντι διαπειρωμένῳ, ἆρα γνώσεται Σωκράτης ὁ σοφὸς δὴ ἐμοῦ χαριεντιζομένου καὶ ἐναντί' ἐμαυτῷ λέγοντος, ἢ ἐξαπατήσω αὐτὸν καὶ τοὺς ἄλλους τοὺς ἀκούοντας; οὗτος γὰρ ἐμοὶ φαίνεται τὰ ἐναντία λέγειν αὐτὸς ἑαυτῷ ἐν τῇ γραφῇ, ὥσπερ ἂν εἰ εἴποι· ἀδικεῖ Σωκράτης θεοὺς οὐ νομίζων, ἀλλὰ θεοὺς νομίζων. καίτοι τοῦτό ἐστι παίζοντος.

XV. Ξυνεπισκέψασθε δή, ὦ ἄνδρες, ᾗ μοι φαίνεται ταῦτα λέγειν· σὺ δὲ ἡμῖν ἀπόκριναι, ὦ Μέλητε· ὑμεῖς δέ, ὅπερ κατ' ἀρχὰς ὑμᾶς παρῃτησάμην, μέμνησθέ
B μοι μὴ θορυβεῖν, ἐὰν ἐν τῷ εἰωθότι τρόπῳ τοὺς λόγους ποιῶμαι. ἔστιν ὅστις ἀνθρώπων, ὦ Μέλητε, ἀνθρώπεια μὲν νομίζει πράγματ' εἶναι, ἀνθρώπους δὲ οὐ νομίζει; ἀποκρινέσθω, ὦ ἄνδρες, καὶ μὴ ἄλλα καὶ ἄλλα θορυβείτω· ἔσθ' ὅστις ἵππους μὲν οὐ νομίζει, ἱππικὰ δὲ πράγματα; ἢ αὐλητὰς μὲν οὐ νομίζει εἶναι,

αὐλητικὰ δὲ πράγματα; οὐκ ἔστιν, ὦ ἄριστε ἀνδρῶν·
εἰ μὴ σὺ βούλει ἀποκρίνασθαι, ἐγώ σοι λέγω καὶ τοῖς
ἄλλοις τουτοισί. ἀλλὰ τὸ ἐπὶ τούτῳ γε ἀπόκριναι·
ἔσθ' ὅστις δαιμόνια μὲν νομίζει πράγματ' εἶναι, δαίμο- C
νας δὲ οὐ νομίζει; Οὐκ ἔστιν. Ὡς ὤνησας ὅτι μόγις
ἀπεκρίνω ὑπὸ τουτωνὶ ἀναγκαζόμενος. οὐκοῦν δαιμό-
νια μὲν φῄς με καὶ νομίζειν καὶ διδάσκειν, εἴτ' οὖν
καινὰ εἴτε παλαιά· ἀλλ' οὖν δαιμόνιά γε νομίζω κατὰ
τὸν σὸν λόγον, καὶ ταῦτα καὶ διωμόσω ἐν τῇ ἀντι-
γραφῇ. εἰ δὲ δαιμόνια νομίζω καὶ δαίμονας δήπου
πολλὴ ἀνάγκη νομίζειν μέ ἐστιν· οὐχ οὕτως ἔχει;
ἔχει δή· τίθημι γάρ σε ὁμολογοῦντα, ἐπειδὴ οὐκ
ἀποκρίνει. τοὺς δὲ δαίμονας οὐχὶ ἤτοι θεούς γε ἡγού- D
μεθα ἢ θεῶν παῖδας; φῂς ἢ οὔ; Πάνυ γε. Οὐκοῦν
εἴπερ δαίμονας ἡγοῦμαι, ὡς σὺ φῄς, εἰ μὲν θεοί τινές
εἰσιν οἱ δαίμονες, τοῦτ' ἂν εἴη ὃ ἐγὼ φημί σε αἰνίτ-
τεσθαι καὶ χαριεντίζεσθαι, θεοὺς οὐχ ἡγούμενον φάναι
ἐμὲ θεοὺς αὖ ἡγεῖσθαι πάλιν, ἐπειδήπερ γε δαίμονας
ἡγοῦμαι· εἰ δ' αὖ οἱ δαίμονες θεῶν παῖδές εἰσι νόθοι
τινὲς ἢ ἐκ νυμφῶν ἢ ἔκ τινων ἄλλων, ὧν δὴ καὶ
λέγονται, τίς ἂν ἀνθρώπων θεῶν μὲν παῖδας ἡγοῖτο
εἶναι, θεοὺς δὲ μή; ὁμοίως γὰρ ἂν ἄτοπον εἴη, ὥσπερ E
ἂν εἴ τις ἵππων μὲν παῖδας ἡγοῖτο ἢ [καὶ] ὄνων [τοὺς
ἡμιόνους], ἵππους δὲ καὶ ὄνους μὴ ἡγοῖτο εἶναι. ἀλλ',
ὦ Μέλητε, οὐκ ἔστιν ὅπως σὺ ταῦτα οὐχὶ ἀποπειρώ-
μενος ἡμῶν ἐγράψω [τὴν γραφὴν ταύτην] ἢ ἀπορῶν
ὅτι ἐγκαλοῖς ἐμοὶ ἀληθὲς ἀδίκημα· ὅπως δὲ σύ τινα
πείθοις ἂν καὶ σμικρὸν νοῦν ἔχοντα ἀνθρώπων, ὡς

[οὐ] τοῦ αὐτοῦ ἐστὶ καὶ δαιμόνια καὶ θεῖα ἡγεῖσθαι, καὶ αὖ τοῦ αὐτοῦ μήτε δαίμονας μήτε θεοὺς μήτε ἥρωας, οὐδεμία μηχανή ἐστιν.

28 XVI. Ἀλλὰ γάρ, ὦ ἄνδρες Ἀθηναῖοι, ὡς μὲν ἐγὼ οὐκ ἀδικῶ κατὰ τὴν Μελήτου γραφήν, οὐ πολλῆς μοι δοκεῖ εἶναι ἀπολογίας, ἀλλὰ ἱκανὰ καὶ ταῦτα· ὃ δὲ καὶ ἐν τοῖς ἔμπροσθεν ἔλεγον, ὅτι πολλή μοι ἀπέχθεια γέγονε καὶ πρὸς πολλούς, εὖ ἴστε ὅτι ἀληθές ἐστι. καὶ τοῦτ' ἔστιν ὃ ἐμὲ αἱρήσει, ἐάνπερ αἱρῇ, οὐ Μέλητος οὐδὲ Ἄνυτος, ἀλλ' ἡ τῶν πολλῶν διαβολή τε καὶ φθόνος. ἃ δὴ πολλοὺς καὶ ἄλλους καὶ ἀγαθοὺς ἄνδρας
B ᾕρηκεν, οἶμαι δὲ καὶ αἱρήσειν· οὐδὲν δὲ δεινὸν μὴ ἐν ἐμοὶ στῇ. ἴσως δ' ἂν οὖν εἴποι τις· εἶτ' οὐκ αἰσχύνει, ὦ Σώκρατες, τοιοῦτον ἐπιτήδευμα ἐπιτηδεύσας, ἐξ οὗ κινδυνεύεις νυνὶ ἀποθανεῖν; ἐγὼ δὲ τούτῳ ἂν δίκαιον λόγον ἀντείποιμι, ὅτι οὐ καλῶς λέγεις, ὦ ἄνθρωπε, εἰ οἴει δεῖν κίνδυνον ὑπολογίζεσθαι τοῦ ζῆν ἢ τεθνάναι ἄνδρα ὅτου τι καὶ σμικρὸν ὄφελός ἐστιν, ἀλλ' οὐκ ἐκεῖνο μόνον σκοπεῖν, ὅταν πράττῃ, πότερα δίκαια ἢ ἄδικα πράττει καὶ ἀνδρὸς ἀγαθοῦ ἔργα ἢ κακοῦ.
C φαῦλοι γὰρ ἂν τῷ γε σῷ λόγῳ εἶεν τῶν ἡμιθέων ὅσοι ἐν Τροίᾳ τετελευτήκασιν οἵ τε ἄλλοι καὶ ὁ τῆς Θέτιδος υἱός, ὃς τοσοῦτον τοῦ κινδύνου κατεφρόνησε παρὰ τὸ αἰσχρόν τι ὑπομεῖναι, ὥστε ἐπειδὴ εἶπεν ἡ μήτηρ αὐτῷ προθυμουμένῳ Ἕκτορα ἀποκτεῖναι, θεὸς οὖσα, οὑτωσί πως ὡς ἐγὼ οἶμαι· ὦ παῖ, εἰ τιμωρήσεις Πατρόκλῳ τῷ ἑταίρῳ τὸν φόνον καὶ Ἕκτορα ἀποκτενεῖς, αὐτὸς ἀποθανεῖ· αὐτίκα γάρ τοι, φησί, μεθ'

Ἕκτορα πότμος ἑτοῖμος· ὁ δὲ ταῦτα ἀκούσας τοῦ μὲν
θανάτου καὶ τοῦ κινδύνου ὠλιγώρησε, πολὺ δὲ μᾶλλον
δείσας τὸ ζῆν κακὸς ὢν καὶ τοῖς φίλοις μὴ τιμωρεῖν, D
αὐτίκα, φησί, τεθναίην δίκην ἐπιθεὶς τῷ ἀδικοῦντι, ἵνα
μὴ ἐνθάδε μένω καταγέλαστος παρὰ νηυσὶ κορωνίσιν
ἄχθος ἀρούρης. μὴ αὐτὸν οἴει φροντίσαι θανάτου καὶ
κινδύνου; οὕτω γὰρ ἔχει, ὦ ἄνδρες Ἀθηναῖοι, τῇ
ἀληθείᾳ· οὗ ἄν τις ἑαυτὸν τάξῃ ἡγησάμενος βέλτιστον
εἶναι ἢ ὑπ' ἄρχοντος ταχθῇ, ἐνταῦθα δεῖ ὡς ἐμοὶ
δοκεῖ μένοντα κινδυνεύειν μηδὲν ὑπολογιζόμενον μήτε
θάνατον μήτε ἄλλο μηδὲν πρὸ τοῦ αἰσχροῦ.

XVII. Ἐγὼ οὖν δεινὰ ἂν εἴην εἰργασμένος, ὦ
ἄνδρες Ἀθηναῖοι, εἰ, ὅτε μέν με οἱ ἄρχοντες ἔταττον, E
οὓς ὑμεῖς εἵλεσθε ἄρχειν μου, καὶ ἐν Ποτιδαίᾳ καὶ ἐν
Ἀμφιπόλει καὶ ἐπὶ Δηλίῳ, τότε μὲν οὗ ἐκεῖνοι ἔταττον
ἔμενον ὥσπερ καὶ ἄλλος τις καὶ ἐκινδύνευον ἀποθανεῖν,
τοῦ δὲ θεοῦ τάττοντος, ὡς ἐγὼ ᾠήθην τε καὶ ὑπέλαβον,
φιλοσοφοῦντά με δεῖν ζῆν καὶ ἐξετάζοντα ἐμαυτὸν καὶ
τοὺς ἄλλους, ἐνταῦθα δὲ φοβηθεὶς ἢ θάνατον ἢ ἄλλο
ὁτιοῦν πρᾶγμα λίποιμι τὴν τάξιν. δεινόν τἂν εἴη, καὶ 29
ὡς ἀληθῶς τότ' ἄν με δικαίως εἰσάγοι τις εἰς δικαστήριον, ὅτι οὐ νομίζω θεοὺς εἶναι ἀπειθῶν τῇ μαντείᾳ καὶ
δεδιὼς θάνατον καὶ οἰόμενος σοφὸς εἶναι οὐκ ὤν. τὸ
γάρ τοι θάνατον δεδιέναι, ὦ ἄνδρες, οὐδὲν ἄλλο ἐστὶν
ἢ δοκεῖν σοφὸν εἶναι μὴ ὄντα· δοκεῖν γὰρ εἰδέναι ἐστὶν
ἃ οὐκ οἶδεν. οἶδε μὲν γὰρ οὐδεὶς τὸν θάνατον οὐδ' εἰ
τυγχάνει τῷ ἀνθρώπῳ πάντων μέγιστον ὂν τῶν ἀγαθῶν, δεδίασι δ' ὡς εὖ εἰδότες ὅτι μέγιστον τῶν κακῶν

B ἐστι. καὶ τοῦτο πῶς οὐκ ἀμαθία ἐστὶν αὕτη ἡ ἐπονείδιστος ἡ τοῦ οἴεσθαι εἰδέναι ἃ οὐκ οἶδεν; ἐγὼ δ', ὦ ἄνδρες, τούτῳ καὶ ἐνταῦθα ἴσως διαφέρω τῶν πολλῶν ἀνθρώπων, καὶ εἰ δή τῳ σοφώτερός του φαίην εἶναι, τούτῳ ἄν, ὅτι οὐκ εἰδὼς ἱκανῶς περὶ τῶν ἐν Ἅιδου οὕτω καὶ οἴομαι οὐκ εἰδέναι· τὸ δὲ ἀδικεῖν καὶ ἀπειθεῖν τῷ βελτίονι, καὶ θεῷ καὶ ἀνθρώπῳ, ὅτι κακὸν καὶ αἰσχρόν ἐστιν οἶδα. πρὸ οὖν τῶν κακῶν ὧν οἶδα ὅτι κακά ἐστιν, ἃ μὴ οἶδα εἰ ἀγαθὰ ὄντα τυγχάνει οὐδέ-
C ποτε φοβήσομαι οὐδὲ φεύξομαι· ὥστε οὐδ' εἴ με νῦν ὑμεῖς ἀφίετε Ἀνύτῳ ἀπιστήσαντες, ὃς ἔφη ἢ τὴν ἀρχὴν οὐ δεῖν ἐμὲ δεῦρο εἰσελθεῖν ἤ, ἐπειδὴ εἰσῆλθον, οὐχ οἷόν τε εἶναι τὸ μὴ ἀποκτεῖναί με, λέγων πρὸς ὑμᾶς ὡς, εἰ διαφευξοίμην, ἤδη ἂν ὑμῶν οἱ υἱεῖς ἐπιτηδεύοντες ἃ Σωκράτης διδάσκει πάντες παντάπασι διαφθαρήσονται — εἴ μοι πρὸς ταῦτα εἴποιτε· ὦ Σώκρατες, νῦν μὲν Ἀνύτῳ οὐ πεισόμεθα, ἀλλ' ἀφίεμέν σε, ἐπὶ τούτῳ μέντοι ἐφ' ᾧτε μηκέτι ἐν ταύτῃ τῇ ζητήσει διατρίβειν μηδὲ φιλοσοφεῖν· ἐὰν δὲ ἁλῷς ἔτι
D τοῦτο πράττων, ἀποθανεῖ· εἰ οὖν με, ὅπερ εἶπον, ἐπὶ τούτοις ἀφίοιτε, εἴποιμ' ἂν ὑμῖν ὅτι ἐγὼ ὑμᾶς, ἄνδρες Ἀθηναῖοι, ἀσπάζομαι μὲν καὶ φιλῶ, πείσομαι δὲ μᾶλλον τῷ θεῷ ἢ ὑμῖν, καὶ ἕωσπερ ἂν ἐμπνέω καὶ οἷός τε ὦ, οὐ μὴ παύσωμαι φιλοσοφῶν καὶ ὑμῖν παρακελευόμενός τε καὶ ἐνδεικνύμενος ὅτῳ ἂν ἀεὶ ἐντυγχάνω ὑμῶν, λέγων οἷάπερ εἴωθα, ὅτι ὦ ἄριστε ἀνδρῶν, Ἀθηναῖος ὤν, πόλεως τῆς μεγίστης καὶ εὐδοκιμωτάτης εἰς σοφίαν καὶ ἰσχύν, χρημάτων μὲν οὐκ αἰσχύνει ἐπιμελούμενος

ὅπως σοι ἔσται ὡς πλεῖστα καὶ δόξης καὶ τιμῆς, φρονή- E
σεως δὲ καὶ ἀληθείας καὶ τῆς ψυχῆς ὅπως ὡς βελτίστη
ἔσται οὐκ ἐπιμελεῖ οὐδὲ φροντίζεις; καὶ ἐάν τις ὑμῶν
ἀμφισβητῇ καὶ φῇ ἐπιμελεῖσθαι, οὐκ εὐθὺς ἀφήσω
αὐτὸν οὐδ᾽ ἄπειμι, ἀλλ᾽ ἐρήσομαι αὐτὸν καὶ ἐξετάσω
καὶ ἐλέγξω, καὶ ἐάν μοι μὴ δοκῇ κεκτῆσθαι ἀρετήν,
φάναι δέ, ὀνειδιῶ ὅτι τὰ πλείστου ἄξια περὶ ἐλαχίστου
ποιεῖται, τὰ δὲ φαυλότερα περὶ πλείονος. ταῦτα καὶ 30
νεωτέρῳ καὶ πρεσβυτέρῳ, ὅτῳ ἂν ἐντυγχάνω, ποιήσω,
καὶ ξένῳ καὶ ἀστῷ, μᾶλλον δὲ τοῖς ἀστοῖς, ὅσῳ μου
ἐγγυτέρω ἐστὲ γένει. ταῦτα γὰρ κελεύει ὁ θεός, εὖ
ἴστε, καὶ ἐγὼ οἴομαι οὐδέν πω ὑμῖν μεῖζον ἀγαθὸν
γενέσθαι ἐν τῇ πόλει ἢ τὴν ἐμὴν τῷ θεῷ ὑπηρεσίαν.
οὐδὲν γὰρ ἄλλο πράττων ἐγὼ περιέρχομαι ἢ πείθων
ὑμῶν καὶ νεωτέρους καὶ πρεσβυτέρους μήτε σωμάτων B
ἐπιμελεῖσθαι μήτε χρημάτων πρότερον μηδὲ οὕτω
σφόδρα ὡς τῆς ψυχῆς ὅπως ὡς ἀρίστη ἔσται, λέγων·
οὐκ ἐκ χρημάτων ἀρετὴ γίγνεται, ἀλλ᾽ ἐξ ἀρετῆς χρή-
ματα καὶ τὰ ἄλλα ἀγαθὰ τοῖς ἀνθρώποις ἅπαντα καὶ
ἰδίᾳ καὶ δημοσίᾳ. εἰ μὲν οὖν ταῦτα λέγων διαφθείρω
τοὺς νέους, ταῦτ᾽ ἂν εἴη βλαβερά· εἰ δέ τίς μέ φησιν
ἄλλα λέγειν ἢ ταῦτα, οὐδὲν λέγει. πρὸς ταῦτα, φαίην
ἄν, ὦ Ἀθηναῖοι, ἢ πείθεσθε Ἀνύτῳ ἢ μή, καὶ ἢ ἀφίετε
ἢ μὴ ἀφίετε, ὡς ἐμοῦ οὐκ ἂν ποιήσοντος ἄλλα, οὐδ᾽ εἰ
μέλλω πολλάκις τεθνάναι. C

XVIII. Μὴ θορυβεῖτε, ἄνδρες Ἀθηναῖοι, ἀλλὰ ἐμμείνατέ μοι οἷς ἐδεήθην ὑμῶν, μὴ θορυβεῖν ἐφ᾽ οἷς ἂν λέγω, ἀλλ᾽ ἀκούειν· καὶ γάρ, ὡς ἐγὼ οἶμαι, ὀνήσεσθε

ἀκούοντες. μέλλω γὰρ οὖν ἄττα ὑμῖν ἐρεῖν καὶ ἄλλα,
ἐφ' οἷς ἴσως βοήσεσθε· ἀλλὰ μηδαμῶς ποιεῖτε τοῦτο.
εὖ γὰρ ἴστε, ἐὰν ἐμὲ ἀποκτείνητε τοιοῦτον ὄντα οἷον
ἐγὼ λέγω, οὐκ ἐμὲ μείζω βλάψετε ἢ ὑμᾶς αὐτούς·
ἐμὲ μὲν γὰρ οὐδὲν ἂν βλάψειεν οὔτε Μέλητος οὔτε
Ἄνυτος· οὐδὲ γὰρ ἂν δύναιντο· οὐ γὰρ οἴομαι θεμιτὸν
D εἶναι ἀμείνονι ἀνδρὶ ὑπὸ χείρονος βλάπτεσθαι. ἀποκ-
τείνειε μεντἂν ἴσως ἢ ἐξελάσειεν ἢ ἀτιμώσειεν· ἀλλὰ
ταῦτα οὗτος μὲν ἴσως οἴεται καὶ ἄλλος τίς που μεγάλα
κακά, ἐγὼ δ' οὐκ οἴομαι, ἀλλὰ πολὺ μᾶλλον ποιεῖν ἃ
οὗτος νυνὶ ποιεῖ, ἄνδρα ἀδίκως ἐπιχειρεῖν ἀποκτιννύναι.
νῦν οὖν, ὦ ἄνδρες Ἀθηναῖοι, πολλοῦ δέω ἐγὼ ὑπὲρ
ἐμαυτοῦ ἀπολογεῖσθαι, ὥς τις ἂν οἴοιτο, ἀλλ' ὑπὲρ
ὑμῶν, μή τι ἐξαμάρτητε περὶ τὴν τοῦ θεοῦ δόσιν ὑμῖν
E ἐμοῦ καταψηφισάμενοι. ἐὰν γὰρ ἐμὲ ἀποκτείνητε, οὐ
ῥᾳδίως ἄλλον τοιοῦτον εὑρήσετε, ἀτεχνῶς, εἰ καὶ γε-
λοιότερον εἰπεῖν, προσκείμενον τῇ πόλει [ὑπὸ τοῦ θεοῦ],
ὥσπερ ἵππῳ μεγάλῳ μὲν καὶ γενναίῳ, ὑπὸ μεγέθους δὲ
νωθεστέρῳ καὶ δεομένῳ ἐγείρεσθαι ὑπὸ μύωπός τινος·
οἷον δή μοι δοκεῖ ὁ θεὸς ἐμὲ τῇ πόλει προστεθεικέναι
τοιοῦτόν τινα, ὃς ὑμᾶς ἐγείρων καὶ πείθων καὶ ὀνει-
31 δίζων ἕνα ἕκαστον οὐδὲν παύομαι τὴν ἡμέραν ὅλην
πανταχοῦ προσκαθίζων. τοιοῦτος οὖν ἄλλος οὐ ῥᾳδίως
ὑμῖν γενήσεται, ὦ ἄνδρες, ἀλλ' ἐὰν ἐμοὶ πείθησθε,
φείσεσθέ μου· ὑμεῖς δ' ἴσως τάχ' ἂν ἀχθόμενοι, ὥσπερ
οἱ νυστάζοντες ἐγειρόμενοι, κρούσαντες ἄν με, πειθό-
μενοι Ἀνύτῳ, ῥᾳδίως ἂν ἀποκτείναιτε, εἶτα τὸν λοιπὸν
βίον καθεύδοντες διατελοῖτε ἄν, εἰ μή τινα ἄλλον ὁ

θεὸς ὑμῖν ἐπιπέμψειεν κηδόμενος ὑμῶν. ὅτι δ' ἐγὼ
τυγχάνω ὢν τοιοῦτος, οἷος ὑπὸ τοῦ θεοῦ τῇ πόλει
δεδόσθαι, ἐνθένδε ἂν κατανοήσαιτε· οὐ γὰρ ἀνθρωπίνῳ B
ἔοικε τὸ ἐμὲ τῶν μὲν ἐμαυτοῦ ἁπάντων ἠμεληκέναι καὶ
ἀνέχεσθαι τῶν οἰκείων ἀμελουμένων τοσαῦτα ἤδη ἔτη,
τὸ δὲ ὑμέτερον πράττειν ἀεί, ἰδίᾳ ἑκάστῳ προσιόντα
ὥσπερ πατέρα ἢ ἀδελφὸν πρεσβύτερον, πείθοντα ἐπι-
μελεῖσθαι ἀρετῆς. καὶ εἰ μέντοι τι ἀπὸ τούτων ἀπέ-
λαυον καὶ μισθὸν λαμβάνων ταῦτα παρεκελευόμην,
εἶχον ἄν τινα λόγον· νῦν δὲ ὁρᾶτε δὴ καὶ αὐτοί, ὅτι
οἱ κατήγοροι τἆλλα πάντα ἀναισχύντως οὕτω κατη-
γοροῦντες τοῦτό γε οὐχ οἷοί τε ἐγένοντο ἀπαναισχυντῆ-
σαι, παρασχόμενοι μάρτυρα, ὥς ἐγώ ποτέ τινα ἢ C
ἐπραξάμην μισθὸν ἢ ᾔτησα. ἱκανὸν γάρ, οἶμαι, ἐγὼ
παρέχομαι τὸν μάρτυρα, ὡς ἀληθῆ λέγω, τὴν πενίαν.

XIX. Ἴσως ἂν οὖν δόξειεν ἄτοπον εἶναι ὅτι δὴ
ἐγὼ ἰδίᾳ μὲν ταῦτα ξυμβουλεύω περιιὼν καὶ πολυ-
πραγμονῶ, δημοσίᾳ δὲ οὐ τολμῶ ἀναβαίνων εἰς τὸ
πλῆθος τὸ ὑμέτερον ξυμβουλεύειν τῇ πόλει. τούτου
δὲ αἴτιόν ἐστιν ὃ ὑμεῖς ἐμοῦ πολλάκις ἀκηκόατε πολ-
λαχοῦ λέγοντος, ὅτι μοι θεῖόν τι καὶ δαιμόνιον γίγνεται, D
ὃ δὴ καὶ ἐν τῇ γραφῇ ἐπικωμῳδῶν Μέλητος ἐγρά-
ψατο· ἐμοὶ δὲ τοῦτό ἐστιν ἐκ παιδὸς ἀρξάμενον φωνή
τις γιγνομένη, ἣ ὅταν γένηται ἀεὶ ἀποτρέπει με τοῦτο
ὃ ἂν μέλλω πράττειν, προτρέπει δὲ οὔποτε· τοῦτό
ἐστιν ὅ μοι ἐναντιοῦται τὰ πολιτικὰ πράττειν. καὶ
παγκάλως γέ μοι δοκεῖ ἐναντιοῦσθαι· εὖ γὰρ ἴστε, ὦ
ἄνδρες Ἀθηναῖοι, εἰ ἐγὼ πάλαι ἐπεχείρησα πράττειν

τὰ πολιτικὰ πράγματα, πάλαι ἂν ἀπολώλη καὶ οὔτ'
E ἂν ὑμᾶς ὠφελήκη οὐδὲν οὔτ' ἂν ἐμαυτόν. καί μοι μὴ
ἄχθεσθε λέγοντι τἀληθῆ· οὐ γάρ ἐστιν ὅστις ἀνθρώ-
πων σωθήσεται οὔτε ὑμῖν οὔτε ἄλλῳ πλήθει οὐδενὶ
γνησίως ἐναντιούμενος καὶ διακωλύων πολλὰ ἄδικα καὶ
παράνομα ἐν τῇ πόλει γίγνεσθαι, ἀλλ' ἀναγκαῖόν ἐστι
32 τὸν τῷ ὄντι μαχούμενον ὑπὲρ τοῦ δικαίου, καὶ εἰ
μέλλει ὀλίγον χρόνον σωθήσεσθαι, ἰδιωτεύειν, ἀλλὰ μὴ
δημοσιεύειν.

XX. Μεγάλα δ' ἔγωγε ὑμῖν τεκμήρια παρέξομαι
τούτων, οὐ λόγους, ἀλλ' ὃ ὑμεῖς τιμᾶτε, ἔργα. ἀκού-
σατε δή μου τὰ ἐμοὶ ξυμβεβηκότα, ἵνα εἰδῆτε ὅτι οὐδ'
ἂν ἑνὶ ὑπεικάθοιμι παρὰ τὸ δίκαιον δείσας θάνατον, μὴ
ὑπείκων δὲ ἅμα καὶ ἅμα ἂν ἀπολοίμην. ἐρῶ δὲ ὑμῖν
φορτικὰ μὲν καὶ δικανικά, ἀληθῆ δέ. ἐγὼ γάρ, ὦ
B Ἀθηναῖοι, ἄλλην μὲν ἀρχὴν οὐδεμίαν πώποτε ἦρξα ἐν
τῇ πόλει, ἐβούλευσα δέ· καὶ ἔτυχεν ἡμῶν ἡ φυλὴ
Ἀντιοχὶς πρυτανεύουσα, ὅτε ὑμεῖς τοὺς δέκα στρατη-
γοὺς τοὺς οὐκ ἀνελομένους τοὺς ἐκ τῆς ναυμαχίας
ἐβούλεσθε ἀθρόους κρίνειν, παρανόμως, ὡς ἐν τῷ
ὑστέρῳ χρόνῳ πᾶσιν ὑμῖν ἔδοξε. τότ' ἐγὼ μόνος τῶν
πρυτάνεων ἠναντιώθην μηδὲν ποιεῖν παρὰ τοὺς νό-
μους [καὶ ἐναντία ἐψηφισάμην], καὶ ἑτοίμων ὄντων
ἐνδεικνύναι με καὶ ἀπάγειν τῶν ῥητόρων καὶ ὑμῶν
C κελευόντων καὶ βοώντων, μετὰ τοῦ νόμου καὶ τοῦ
δικαίου ᾤμην μᾶλλόν με δεῖν διακινδυνεύειν ἢ μεθ'
ὑμῶν γενέσθαι μὴ δίκαια βουλευομένων φοβηθέντα
δεσμὸν ἢ θάνατον. καὶ ταῦτα μὲν ἦν ἔτι δημοκρα-

τουμένης τῆς πόλεως· ἐπειδὴ δὲ ὀλιγαρχία ἐγένετο, οἱ τριάκοντα αὖ μεταπεμψάμενοί με πέμπτον αὐτὸν εἰς τὴν θόλον προσέταξαν ἀγαγεῖν ἐκ Σαλαμῖνος Λέοντα τὸν Σαλαμίνιον ἵνα ἀποθάνοι· οἷα δὴ καὶ ἄλλοις ἐκεῖνοι πολλοῖς πολλὰ προσέταττον βουλόμενοι ὡς πλείστους ἀναπλῆσαι αἰτιῶν· τότε μέντοι ἐγὼ οὐ
λόγῳ ἀλλ' ἔργῳ αὖ ἐνεδειξάμην, ὅτι ἐμοὶ θανάτου μὲν D
μέλει, εἰ μὴ ἀγροικότερον ἦν εἰπεῖν, οὐδ' ὁτιοῦν, τοῦ δὲ μηδὲν ἄδικον μηδ' ἀνόσιον ἐργάζεσθαι, τούτου δὲ τὸ πᾶν μέλει. ἐμὲ γὰρ ἐκείνη ἡ ἀρχὴ οὐκ ἐξέπληξεν οὕτως ἰσχυρὰ οὖσα ὥστε ἄδικόν τι ἐργάσασθαι, ἀλλ' ἐπειδὴ ἐκ τῆς θόλου ἐξήλθομεν, οἱ μὲν τέτταρες ᾤχοντο εἰς Σαλαμῖνα καὶ ἤγαγον Λέοντα, ἐγὼ δὲ ᾠχόμην ἀπιὼν οἴκαδε. καὶ ἴσως ἂν διὰ ταῦτ' ἀπέθανον, εἰ μὴ ἡ ἀρχὴ διὰ ταχέων κατελύθη· καὶ τούτων ὑμῖν ἔσονται πολλοὶ μάρτυρες.

XXI. Ἆρ' οὖν ἄν με οἴεσθε τοσάδε ἔτη διαγενέ- E
σθαι, εἰ ἔπραττον τὰ δημόσια καὶ πράττων ἀξίως ἀνδρὸς ἀγαθοῦ ἐβοήθουν τοῖς δικαίοις καὶ ὥσπερ χρὴ τοῦτο περὶ πλείστου ἐποιούμην; πολλοῦ γε δεῖ, ὦ ἄνδρες
Ἀθηναῖοι· οὐδὲ γὰρ ἂν ἄλλος ἀνθρώπων οὐδείς. ἀλλ' 33
ἐγὼ διὰ παντὸς τοῦ βίου δημοσίᾳ τε, εἴ πού τι ἔπραξα, τοιοῦτος φανοῦμαι, καὶ ἰδίᾳ ὁ αὐτὸς οὗτος, οὐδενὶ πώποτε ξυγχωρήσας οὐδὲν παρὰ τὸ δίκαιον οὔτε ἄλλῳ οὔτε τούτων οὐδενί, οὓς οἱ διαβάλλοντες ἐμέ φασιν ἐμοὺς μαθητὰς εἶναι. ἐγὼ δὲ διδάσκαλος μὲν οὐδενὸς πώποτ' ἐγενόμην· εἰ δέ τίς μου λέγοντος καὶ τὰ ἐμαυτοῦ πράττοντος ἐπιθυμεῖ ἀκούειν, εἴτε νεώτερος εἴτε

πρεσβύτερος, οὐδενὶ πώποτε ἐφθόνησα, οὐδὲ χρήματα
μὲν λαμβάνων διαλέγομαι, μὴ λαμβάνων δὲ οὔ, ἀλλ'
ὁμοίως καὶ πλουσίῳ καὶ πένητι παρέχω ἐμαυτὸν ἐρω-
B τᾶν, καὶ ἐάν τις βούληται ἀποκρινόμενος ἀκούειν ὧν ἂν
λέγω. καὶ τούτων ἐγὼ εἴτε τις χρηστὸς γίγνεται εἴτε
μή, οὐκ ἂν δικαίως τὴν αἰτίαν ὑπέχοιμι, ὧν μήτε
ὑπεσχόμην μηδενὶ μηδὲν πώποτε μάθημα μήτε ἐδί-
δαξα· εἰ δέ τίς φησι παρ' ἐμοῦ πώποτέ τι μαθεῖν ἢ
ἀκοῦσαι ἰδίᾳ ὅτι μὴ καὶ ἄλλοι πάντες, εὖ ἴστε ὅτι οὐκ
ἀληθῆ λέγει.

XXII. Ἀλλὰ διὰ τί δή ποτε μετ' ἐμοῦ χαίρουσί
τινες πολὺν χρόνον διατρίβοντες; ἀκηκόατε, ὦ ἄνδρες
C Ἀθηναῖοι· πᾶσαν ὑμῖν τὴν ἀλήθειαν ἐγὼ εἶπον, ὅτι
ἀκούοντες χαίρουσιν ἐξεταζομένοις τοῖς οἰομένοις μὲν
εἶναι σοφοῖς, οὖσι δ' οὔ· ἔστι γὰρ οὐκ ἀηδές. ἐμοὶ δὲ
τοῦτο, ὡς ἐγώ φημι, προστέτακται ὑπὸ τοῦ θεοῦ πράτ-
τειν καὶ ἐκ μαντείων καὶ ἐξ ἐνυπνίων καὶ παντὶ τρόπῳ,
ᾧπερ τίς ποτε καὶ ἄλλη θεία μοῖρα ἀνθρώπῳ καὶ ὁτιοῦν
προσέταξε πράττειν. ταῦτα, ὦ Ἀθηναῖοι, καὶ ἀληθῆ
ἐστι καὶ εὐέλεγκτα. εἰ γὰρ δὴ ἔγωγε τῶν νέων τοὺς
D μὲν διαφθείρω, τοὺς δὲ διέφθαρκα, χρῆν δήπου, εἴτε
τινὲς αὐτῶν πρεσβύτεροι γενόμενοι ἔγνωσαν ὅτι νέοις
οὖσιν αὐτοῖς ἐγὼ κακὸν πώποτέ τι ξυνεβούλευσα, νυνὶ
αὐτοὺς ἀναβαίνοντας ἐμοῦ κατηγορεῖν καὶ τιμωρεῖσθαι·
εἰ δὲ μὴ αὐτοὶ ἤθελον, τῶν οἰκείων τινὰς τῶν ἐκείνων,
πατέρας καὶ ἀδελφοὺς καὶ ἄλλους τοὺς προσήκοντας,
εἴπερ ὑπ' ἐμοῦ τι κακὸν ἐπεπόνθεσαν αὐτῶν οἱ οἰκεῖοι,
νῦν μεμνῆσθαι [καὶ τιμωρεῖσθαι]. πάντως δέ πάρεισιν

αὐτῶν πολλοὶ ἐνταυθοῖ οὓς ἐγὼ ὁρῶ, πρῶτον μὲν
Κρίτων οὑτοσί, ἐμὸς ἡλικιώτης καὶ δημότης, Κριτο- E
βούλου τοῦδε πατήρ· ἔπειτα Λυσανίας ὁ Σφήττιος,
Αἰσχίνου τοῦδε πατήρ· ἔτι Ἀντιφῶν ὁ Κηφισιεὺς
οὑτοσί, Ἐπιγένους πατήρ· ἄλλοι τοίνυν οὗτοι ὧν οἱ
ἀδελφοὶ ἐν ταύτῃ τῇ διατριβῇ γεγόνασι, Νικόστρατος
Θεοζοτίδου, ἀδελφὸς Θεοδότου — καὶ ὁ μὲν Θεόδοτος
τετελεύτηκεν, ὥστε οὐκ ἂν ἐκεῖνός γε αὐτοῦ κατα-
δεηθείη — καὶ Πάραλος ὅδε ὁ Δημοδόκου οὗ ἦν Θεάγης 34
ἀδελφός· ὅδε δὲ Ἀδείμαντος ὁ Ἀρίστωνος οὗ ἀδελφὸς
οὑτοσὶ Πλάτων, καὶ Αἰαντόδωρος οὗ Ἀπολλόδωρος ὅδε
ἀδελφός. καὶ ἄλλους πολλοὺς ἐγὼ ἔχω ὑμῖν εἰπεῖν
ὧν τινα ἐχρῆν μάλιστα μὲν ἐν τῷ ἑαυτοῦ λόγῳ παρα-
σχέσθαι Μέλητον μάρτυρα· εἰ δὲ τότε ἐπελάθετο, νῦν
παρασχέσθω, ἐγὼ παραχωρῶ, καὶ λεγέτω, εἴ τι ἔχει
τοιοῦτον. ἀλλὰ τούτου πᾶν τοὐναντίον εὑρήσετε, ὦ
ἄνδρες, πάντας ἐμοὶ βοηθεῖν ἑτοίμους τῷ διαφθείροντι,
τῷ κακὰ ἐργαζομένῳ τοὺς οἰκείους αὐτῶν, ὥς φασι
Μέλητος καὶ Ἄνυτος. αὐτοὶ μὲν γὰρ οἱ διεφθαρμένοι B
τάχ' ἂν λόγον ἔχοιεν βοηθοῦντες· οἱ δὲ ἀδιάφθαρτοι,
πρεσβύτεροι ἤδη ἄνδρες, οἱ τούτων προσήκοντες, τίνα
ἄλλον ἔχουσι λόγον βοηθοῦντες ἐμοὶ ἀλλ' ἢ τὸν ὀρθόν
τε καὶ δίκαιον, ὅτι ξυνίσασι Μελήτῳ μὲν ψευδομένῳ,
ἐμοὶ δὲ ἀληθεύοντι;

XXIII. Εἶεν δή, ὦ ἄνδρες· ἃ μὲν ἐγὼ ἔχοιμ' ἂν
ἀπολογεῖσθαι, σχεδόν ἐστι ταῦτα καὶ ἄλλα ἴσως τοιαῦ-
τα. τάχα δ' ἄν τις ὑμῶν ἀγανακτήσειεν ἀναμνησθεὶς C
ἑαυτοῦ, εἰ ὁ μὲν καὶ ἐλάττω τουτουὶ τοῦ ἀγῶνος ἀγῶνα

ἀγωνιζόμενος ἐδεήθη τε καὶ ἱκέτευσε τοὺς δικαστὰς
μετὰ πολλῶν δακρύων, παιδία τε αὑτοῦ ἀναβιβασά-
μενος, ἵνα ὅτι μάλιστα ἐλεηθείη, καὶ ἄλλους τῶν οἰ-
κείων καὶ φίλων πολλούς, ἐγὼ δὲ οὐδὲν ἄρα τούτων
ποιήσω, καὶ ταῦτα κινδυνεύων ὡς ἂν δόξαιμι τὸν ἔσχα-
τον κίνδυνον. τάχ' οὖν τις ταῦτα ἐννοήσας αὐθαδέστε-
ρον ἂν πρός με σχοίη, καὶ ὀργισθεὶς αὐτοῖς τούτοις
θεῖτο ἂν μετ' ὀργῆς τὴν ψῆφον. εἰ δή τις ὑμῶν οὕτως
D ἔχει — οὐκ ἀξιῶ μὲν γὰρ ἔγωγε· εἰ δ' οὖν, ἐπιεικῆ ἄν
μοι δοκῶ πρὸς τοῦτον λέγειν λέγων ὅτι ἐμοί, ὦ ἄριστε,
εἰσὶ μέν πού τινες καὶ οἰκεῖοι· καὶ γὰρ τοῦτο αὐτὸ
τὸ τοῦ Ὁμήρου, οὐδ' ἐγὼ ἀπὸ δρυὸς οὐδ' ἀπὸ πέτρης
πέφυκα, ἀλλ' ἐξ ἀνθρώπων, ὥστε καὶ οἰκεῖοί μοί εἰσι
καὶ υἱεῖς, ὦ ἄνδρες Ἀθηναῖοι, τρεῖς, εἷς μὲν μειράκιον
ἤδη, δύο δὲ παιδία· ἀλλ' ὅμως οὐδένα αὐτῶν δεῦρο
ἀναβιβασάμενος δεήσομαι ὑμῶν ἀποψηφίσασθαι. τί
δὴ οὖν οὐδὲν τούτων ποιήσω; οὐκ αὐθαδιζόμενος, ὦ
E ἄνδρες Ἀθηναῖοι, οὐδ' ὑμᾶς ἀτιμάζων, ἀλλ' εἰ μὲν
θαρραλέως ἐγὼ ἔχω πρὸς θάνατον ἢ μή, ἄλλος λόγος,
πρὸς δ' οὖν δόξαν καὶ ἐμοὶ καὶ ὑμῖν καὶ ὅλῃ τῇ πόλει
οὔ μοι δοκεῖ καλὸν εἶναι ἐμὲ τούτων οὐδὲν ποιεῖν καὶ
τηλικόνδε ὄντα καὶ τοῦτο τοὔνομα ἔχοντα, εἴτ' οὖν
ἀληθὲς εἴτ' οὖν ψεῦδος· ἀλλ' οὖν δεδογμένον γέ ἐστι
τὸ Σωκράτη διαφέρειν τινὶ τῶν πολλῶν ἀνθρώπων.
35 εἰ οὖν ὑμῶν οἱ δοκοῦντες διαφέρειν εἴτε σοφίᾳ εἴτε
ἀνδρείᾳ εἴτε ἄλλῃ ᾑτινιοῦν ἀρετῇ τοιοῦτοι ἔσονται,
αἰσχρὸν ἂν εἴη· οἵουσπερ ἐγὼ πολλάκις ἑώρακά τινας,
ὅταν κρίνωνται, δοκοῦντας μέν τι εἶναι, θαυμάσια δὲ

ἐργαζομένους, ὡς δεινόν τι οἰομένους πείσεσθαι εἰ ἀποθανοῦνται, ὥσπερ ἀθανάτων ἐσομένων, ἂν ὑμεῖς αὐτοὺς μὴ ἀποκτείνητε· οἳ ἐμοὶ δοκοῦσιν αἰσχύνην τῇ πόλει περιάπτειν, ὥστ' ἄν τινα καὶ τῶν ξένων ὑπολαβεῖν ὅτι οἱ διαφέροντες Ἀθηναίων εἰς ἀρετήν, οὓς αὐτοὶ ἑαυτῶν ἔν τε ταῖς ἀρχαῖς καὶ ταῖς ἄλλαις B
τιμαῖς προκρίνουσιν, οὗτοι γυναικῶν οὐδὲν διαφέρουσι. ταῦτα γάρ, ὦ ἄνδρες Ἀθηναῖοι, οὔτε ὑμᾶς χρὴ ποιεῖν τοὺς δοκοῦντας καὶ ὁτιοῦν εἶναι, οὔτ' ἂν ἡμεῖς ποιῶμεν ὑμᾶς ἐπιτρέπειν, ἀλλὰ τοῦτο αὐτὸ ἐνδείκνυσθαι, ὅτι πολὺ μᾶλλον καταψηφιεῖσθε τοῦ τὰ ἐλεεινὰ ταῦτα δράματα εἰσάγοντος καὶ καταγέλαστον τὴν πόλιν ποιοῦντος ἢ τοῦ ἡσυχίαν ἄγοντος.

XXIV. Χωρὶς δὲ τῆς δόξης, ὦ ἄνδρες, οὐδὲ δίκαιόν μοι δοκεῖ εἶναι δεῖσθαι τοῦ δικαστοῦ οὐδὲ δεόμενον C
ἀποφεύγειν, ἀλλὰ διδάσκειν καὶ πείθειν. οὐ γὰρ ἐπὶ τούτῳ κάθηται ὁ δικαστής, ἐπὶ τῷ καταχαρίζεσθαι τὰ δίκαια, ἀλλ' ἐπὶ τῷ κρίνειν ταῦτα· καὶ ὀμώμοκεν οὐ χαριεῖσθαι οἷς ἂν δοκῇ αὐτῷ, ἀλλὰ δικάσειν κατὰ τοὺς νόμους. οὔκουν χρὴ οὔτε ἡμᾶς ἐθίζειν ὑμᾶς ἐπιορκεῖν οὔθ' ὑμᾶς ἐθίζεσθαι· οὐδέτεροι γὰρ ἂν ἡμῶν εὐσεβοῖεν. μὴ οὖν ἀξιοῦτέ με, ὦ ἄνδρες Ἀθηναῖοι, τοιαῦτα δεῖν πρὸς ὑμᾶς πράττειν, ἃ μήτε ἡγοῦμαι καλὰ εἶναι μήτε δίκαια μήτε ὅσια, ἄλλως τε μέντοι νὴ Δία πάντως D
καὶ ἀσεβείας φεύγοντα ὑπὸ Μελήτου τουτουΐ. σαφῶς γὰρ ἄν, εἰ πείθοιμι ὑμᾶς καὶ τῷ δεῖσθαι βιαζοίμην ὀμωμοκότας, θεοὺς ἂν διδάσκοιμι μὴ ἡγεῖσθαι ὑμᾶς εἶναι, καὶ ἀτεχνῶς ἀπολογούμενος κατηγοροίην ἂν

ἐμαυτοῦ ὡς θεοὺς οὐ νομίζω. ἀλλὰ πολλοῦ δεῖ οὕτως
ἔχειν· νομίζω τε γάρ, ὦ ἄνδρες Ἀθηναῖοι, ὡς οὐδεὶς
τῶν ἐμῶν κατηγόρων, καὶ ὑμῖν ἐπιτρέπω καὶ τῷ θεῷ
κρῖναι περὶ ἐμοῦ ὅπῃ μέλλει ἐμοί τε ἄριστα εἶναι καὶ
ὑμῖν.

E XXV. Τὸ μὲν μὴ ἀγανακτεῖν, ὦ ἄνδρες Ἀθηναῖοι,
36 ἐπὶ τούτῳ τῷ γεγονότι, ὅτι μου κατεψηφίσασθε, ἄλλα
τέ μοι πολλὰ ξυμβάλλεται, καὶ οὐκ ἀνέλπιστόν μοι
γέγονε τὸ γεγονὸς τοῦτο, ἀλλὰ πολὺ μᾶλλον θαυμάζω
ἑκατέρων τῶν ψήφων τὸν γεγονότα ἀριθμόν. οὐ γὰρ
ᾠόμην ἔγωγε οὕτω παρ' ὀλίγον ἔσεσθαι, ἀλλὰ παρὰ
πολύ· νῦν δέ, ὡς ἔοικεν, εἰ τριάκοντα μόναι μετέπεσον
τῶν ψήφων, ἀποπεφεύγη ἄν. Μέλητον μὲν οὖν, ὡς
ἐμοὶ δοκῶ, καὶ νῦν ἀποπέφευγα, καὶ οὐ μόνον ἀποπέ-
φευγα, ἀλλὰ παντὶ δῆλον τοῦτό γε, ὅτι, εἰ μὴ ἀνέβη
Ἄνυτος καὶ Λύκων κατηγορήσοντες ἐμοῦ, κἂν ὦφλε
B χιλίας δραχμὰς οὐ μεταλαβὼν τὸ πέμπτον μέρος τῶν
ψήφων.

XXVI. Τιμᾶται δ' οὖν μοι ὁ ἀνὴρ θανάτου. εἶεν·
ἐγὼ δὲ δὴ τίνος ὑμῖν ἀντιτιμήσομαι, ὦ ἄνδρες Ἀθη-
ναῖοι; ἢ δῆλον ὅτι τῆς ἀξίας; τί οὖν; τί ἄξιός εἰμι
παθεῖν ἢ ἀποτῖσαι, ὅτι μαθὼν ἐν τῷ βίῳ οὐχ ἡσυχίαν
ἦγον, ἀλλ' ἀμελήσας ὧνπερ οἱ πολλοί, χρηματισμοῦ
τε καὶ οἰκονομίας καὶ στρατηγιῶν καὶ δημηγοριῶν καὶ
τῶν ἄλλων ἀρχῶν καὶ ξυνωμοσιῶν καὶ στάσεων τῶν
ἐν τῇ πόλει γιγνομένων, ἡγησάμενος ἐμαυτὸν τῷ ὄντι
C ἐπιεικέστερον εἶναι ἢ ὥστε εἰς ταῦτ' ὄντα σῴζεσθαι,

ἐνταῦθα μὲν οὐκ ᾖα, οἷ ἐλθὼν μήτε ὑμῖν μήτε ἐμαυτῷ
ἔμελλον μηδὲν ὄφελος εἶναι, ἐπὶ δὲ τὸ ἰδίᾳ ἕκαστον
ἰὼν εὐεργετεῖν τὴν μεγίστην εὐεργεσίαν, ὥς ἐγώ φημι,
ἐνταῦθα ᾖα, ἐπιχειρῶν ἕκαστον ὑμῶν πείθειν μὴ πρό-
τερον μήτε τῶν ἑαυτοῦ μηδενὸς ἐπιμελεῖσθαι, πρὶν
ἑαυτοῦ ἐπιμεληθείη ὅπως ὡς βέλτιστος καὶ φρονιμώ-
τατος ἔσοιτο, μήτε τῶν τῆς πόλεως πρὶν αὐτῆς τῆς
πόλεως, τῶν τε ἄλλων οὕτω κατὰ τὸν αὐτὸν τρόπον
ἐπιμελεῖσθαι· τί οὖν εἰμι ἄξιος παθεῖν τοιοῦτος ὤν; D
ἀγαθόν τι, ὦ ἄνδρες Ἀθηναῖοι, εἰ δεῖ γε κατὰ τὴν
ἀξίαν τῇ ἀληθείᾳ τιμᾶσθαι· καὶ ταῦτά γε ἀγαθὸν
τοιοῦτον, ὅτι ἂν πρέποι ἐμοί. τί οὖν πρέπει ἀνδρὶ
πένητι εὐεργέτῃ δεομένῳ ἄγειν σχολὴν ἐπὶ τῇ ὑμετέρᾳ
παρακελεύσει; οὐκ ἔσθ᾽ ὅτι μᾶλλον, ὦ ἄνδρες Ἀθη-
ναῖοι, πρέπει οὕτως, ὡς τὸν τοιοῦτον ἄνδρα ἐν πρυτα-
νείῳ σιτεῖσθαι, πολύ γε μᾶλλον ἢ εἴ τις ὑμῶν ἵππῳ
ἢ ξυνωρίδι ἢ ζεύγει νενίκηκεν Ὀλυμπίασιν. ὁ μὲν γὰρ
ὑμᾶς ποιεῖ εὐδαίμονας δοκεῖν εἶναι, ἐγὼ δὲ εἶναι· καὶ E
ὁ μὲν τροφῆς οὐδὲν δεῖται, ἐγὼ δὲ δέομαι. εἰ οὖν δεῖ
με κατὰ τὸ δίκαιον τῆς ἀξίας τιμᾶσθαι, τούτου τιμῶμαι, 37
ἐν πρυτανείῳ σιτήσεως.

XXVII. Ἴσως οὖν ὑμῖν καὶ ταυτὶ λέγων παρα-
πλησίως δοκῶ λέγειν ὥσπερ περὶ τοῦ οἴκτου καὶ τῆς
ἀντιβολήσεως, ἀπαυθαδιζόμενος· τὸ δὲ οὐκ ἔστιν, ὦ
Ἀθηναῖοι, τοιοῦτον, ἀλλὰ τοιόνδε μᾶλλον. πέπεισμαι
ἐγὼ ἑκὼν εἶναι μηδένα ἀδικεῖν ἀνθρώπων, ἀλλὰ ὑμᾶς
τοῦτο οὐ πείθω· ὀλίγον γὰρ χρόνον ἀλλήλοις διει-
λέγμεθα· ἐπεί, ὡς ἐγῷμαι, εἰ ἦν ὑμῖν νόμος, ὥσπερ καὶ B

ἄλλοις ἀνθρώποις, περὶ θανάτου μὴ μίαν ἡμέραν μόνον κρίνειν, ἀλλὰ πολλάς, ἐπείσθητε ἄν· νῦν δ' οὐ ῥᾴδιον ἐν χρόνῳ ὀλίγῳ μεγάλας διαβολὰς ἀπολύεσθαι. πεπεισμένος δὴ ἐγὼ μηδένα ἀδικεῖν πολλοῦ δέω ἐμαυτόν γε ἀδικήσειν καὶ κατ' ἐμαυτοῦ ἐρεῖν αὐτός, ὡς ἄξιός εἰμί του κακοῦ, καὶ τιμήσεσθαι τοιούτου τινὸς ἐμαυτῷ. τί δείσας; ἢ μὴ πάθω τοῦτο οὗ Μέλητός μοι τιμᾶται, ὅ φημι οὐκ εἰδέναι οὔτ' εἰ ἀγαθὸν οὔτ' εἰ κακόν ἐστιν; ἀντὶ τούτου δὴ ἕλωμαι ὧν εὖ οἶδ' ὅτι κακῶν ὄντων, τούτου τιμησάμενος; πότερον δεσμοῦ; καὶ τί με δεῖ
C ζῆν ἐν δεσμωτηρίῳ, δουλεύοντα τῇ ἀεὶ καθισταμένῃ ἀρχῇ, τοῖς ἕνδεκα; ἀλλὰ χρημάτων, καὶ δεδέσθαι ἕως ἂν ἐκτίσω; ἀλλὰ ταὐτόν μοί ἐστιν ὅπερ νῦν δὴ ἔλεγον· οὐ γὰρ ἔστι μοι χρήματα ὁπόθεν ἐκτίσω. ἀλλὰ δὴ φυγῆς τιμήσωμαι; ἴσως γὰρ ἄν μοι τούτου τιμήσαιτε. πολλὴ μεντἄν με φιλοψυχία ἔχοι, εἰ οὕτως ἀλόγιστός εἰμι ὥστε μὴ δύνασθαι λογίζεσθαι, ὅτι ὑμεῖς μὲν ὄντες πολῖταί μου οὐχ οἷοί τε ἐγένεσθε ἐνεγκεῖν τὰς ἐμὰς διατριβὰς καὶ τοὺς λόγους, ἀλλ'
D ὑμῖν βαρύτεραι γεγόνασι καὶ ἐπιφθονώτεραι, ὥστε ζητεῖτε αὐτῶν νυνὶ ἀπαλλαγῆναι· ἄλλοι δὲ ἄρα αὐτὰς οἴσουσι ῥᾳδίως; πολλοῦ γε δεῖ, ὦ Ἀθηναῖοι. καλὸς οὖν ἄν μοι ὁ βίος εἴη ἐξελθόντι τηλικῷδε ἀνθρώπῳ ἄλλην ἐξ ἄλλης πόλεως ἀμειβομένῳ καὶ ἐξελαυνομένῳ ζῆν. εὖ γὰρ οἶδ' ὅτι, ὅποι ἂν ἔλθω, λέγοντος ἐμοῦ ἀκροάσονται οἱ νέοι ὥσπερ ἐνθάδε. κἂν μὲν τούτους ἀπελαύνω, οὗτοι ἐμὲ αὐτοὶ ἐξελῶσι πείθοντες τοὺς πρεσβυτέρους· ἐὰν δὲ μὴ ἀπε-

λαύνω, οἱ τούτων πατέρες τε καὶ οἰκεῖοι δι' αὐτοὺς
τούτους.

XXVIII. Ἴσως οὖν ἄν τις εἴποι· σιγῶν δὲ καὶ E
ἡσυχίαν ἄγων, ὦ Σώκρατες, οὐχ οἷός τ' ἔσει ἡμῖν
ἐξελθὼν ζῆν; τουτὶ δή ἐστι πάντων χαλεπώτατον
πεῖσαί τινας ὑμῶν. ἐάν τε γὰρ λέγω ὅτι τῷ θεῷ
ἀπειθεῖν τοῦτ' ἐστὶν καὶ διὰ τοῦτο ἀδύνατον ἡσυχίαν
ἄγειν, οὐ πείσεσθέ μοι ὡς εἰρωνευομένῳ· ἐάν τ' αὖ
λέγω ὅτι καὶ τυγχάνει μέγιστον ἀγαθὸν ὂν ἀνθρώπῳ 38
τοῦτο, ἑκάστης ἡμέρας περὶ ἀρετῆς τοὺς λόγους ποι-
εῖσθαι καὶ τῶν ἄλλων περὶ ὧν ὑμεῖς ἐμοῦ ἀκούετε
διαλεγομένου καὶ ἐμαυτὸν καὶ ἄλλους ἐξετάζοντος, ὁ
δὲ ἀνεξέταστος βίος οὐ βιωτὸς ἀνθρώπῳ, ταῦτα δ'
ἔτι ἧττον πείσεσθέ μοι λέγοντι. τὰ δὲ ἔχει μὲν
οὕτως ὡς ἐγώ φημι, ὦ ἄνδρες, πείθειν δὲ οὐ ῥᾴδιον.
καὶ ἐγὼ ἅμα οὐκ εἴθισμαι ἐμαυτὸν ἀξιοῦν κακοῦ
οὐδενός. εἰ μὲν γὰρ ἦν μοι χρήματα, ἐτιμησάμην
ἂν χρημάτων ὅσα ἔμελλον ἐκτίσειν· οὐδὲν γὰρ ἂν
ἐβλάβην· νῦν δὲ οὐ γὰρ ἔστιν, εἰ μὴ ἄρα ὅσον ἂν B
ἐγὼ δυναίμην ἐκτῖσαι, τοσούτου βούλεσθέ μοι τιμῆσαι.
ἴσως δ' ἂν δυναίμην ἐκτῖσαι ὑμῖν μνᾶν ἀργυρίου·
τοσούτου οὖν τιμῶμαι. Πλάτων δὲ ὅδε, ὦ ἄνδρες
Ἀθηναῖοι, καὶ Κρίτων καὶ Κριτόβουλος καὶ Ἀπολ-
λόδωρος κελεύουσί με τριάκοντα μνῶν τιμήσασθαι,
αὐτοὶ δ' ἐγγυᾶσθαι· τιμῶμαι οὖν τοσούτου, ἐγγυηταὶ
δ' ὑμῖν ἔσονται τοῦ ἀργυρίου οὗτοι ἀξιόχρεῳ. C

XXIX. Οὐ πολλοῦ γ' ἕνεκα χρόνου, ὦ ἄνδρες
Ἀθηναῖοι, ὄνομα ἕξετε καὶ αἰτίαν ὑπὸ τῶν βουλομένων
τὴν πόλιν λοιδορεῖν, ὡς Σωκράτη ἀπεκτόνατε, ἄνδρα
σοφόν· φήσουσι γὰρ δὴ σοφὸν εἶναι, εἰ καὶ μὴ εἰμί, οἱ
βουλόμενοι ὑμῖν ὀνειδίζειν. εἰ οὖν περιεμείνατε ὀλίγον
χρόνον, ἀπὸ τοῦ αὐτομάτου ἂν ὑμῖν τοῦτο ἐγένετο·
ὁρᾶτε γὰρ δή τὴν ἡλικίαν ὅτι πόρρω ἤδη ἐστὶ τοῦ
βίου, θανάτου δὲ ἐγγύς. λέγω δὲ τοῦτο οὐ πρὸς
D πάντας ὑμᾶς, ἀλλὰ πρὸς τοὺς ἐμοῦ καταψηφισαμέ-
νους θάνατον. λέγω δὲ καὶ τόδε πρὸς τοὺς αὐτοὺς
τούτους. ἴσως με οἴεσθε, ὦ ἄνδρες, ἀπορίᾳ λόγων
ἑαλωκέναι τοιούτων, οἷς ἂν ὑμᾶς ἔπεισα, εἰ ᾤμην δεῖν
ἅπαντα ποιεῖν καὶ λέγειν ὥστε ἀποφυγεῖν τὴν δίκην.
πολλοῦ γε δεῖ. ἀλλ' ἀπορίᾳ μὲν ἑάλωκα, οὐ μέντοι
λόγων, ἀλλὰ τόλμης καὶ ἀναισχυντίας καὶ τοῦ ἐθέλειν
λέγειν πρὸς ὑμᾶς τοιαῦτα, οἷ' ἂν ὑμῖν ἥδιστα ἦν
E ἀκούειν, θρηνοῦντός τέ μου καὶ ὀδυρομένου καὶ ἄλλα
ποιοῦντος καὶ λέγοντος πολλὰ καὶ ἀνάξια ἐμοῦ, ὡς
ἐγώ φημι· οἷα δὴ καὶ εἴθισθε ὑμεῖς τῶν ἄλλων ἀκού-
ειν. ἀλλ' οὔτε τότε ᾠήθην δεῖν ἕνεκα τοῦ κινδύνου
πρᾶξαι οὐδὲν ἀνελεύθερον, οὔτε νῦν μοι μεταμέλει
οὕτως ἀπολογησαμένῳ, ἀλλὰ πολὺ μᾶλλον αἱροῦμαι
ὧδε ἀπολογησάμενος τεθνάναι ἢ ἐκείνως ζῆν· οὔτε
γὰρ ἐν δίκῃ οὔτ' ἐν πολέμῳ οὔτ' ἐμὲ οὔτ' ἄλλον
39 οὐδένα δεῖ τοῦτο μηχανᾶσθαι, ὅπως ἀποφεύξεται πᾶν
ποιῶν θάνατον. καὶ γὰρ ἐν ταῖς μάχαις πολλάκις
δῆλον γίγνεται ὅτι τό γε ἀποθανεῖν ἄν τις ἐκφύγοι καὶ
ὅπλα ἀφεὶς καὶ ἐφ' ἱκετείαν τραπόμενος τῶν διωκόντων·

καὶ ἄλλαι μηχαναὶ πολλαί εἰσιν ἐν ἑκάστοις τοῖς κινδύνοις ὥστε διαφεύγειν θάνατον, ἐάν τις τολμᾷ πᾶν ποιεῖν καὶ λέγειν. ἀλλὰ μὴ οὐ τοῦτ᾽ ᾖ χαλεπόν, ὦ ἄνδρες, θάνατον ἐκφυγεῖν, ἀλλὰ πολὺ χαλεπώτερον πονηρίαν· θᾶττον γὰρ θανάτου θεῖ. καὶ νῦν ἐγὼ μὲν B ἅτε βραδὺς ὢν καὶ πρεσβύτης ὑπὸ τοῦ βραδυτέρου ἑάλων, οἱ δ᾽ ἐμοὶ κατήγοροι ἅτε δεινοὶ καὶ ὀξεῖς ὄντες ὑπὸ τοῦ θάττονος, τῆς κακίας. καὶ νῦν ἐγὼ μὲν ἄπειμι ὑφ᾽ ὑμῶν θανάτου δίκην ὀφλών, οὗτοι δ᾽ ὑπὸ τῆς ἀληθείας ὠφληκότες μοχθηρίαν καὶ ἀδικίαν. καὶ ἐγώ τε τῷ τιμήματι ἐμμένω καὶ οὗτοι. ταῦτα μέν που ἴσως οὕτω καὶ ἔδει σχεῖν, καὶ οἶμαι αὐτὰ μετρίως ἔχειν.

XXX. Τὸ δὲ δὴ μετὰ τοῦτο ἐπιθυμῶ ὑμῖν χρησ- C μῳδῆσαι, ὦ καταψηφισάμενοί μου. καὶ γάρ εἰμι ἤδη ἐνταῦθα, ἐν ᾧ μάλιστ᾽ ἄνθρωποι χρησμῳδοῦσιν, ὅταν μέλλωσιν ἀποθανεῖσθαι. φημὶ γάρ, ἄνδρες, οἳ ἐμὲ ἀπεκτόνατε, τιμωρίαν ὑμῖν ἥξειν εὐθὺς μετὰ τὸν ἐμὸν θάνατον πολὺ χαλεπωτέραν νὴ Δία ἢ οἵαν ἐμὲ ἀπεκτόνατε· νῦν γὰρ τοῦτο εἰργάσασθε οἰόμενοι ἀπαλλάξεσθαι τοῦ διδόναι ἔλεγχον τοῦ βίου, τὸ δὲ ὑμῖν πολὺ ἐναντίον ἀποβήσεται, ὡς ἐγώ φημι. πλείους ἔσονται ὑμᾶς οἱ ἐλέγχοντες, οὓς νῦν ἐγὼ κατεῖχον, ὑμεῖς δὲ D οὐκ ᾐσθάνεσθε· καὶ χαλεπώτεροι ἔσονται ὅσῳ νεώτεροί εἰσι, καὶ ὑμεῖς μᾶλλον ἀγανακτήσετε. εἰ γὰρ οἴεσθε ἀποκτείνοντες ἀνθρώπους ἐπισχήσειν τοῦ ὀνειδίζειν τινὰ ὑμῖν ὅτι οὐκ ὀρθῶς ζῆτε, οὐκ ὀρθῶς διανοεῖσθε. οὐ γὰρ ἔσθ᾽ αὕτη ἡ ἀπαλλαγὴ οὔτε πάνυ δυνατὴ οὔτε καλή, ἀλλ' ἐκείνη καὶ καλλίστη καὶ ῥᾴστη, μὴ τοὺς ἄλλους κολούειν, ἀλλ' ἑαυτὸν παρασκευάζειν ὅπως ἔσται ὡς βέλτιστος. ταῦτα μὲν οὖν ὑμῖν τοῖς καταψηφισαμένοις μαντευσάμενος ἀπαλλάττομαι.

XXXI. Τοῖς δὲ ἀποψηφισαμένοις ἡδέως ἂν δια-
E λεχθείην ὑπὲρ τοῦ γεγονότος τουτουῒ πράγματος, ἐν ᾧ οἱ ἄρχοντες ἀσχολίαν ἄγουσι καὶ οὔπω ἔρχομαι οἶ ἐλθόντα με δεῖ τεθνάναι. ἀλλά μοι, ὦ ἄνδρες, παραμείνατε τοσοῦτον χρόνον· οὐδὲν γὰρ κωλύει διαμυθολογῆσαι πρὸς ἀλλήλους ἕως ἔξεστιν· ὑμῖν γὰρ ὡς
40 φίλοις οὖσιν ἐπιδεῖξαι ἐθέλω τὸ νυνί μοι ξυμβεβηκὸς τί ποτε νοεῖ. ἐμοὶ γάρ, ὦ ἄνδρες δικασταί—ὑμᾶς γὰρ δικαστὰς καλῶν ὀρθῶς ἂν καλοίην—θαυμάσιόν τι γέγονεν. ἡ γὰρ εἰωθυῖά μοι μαντικὴ ἡ τοῦ δαιμονίου ἐν μὲν τῷ πρόσθεν χρόνῳ παντὶ πάνυ πυκνὴ ἀεὶ ἦν καὶ πάνυ ἐπὶ σμικροῖς ἐναντιουμένη, εἴ τι μέλλοιμι μὴ ὀρθῶς πράξειν· νυνὶ δὲ ξυμβέβηκέ μοι, ἅπερ ὁρᾶτε καὶ αὐτοί, ταυτὶ ἅ γε δὴ οἰηθείη ἄν τις καὶ νομίζεται
B ἔσχατα κακῶν εἶναι, ἐμοὶ δὲ οὔτε ἐξιόντι ἕωθεν οἴκοθεν ἠναντιώθη τὸ τοῦ θεοῦ σημεῖον, οὔτε ἡνίκα ἀνέβαινον ἐνταυθοῖ ἐπὶ τὸ δικαστήριον, οὔτε ἐν τῷ λόγῳ οὐδαμοῦ μέλλοντί τι ἐρεῖν· καίτοι ἐν ἄλλοις λόγοις πολλαχοῦ δή με ἐπέσχε λέγοντα μεταξύ· νῦν δὲ οὐδαμοῦ περὶ ταύτην τὴν πρᾶξιν οὔτ' ἐν ἔργῳ οὐδενὶ οὔτ' ἐν λόγῳ ἠναντίωταί μοι. τί οὖν αἴτιον εἶναι ὑπολαμβάνω; ἐγὼ ὑμῖν ἐρῶ· κινδυνεύει γάρ μοι τὸ ξυμβεβηκὸς τοῦτο ἀγαθὸν γεγονέναι, καὶ οὐκ ἔσθ' ὅπως ἡμεῖς
C ὀρθῶς ὑπολαμβάνομεν ὅσοι οἰόμεθα κακὸν εἶναι τὸ

τεθνάναι. μέγα μοι τεκμήριον τούτου γέγονεν· οὐ γὰρ ἔσθ' ὅπως οὐκ ἠναντιώθη ἄν μοι τὸ εἰωθὸς σημεῖον, εἰ μή τι ἔμελλον ἐγὼ ἀγαθὸν πράξειν.

XXXII. Ἐννοήσωμεν δὲ καὶ τῇδε ὡς πολλὴ ἐλπίς ἐστιν ἀγαθὸν αὐτὸ εἶναι. δυοῖν γὰρ θάτερόν ἐστι τὸ τεθνάναι· ἢ γὰρ οἷον μηδὲν εἶναι μηδ' αἴσθησιν μηδεμίαν μηδενὸς ἔχειν τὸν τεθνεῶτα, ἢ κατὰ τὰ λεγόμενα μεταβολή τις τυγχάνει οὖσα καὶ μετοίκησις τῇ ψυχῇ τοῦ τόπου τοῦ ἐνθένδε εἰς ἄλλον τόπον. καὶ εἴτε D μηδεμία αἴσθησίς ἐστιν, ἀλλ' οἷον ὕπνος ἐπειδάν τις καθεύδων μηδ' ὄναρ μηδὲν ὁρᾷ, θαυμάσιον κέρδος ἂν εἴη ὁ θάνατος. ἐγὼ γὰρ ἂν οἶμαι, εἴ τινα ἐκλεξάμενον δέοι ταύτην τὴν νύκτα, ἐν ᾗ οὕτω κατέδαρθεν ὥστε μηδὲ ὄναρ ἰδεῖν, καὶ τὰς ἄλλας νύκτας τε καὶ ἡμέρας τὰς τοῦ βίου τοῦ ἑαυτοῦ ἀντιπαραθέντα ταύτῃ τῇ νυκτὶ δέοι σκεψάμενον εἰπεῖν, πόσας ἄμεινον καὶ ἥδιον ἡμέρας καὶ νύκτας ταύτης τῆς νυκτὸς βεβίωκεν ἐν τῷ ἑαυτοῦ βίῳ, οἶμαι ἂν μὴ ὅτι ἰδιώτην τινά, ἀλλὰ τὸν μέγαν βασιλέα εὐαριθμήτους ἂν εὑρεῖν αὐτὸν ταύτας E πρὸς τὰς ἄλλας ἡμέρας καὶ νύκτας. εἰ οὖν τοιοῦτον ὁ θάνατός ἐστι, κέρδος ἔγωγε λέγω· καὶ γὰρ οὐδὲν πλείων ὁ πᾶς χρόνος φαίνεται οὕτω δὴ εἶναι ἢ μία νύξ. εἰ δ' αὖ οἷον ἀποδημῆσαί ἐστιν ὁ θάνατος ἐνθένδε εἰς ἄλλον τόπον, καὶ ἀληθῆ ἐστι τὰ λεγόμενα ὡς ἄρα ἐκεῖ εἰσιν ἅπαντες οἱ τεθνεῶτες, τί μεῖζον ἀγαθὸν τούτου εἴη ἄν, ὦ ἄνδρες δικασταί; εἰ γάρ τις ἀφικόμενος εἰς Ἅιδου, ἀπαλλαγεὶς τούτων τῶν φασκόντων δικαστῶν 41 εἶναι, εὑρήσει τοὺς ἀληθῶς δικαστάς, οἵπερ καὶ λέγονται

ἐκεῖ δικάζειν, Μίνως τε καὶ Ῥαδάμανθυς καὶ Αἰακὸς καὶ Τριπτόλεμος καὶ ἄλλοι ὅσοι τῶν ἡμιθέων δίκαιοι ἐγένοντο ἐν τῷ ἑαυτῶν βίῳ, ἆρα φαύλη ἂν εἴη ἡ ἀποδημία; ἢ αὖ Ὀρφεῖ ξυγγενέσθαι καὶ Μουσαίῳ καὶ Ἡσιόδῳ καὶ Ὁμήρῳ ἐπὶ πόσῳ ἄν τις δέξαιτ' ἂν ὑμῶν; ἐγὼ μὲν γὰρ πολλάκις θέλω τεθνάναι, εἰ ταῦτ' ἐστὶν ἀληθῆ· ἐπεὶ ἔμοιγε καὶ αὐτῷ θαυμαστὴ ἂν εἴη ἡ διατριβὴ αὐ-
B τόθι, ὁπότε ἐντύχοιμι Παλαμήδει καὶ Αἴαντι τῷ Τελαμῶνος καὶ εἴ τις ἄλλος τῶν παλαιῶν διὰ κρίσιν ἄδικον τέθνηκεν. ἀντιπαραβάλλοντι τὰ ἐμαυτοῦ πάθη πρὸς τὰ ἐκείνων, ὡς ἐγὼ οἶμαι, οὐκ ἂν ἀηδὲς εἴη. καὶ δὴ τὸ μέγιστον, τοὺς ἐκεῖ ἐξετάζοντα καὶ ἐρευνῶντα ὥσπερ τοὺς ἐνταῦθα διάγειν, τίς δὴ αὐτῶν σοφός ἐστιν καὶ τίς οἴεται μέν, ἔστιν δ' οὔ. ἐπὶ πόσῳ δ' ἄν τις, ὦ ἄνδρες δικασταί, δέξαιτο ἐξετάσαι τὸν ἐπὶ Τροίαν
C ἄγοντα τὴν πολλὴν στρατιὰν ἢ Ὀδυσσέα ἢ Σίσυφον, ἢ ἄλλους μυρίους ἄν τις εἴποι καὶ ἄνδρας καὶ γυναῖκας, οἷς ἐκεῖ διαλέγεσθαι καὶ ξυνεῖναι καὶ ἐξετάζειν ἀμήχανον ἂν εἴη εὐδαιμονίας. πάντως οὐ δήπου τούτου γε ἕνεκα οἱ ἐκεῖ ἀποκτείνουσι· τά τε γὰρ ἄλλα εὐδαιμονέστεροί εἰσιν οἱ ἐκεῖ τῶν ἐνθάδε, καὶ ἤδη τὸν λοιπὸν χρόνον ἀθάνατοί εἰσιν, εἴπερ γε τὰ λεγόμενα ἀληθῆ ἐστιν.

XXXIII. Ἀλλὰ καὶ ὑμᾶς χρή, ὦ ἄνδρες δικασταί, εὐέλπιδας εἶναι πρὸς τὸν θάνατον, καὶ ἕν τι τοῦτο
D διανοεῖσθαι ἀληθές, ὅτι οὐκ ἔστιν ἀνδρὶ ἀγαθῷ κακὸν οὐδὲν οὔτε ζῶντι οὔτε τελευτήσαντι, οὐδὲ ἀμελεῖται ὑπὸ θεῶν τὰ τούτου πράγματα· οὐδὲ τὰ ἐμὰ νῦν ἀπὸ

τοῦ αὐτομάτου γέγονεν, ἀλλά μοι δῆλόν ἐστι τοῦτο,
ὅτι ἤδη τεθνάναι καὶ ἀπηλλάχθαι πραγμάτων βέλτιον
ἦν μοι. διὰ τοῦτο καὶ ἐμὲ οὐδαμοῦ ἀπέτρεψεν τὸ ση-
μεῖον, καὶ ἔγωγε τοῖς καταψηφισαμένοις μου καὶ τοῖς
κατηγόροις οὐ πάνυ χαλεπαίνω. καίτοι οὐ ταύτῃ τῇ
διανοίᾳ κατεψηφίζοντό μου καὶ κατηγόρουν, ἀλλ' οἰό-
μενοι βλάπτειν· τοῦτο αὐτοῖς ἄξιον μέμφεσθαι. το- E
σόνδε μέντοι δέομαι αὐτῶν· τοὺς υἱεῖς μου ἐπειδὰν
ἡβήσωσι τιμωρήσασθε, ὦ ἄνδρες, ταὐτὰ ταῦτα λυ-
ποῦντες ἅπερ ἐγὼ ὑμᾶς ἐλύπουν, ἐὰν ὑμῖν δοκῶσιν
ἢ χρημάτων ἢ ἄλλου του πρότερον ἐπιμελεῖσθαι ἢ
ἀρετῆς, καὶ ἐὰν δοκῶσί τι εἶναι μηδὲν ὄντες, ὀνειδίζετε
αὐτοῖς ὥσπερ ἐγὼ ὑμῖν, ὅτι οὐκ ἐπιμελοῦνται ὧν δεῖ
καὶ οἴονταί τι εἶναι ὄντες οὐδενὸς ἄξιοι. καὶ ἐὰν
ταῦτα ποιῆτε, δίκαια πεπονθὼς ἐγὼ ἔσομαι ὑφ' ὑμῶν, 42
αὐτός τε καὶ οἱ υἱεῖς. ἀλλὰ γὰρ ἤδη ὥρα ἀπιέναι,
ἐμοὶ μὲν ἀποθανουμένῳ, ὑμῖν δὲ βιωσομένοις· ὁπό-
τεροι δὲ ἡμῶν ἔρχονται ἐπὶ ἄμεινον πρᾶγμα, ἄδηλον
παντὶ πλὴν ἢ τῷ θεῷ.

ΚΡΙΤΩΝ.

ΤΑ ΤΟΥ ΔΙΑΛΟΓΟΥ ΠΡΟΣΩΠΑ.

ΣΩΚΡΑΤΗΣ, ΚΡΙΤΩΝ.

---

48 I. ΣΩ. Τί τηνικάδε ἀφῖξαι, ὦ Κρίτων; ἢ οὐ πρῲ ἔτι ἐστίν;

ΚΡ. Πάνυ μὲν οὖν.

ΣΩ. Πηνίκα μάλιστα;

ΚΡ. Ὄρθρος βαθύς.

ΣΩ. Θαυμάζω ὅπως ἠθέλησέ σοι ὁ τοῦ δεσμωτηρίου φύλαξ ὑπακοῦσαι.

ΚΡ. Ξυνήθης ἤδη μοί ἐστιν, ὦ Σώκρατες, διὰ τὸ πολλάκις δεῦρο φοιτᾶν, καί τι καὶ εὐεργέτηται ὑπ' ἐμοῦ.

ΣΩ. Ἄρτι δὲ ἥκεις ἢ πάλαι;

ΚΡ. Ἐπιεικῶς πάλαι.

B ΣΩ. Εἶτα πῶς οὐκ εὐθὺς ἐπήγειράς με, ἀλλὰ σιγῇ παρακάθησαι;

ΚΡ. Οὐ μὰ τὸν Δία, ὦ Σώκρατες, οὐδ' ἂν αὐτὸς ἤθελον ἐν τοσαύτῃ τε ἀγρυπνίᾳ καὶ λύπῃ εἶναι. ἀλλὰ καὶ σοῦ πάλαι θαυμάζω αἰσθανόμενος ὡς ἡδέως καθεύδεις· καὶ ἐπίτηδές σε οὐκ ἤγειρον, ἵνα ὡς ἥδιστα διάγης. καὶ πολλάκις μὲν δή σε καὶ πρότερον ἐν παντὶ τῷ βίῳ εὐδαιμόνισα τοῦ τρόπου, πολὺ δὲ μάλιστα ἐν τῇ νῦν παρεστώσῃ ξυμφορᾷ ὡς ῥᾳδίως αὐτὴν καὶ πρᾴως φέρεις.

ΣΩ. Καὶ γὰρ ἄν, ὦ Κρίτων, πλημμελὲς εἴη ἀγανακτεῖν τηλικοῦτον ὄντα, εἰ δεῖ ἤδη τελευτᾶν.

ΚΡ. Καὶ ἄλλοι, ὦ Σώκρατες, τηλικοῦτοι ἐν τοιαύ- C
ταις ξυμφοραῖς ἁλίσκονται, ἀλλ' οὐδὲν αὐτοὺς ἐπιλύεται ἡ ἡλικία τὸ μὴ οὐχὶ ἀγανακτεῖν τῇ παρούσῃ τύχῃ.

ΣΩ. Ἔστι ταῦτα. ἀλλὰ τί δὴ οὕτω πρῴ ἀφῖξαι;

ΚΡ. Ἀγγελίαν, ὦ Σώκρατες, φέρων χαλεπήν, οὐ σοί, ὡς ἐμοὶ φαίνεται, ἀλλ' ἐμοὶ καὶ τοῖς σοῖς ἐπιτηδείοις πᾶσιν καὶ χαλεπὴν καὶ βαρεῖαν, ἣν ἐγὼ ὡς ἐμοὶ δοκῶ ἐν τοῖς βαρύτατ' ἂν ἐνέγκαιμι.

ΣΩ. Τίνα ταύτην; ἢ τὸ πλοῖον ἀφῖκται ἐκ Δήλου,
οὗ δεῖ ἀφικομένου τεθνάναι με; D

ΚΡ. Οὔτοι δὴ ἀφῖκται, ἀλλὰ δοκεῖ μέν μοι ἥξειν τήμερον ἐξ ὧν ἀπαγγέλλουσιν ἥκοντές τινες ἀπὸ Σουνίου καὶ καταλιπόντες ἐκεῖ αὐτό. δῆλον οὖν ἐκ τούτων [τῶν ἀγγέλων] ὅτι ἥξει τήμερον, καὶ ἀνάγκη δὴ εἰς αὔριον ἔσται, ὦ Σώκρατες, τὸν βίον σε τελευτᾶν.

II. ΣΩ. Ἀλλ', ὦ Κρίτων, τύχῃ ἀγαθῇ. εἰ ταύτῃ
τοῖς θεοῖς φίλον, ταύτῃ ἔστω. οὐ μέντοι οἶμαι ἥξειν 44
αὐτὸ τήμερον.

ΚΡ. Πόθεν τοῦτο τεκμαίρει;

ΣΩ. Ἐγώ σοι ἐρῶ. τῇ γάρ που ὑστεραίᾳ δεῖ με ἀποθνήσκειν ἢ ᾗ ἂν ἔλθῃ τὸ πλοῖον.

ΚΡ. Φασί γέ τοι δὴ οἱ τούτων κύριοι.

ΣΩ. Οὐ τοίνυν τῆς ἐπιούσης ἡμέρας οἶμαι αὐτὸ ἥξειν, ἀλλὰ τῆς ἑτέρας. τεκμαίρομαι δὲ ἔκ τινος ἐνυπνίου ὃ ἑώρακα ὀλίγον πρότερον ταύτης τῆς νυκτός· καὶ κινδυνεύεις ἐν καιρῷ τινι οὐκ ἐγεῖραί με.

ΚΡ. Ἦν δὲ δὴ τί τὸ ἐνύπνιον;

ΣΩ. Ἐδόκει τίς μοι γυνὴ προσελθοῦσα καλὴ καὶ εὐειδής, λευκὰ ἱμάτια ἔχουσα, καλέσαι με καὶ εἰπεῖν· B ὦ Σώκρατες, ἤματί κεν τριτάτῳ Φθίην ἐρίβωλον ἵκοιο.

ΚΡ. Ἄτοπον τὸ ἐνύπνιον, ὦ Σώκρατες.

ΣΩ. Ἐναργὲς μὲν οὖν ὥς γέ μοι δοκεῖ, ὦ Κρίτων.

III. ΚΡ. Λίαν γε, ὡς ἔοικεν. ἀλλ' ὦ δαιμόνιε Σώκρατες, ἔτι καὶ νῦν ἐμοὶ πείθου καὶ σώθητι· ὡς ἐμοί, ἐὰν σὺ ἀποθάνῃς, οὐ μία ξυμφορά ἐστιν, ἀλλὰ χωρὶς μὲν τοῦ ἐστερῆσθαι τοιούτου ἐπιτηδείου, οἷον ἐγὼ οὐδένα μή ποτε εὑρήσω, ἔτι δὲ καὶ πολλοῖς δόξω, οἳ ἐμὲ καὶ σὲ μὴ σαφῶς ἴσασιν, ὡς οἷός τε ὢν σε σῴζειν, εἰ ἤθελον ἀναλίσκειν χρήματα, ἀμελῆσαι. καίτοι C τίς ἂν αἰσχίων εἴη ταύτης δόξα ἢ δοκεῖν χρήματα περὶ πλείονος ποιεῖσθαι ἢ φίλους; οὐ γὰρ πείσονται οἱ πολλοὶ ὡς σὺ αὐτὸς οὐκ ἠθέλησας ἀπιέναι ἐνθένδε ἡμῶν προθυμουμένων.

ΣΩ. Ἀλλὰ τί ἡμῖν, ὦ μακάριε Κρίτων, οὕτω τῆς τῶν πολλῶν δόξης μέλει; οἱ γὰρ ἐπιεικέστατοι, ὧν μᾶλλον ἄξιον φροντίζειν, ἡγήσονται αὐτὰ οὕτω πεπρᾶχθαι ὥσπερ ἂν πραχθῇ.

D ΚΡ. Ἀλλ' ὁρᾷς δὴ ὅτι ἀνάγκη, ὦ Σώκρατες, καὶ τῆς τῶν πολλῶν δόξης μέλειν. αὐτὰ δὲ δῆλα τὰ παρόντα νυνί, ὅτι οἷοί τέ εἰσιν οἱ πολλοὶ οὐ τὰ σμικρότατα τῶν κακῶν ἐξεργάζεσθαι, ἀλλὰ τὰ μέγιστα σχεδόν, ἐάν τις ἐν αὐτοῖς διαβεβλημένος ᾖ.

ΣΩ. Εἰ γὰρ ὤφελον, ὦ Κρίτων, οἷοί τε εἶναι οἱ πολλοὶ τὰ μέγιστα κακὰ ἐργάζεσθαι, ἵνα οἷοί τε ἦσαν καὶ ἀγαθὰ τὰ μέγιστα, καὶ καλῶς ἂν εἶχεν. νῦν δὲ οὐδέτερα οἷοί τε· οὔτε γὰρ φρόνιμον οὔτε ἄφρονα δυνατοὶ ποιῆσαι, ποιοῦσι δὲ τοῦτο ὅτι ἂν τύχωσιν.

IV. ΚΡ. Ταῦτα μὲν δὴ οὕτως ἐχέτω· τάδε δέ, ὦ Σώκρατες, εἰπέ μοι· ἆρά γε μὴ ἐμοῦ προμηθεῖ καὶ τῶν E ἄλλων ἐπιτηδείων, μή, ἐὰν σὺ ἐνθένδε ἐξέλθῃς, οἱ συκοφάνται ἡμῖν πράγματα παρέχωσιν ὡς σὲ ἐνθένδε ἐκκλέψασιν, καὶ ἀναγκασθῶμεν ἢ καὶ πᾶσαν τὴν οὐσίαν ἀποβαλεῖν ἢ συχνὰ χρήματα, ἢ καὶ ἄλλο τι πρὸς τούτοις παθεῖν; εἰ γάρ τι τοιοῦτον φοβεῖ, ἔασον αὐτὸ χαίρειν· ἡμεῖς γάρ που δίκαιοί ἐσμεν σώσαντές 45 σε κινδυνεύειν τοῦτον τὸν κίνδυνον καὶ ἐὰν δέῃ ἔτι τούτου μείζω. ἀλλ' ἐμοὶ πείθου καὶ μὴ ἄλλως ποίει.

ΣΩ. Καὶ ταῦτα προμηθοῦμαι, ὦ Κρίτων, καὶ ἄλλα πολλά.

ΚΡ. Μήτε τοίνυν ταῦτα φοβοῦ. καὶ γὰρ οὐδὲ πολὺ τἀργύριόν ἐστιν, ὃ θέλουσι λαβόντες τινὲς σῶσαί σε καὶ ἐξαγαγεῖν ἐνθένδε. ἔπειτα οὐχ ὁρᾷς τούτους τοὺς συκοφάντας ὡς εὐτελεῖς, καὶ οὐδὲν ἂν δέοι ἐπ' αὐτοὺς πολλοῦ ἀργυρίου; σοὶ δὲ ὑπάρχει μὲν τὰ ἐμὰ χρήματα B ὡς ἐγὼ οἶμαι ἱκανά· ἔπειτα καὶ εἴ τι ἐμοῦ κηδόμενος οὐκ οἴει δεῖν ἀναλίσκειν τἀμά, ξένοι οὗτοι ἐνθάδε ἕτοιμοι ἀναλίσκειν· εἷς δὲ καὶ κεκόμικεν ἐπ' αὐτὸ τοῦτο

ἀργύριον ἱκανόν, Σιμμίας ὁ Θηβαῖος· ἕτοιμος δὲ καὶ
Κέβης καὶ ἄλλοι πολλοὶ πάνυ. ὥστε, ὅπερ λέγω,
μήτε ταῦτα φοβούμενος ἀποκάμῃς σαυτὸν σῶσαι, μήτε
ὃ ἔλεγες ἐν τῷ δικαστηρίῳ δυσχερές σοι γενέσθω, ὅτι
οὐκ ἂν ἔχοις ἐξελθὼν ὅτι χρῷο σαυτῷ· πολλαχοῦ μὲν
γὰρ καὶ ἄλλοσε ὅποι ἂν ἀφίκῃ ἀγαπήσουσί σε· ἐὰν δὲ
C βούλῃ εἰς Θετταλίαν ἰέναι, εἰσὶν ἐμοὶ ἐκεῖ ξένοι, οἵ σε
περὶ πολλοῦ ποιήσονται καὶ ἀσφάλειάν σοι παρέξονται
ὥστε σε μηδένα λυπεῖν τῶν κατὰ Θετταλίαν.

V. Ἔτι δέ, ὦ Σώκρατες, οὐδὲ δίκαιόν μοι δοκεῖς
ἐπιχειρεῖν πρᾶγμα, σαυτὸν προδοῦναι, ἐξὸν σωθῆναι·
καὶ τοιαῦτα σπεύδεις περὶ σαυτὸν γενέσθαι, ἅπερ ἂν
καὶ οἱ ἐχθροί σου σπεύσαιέν τε καὶ ἔσπευσαν σὲ δια-
φθεῖραι βουλόμενοι. πρὸς δὲ τούτοις καὶ τοὺς υἱεῖς
τοὺς σαυτοῦ ἔμοιγε δοκεῖς προδιδόναι, οὕς σοι ἐξὸν καὶ
D ἐκθρέψαι καὶ ἐκπαιδεῦσαι οἰχήσει καταλιπών, καὶ τὸ
σὸν μέρος, ὅτι ἂν τύχωσι, τοῦτο πράξουσιν· τεύξονται
δὲ ὡς τὸ εἰκός τοιούτων οἷάπερ εἴωθε γίγνεσθαι ἐν ταῖς
ὀρφανίαις περὶ τοὺς ὀρφανούς. ἢ γὰρ οὐ χρὴ ποιεῖσθαι
παῖδας, ἢ ξυνδιαταλαιπωρεῖν καὶ τρέφοντα καὶ παι-
δεύοντα· σὺ δέ μοι δοκεῖς τὰ ῥᾳθυμότατα αἱρεῖσθαι·
χρὴ δέ, ἅπερ ἂν ἀνὴρ ἀγαθὸς καὶ ἀνδρεῖος ἕλοιτο,
ταῦτα αἱρεῖσθαι, φάσκοντά γε δὴ ἀρετῆς διὰ παντὸς
τοῦ βίου ἐπιμελεῖσθαι· ὡς ἔγωγε καὶ ὑπὲρ σοῦ καὶ
E ὑπὲρ ἡμῶν τῶν σῶν ἐπιτηδείων αἰσχύνομαι, μὴ δόξῃ
ἅπαν τὸ πρᾶγμα τὸ περὶ σὲ ἀνανδρίᾳ τινὶ τῇ ἡμετέρᾳ
πεπρᾶχθαι, καὶ ἡ εἴσοδος τῆς δίκης εἰς τὸ δικαστήριον
ὡς εἰσῆλθεν ἐξὸν μὴ εἰσελθεῖν, καὶ αὐτὸς ὁ ἀγὼν τῆς

δίκης ὡς ἐγένετο, καὶ τὸ τελευταῖον δὴ τουτὶ ὥσπερ κατάγελως τῆς πράξεως κακίᾳ τινὶ καὶ ἀνανδρίᾳ τῇ ἡμετέρᾳ διαπεφευγέναι ἡμᾶς δοκεῖν, οἵτινές σε οὐχὶ ἐσώσαμεν οὐδὲ σὺ σαυτόν, οἷόν τε ὂν καὶ δυνατόν, εἴ 46
τι καὶ μικρὸν ἡμῶν ὄφελος ἦν. ταῦτα οὖν, ὦ Σώκρατες, ὅρα μὴ ἅμα τῷ κακῷ καὶ αἰσχρὰ ᾖ σοί τε καὶ ἡμῖν. ἀλλὰ βουλεύου, μᾶλλον δὲ οὐδὲ βουλεύεσθαι ἔτι ὥρα, ἀλλὰ βεβουλεῦσθαι. μία δὲ βουλή· τῆς γὰρ ἐπιούσης νυκτὸς πάντα ταῦτα δεῖ πεπρᾶχθαι. εἰ δέ τι περιμενοῦμεν, ἀδύνατον καὶ οὐκέτι οἷόν τε. ἀλλὰ παντὶ τρόπῳ, ὦ Σώκρατες, πείθου μοι καὶ μηδαμῶς ἄλλως ποίει.

VI. ΣΩ. Ὦ φίλε Κρίτων, ἡ προθυμία σου πολλοῦ ἀξία, εἰ μετά τινος ὀρθότητος εἴη· εἰ δὲ μή, ὅσῳ B
μείζων, τοσούτῳ χαλεπωτέρα. σκοπεῖσθαι οὖν χρὴ ἡμᾶς εἴτε ταῦτα πρακτέον εἴτε μή· ὡς ἐγὼ οὐ μόνον νῦν ἀλλὰ καὶ ἀεὶ τοιοῦτος οἷος τῶν ἐμῶν μηδενὶ ἄλλῳ πείθεσθαι ἢ τῷ λόγῳ, ὃς ἄν μοι λογιζομένῳ βέλτιστος φαίνηται. τοὺς δὲ λόγους οὓς ἐν τῷ ἔμπροσθεν ἔλεγον οὐ δύναμαι νῦν ἐκβαλεῖν, ἐπειδή μοι ἥδε ἡ τύχη γέγονεν, ἀλλὰ σχεδόν τι ὅμοιοι φαίνονταί μοι καὶ τοὺς αὐτοὺς πρεσβεύω καὶ τιμῶ οὕσπερ καὶ πρότερον· ὧν C
ἐὰν μὴ βελτίω ἔχωμεν λέγειν ἐν τῷ παρόντι, εὖ ἴσθι ὅτι οὐ μή σοι ξυγχωρήσω, οὐδ' ἂν πλείω τῶν νῦν παρόντων ἡ τῶν πολλῶν δύναμις ὥσπερ παῖδας ἡμᾶς μορμολύττηται, δεσμοὺς καὶ θανάτους ἐπιπέμπουσα καὶ χρημάτων ἀφαιρέσεις. πῶς οὖν ἂν μετριώτατα σκοποίμεθα αὐτά; εἰ πρῶτον μὲν τοῦτον τὸν λόγον

ἀναλάβοιμεν, ὃν σὺ λέγεις περὶ τῶν δοξῶν, πότερον
καλῶς ἐλέγετο ἑκάστοτε ἢ οὔ, ὅτι ταῖς μὲν δεῖ τῶν
D δοξῶν προσέχειν τὸν νοῦν, ταῖς δὲ οὔ· ἢ πρὶν μὲν ἐμὲ
δεῖν ἀποθνήσκειν καλῶς ἐλέγετο, νῦν δὲ κατάδηλος ἄρα
ἐγένετο ὅτι ἄλλως ἕνεκα λόγου ἐλέγετο, ἦν δὲ παιδιὰ
καὶ φλυαρία ὡς ἀληθῶς; ἐπιθυμῶ δ' ἔγωγ' ἐπισκέ-
ψασθαι, ὦ Κρίτων, κοινῇ μετὰ σοῦ, εἴ τί μοι ἀλλοιό-
τερος φανεῖται ἐπειδὴ ὧδε ἔχω ἢ ὁ αὐτός, καὶ ἐάσομεν
χαίρειν ἢ πεισόμεθα αὐτῷ. ἐλέγετο δέ πως ὡς ἐγῷμαι
ἑκάστοτε ὧδε ὑπὸ τῶν οἰομένων τι λέγειν, ὥσπερ νῦν
δὴ ἐγὼ ἔλεγον, ὅτι τῶν δοξῶν ἃς οἱ ἄνθρωποι δοξάζουσι
δέοι τὰς μὲν περὶ πολλοῦ ποιεῖσθαι, τὰς δὲ μή. τοῦτο
πρὸς θεῶν, ὦ Κρίτων, οὐ δοκεῖ καλῶς σοι λέγεσθαι;
E σὺ γὰρ ὅσα γε τἀνθρώπεια ἐκτὸς εἶ τοῦ μέλλειν ἀποθ-
νήσκειν αὔριον, καὶ οὐκ ἄν σε παρακρούοι ἡ παροῦσα
47 ξυμφορά· σκόπει δή, οὐχ ἱκανῶς δοκεῖ σοι λέγεσθαι,
ὅτι οὐ πάσας χρὴ τὰς δόξας τῶν ἀνθρώπων τιμᾶν,
ἀλλὰ τὰς μέν, τὰς δ' οὔ; [οὐδὲ πάντων, ἀλλὰ τῶν
μέν, τῶν δ' οὔ;] τί φῄς; ταῦτα οὐχὶ καλῶς λέγεται;

ΚΡ. Καλῶς.

ΣΩ. Οὐκοῦν τὰς μὲν χρηστὰς τιμᾶν, τὰς δὲ πονη-ρὰς μή;

ΚΡ. Ναί.

ΣΩ. Χρησταὶ δὲ οὐχ αἱ τῶν φρονίμων, πονηραὶ δὲ αἱ τῶν ἀφρόνων;

ΚΡ. Πῶς δ' οὔ;

VII. ΣΩ. Φέρε δή, πῶς αὖ τὰ τοιαῦτα ἐλέγετο;
B γυμναζόμενος ἀνὴρ καὶ τοῦτο πράττων πότερον παντὸς

ἀνδρὸς ἐπαίνῳ καὶ ψόγῳ καὶ δόξῃ τὸν νοῦν προσέχει, ἢ ἑνὸς μόνου ἐκείνου ὃς ἂν τυγχάνῃ ἰατρὸς ἢ παιδοτρίβης ὤν;

ΚΡ. Ἑνὸς μόνου.

ΣΩ. Οὐκοῦν φοβεῖσθαι χρὴ τοὺς ψόγους καὶ ἀσπάζεσθαι τοὺς ἐπαίνους τοὺς τοῦ ἑνὸς ἐκείνου, ἀλλὰ μὴ τοὺς τῶν πολλῶν;

ΚΡ. Δῆλα δή.

ΣΩ. Ταύτῃ ἄρα αὐτῷ πρακτέον καὶ γυμναστέον καὶ ἐδεστέον γε καὶ ποτέον, ᾗ ἂν τῷ ἑνὶ δοκῇ τῷ ἐπιστάτῃ καὶ ἐπαΐοντι, μᾶλλον ἢ ᾗ ξύμπασι τοῖς ἄλλοις;

ΚΡ. Ἔστι ταῦτα.

ΣΩ. Εἶεν. ἀπειθήσας δὲ τῷ ἑνὶ καὶ ἀτιμάσας C αὐτοῦ τὴν δόξαν καὶ τοὺς ἐπαίνους, τιμήσας δὲ τοὺς τῶν πολλῶν λόγους καὶ μηδὲν ἐπαϊόντων, ἆρα οὐδὲν κακὸν πείσεται;

ΚΡ. Πῶς γὰρ οὔ;

ΣΩ. Τί δ᾽ ἐστὶ τὸ κακὸν τοῦτο καὶ ποῖ τείνει καὶ εἰς τί τῶν τοῦ ἀπειθοῦντος;

ΚΡ. Δῆλον ὅτι εἰς τὸ σῶμα. τοῦτο γὰρ διόλλυσιν.

ΣΩ. Καλῶς λέγεις. οὐκοῦν καὶ τἆλλα, ὦ Κρίτων, οὕτως, ἵνα μὴ πάντα διΐωμεν, καὶ δὴ καὶ περὶ τῶν δικαίων καὶ ἀδίκων καὶ αἰσχρῶν καὶ καλῶν καὶ ἀγαθῶν καὶ κακῶν, περὶ ὧν νῦν ἡ βουλὴ ἡμῖν ἐστιν; πότερον τῇ τῶν πολλῶν δόξῃ δεῖ ἡμᾶς ἕπεσθαι καὶ φοβεῖσθαι D αὐτήν, ἢ τῇ τοῦ ἑνός, εἴ τίς ἐστιν ἐπαΐων, ὃν δεῖ καὶ αἰχύνεσθαι καὶ φοβεῖσθαι μᾶλλον ἢ ξύμπαντας τοὺς ἄλλους, ᾧ εἰ μὴ ἀκολουθήσομεν, διαφθεροῦμεν ἐκεῖνο καὶ λωβησόμεθα, ὃ τῷ μὲν δικαίῳ βέλτιον ἐγίγνετο, τῷ δὲ ἀδίκῳ ἀπώλλυτο; ἢ οὐδέν ἐστι τοῦτο;

ΚΡ. Οἶμαι ἔγωγε, ὦ Σώκρατες.

VIII. ΣΩ. Φέρε δή, ἐὰν τὸ ὑπὸ τοῦ ὑγιεινοῦ μὲν βέλτιον γιγνόμενον, ὑπὸ τοῦ νοσώδους δὲ διαφθειρόμενον διολέσωμεν πειθόμενοι μὴ τῇ τῶν ἐπαϊόντων
E δόξῃ, ἆρα βιωτὸν ἡμῖν ἐστιν διεφθαρμένου αὐτοῦ; ἔστι δέ που τοῦτο τὸ σῶμα· ἢ οὐχί;

ΚΡ. Ναί.

ΣΩ. Ἆρ' οὖν βιωτὸν ἡμῖν ἐστιν μετὰ μοχθηροῦ καὶ διεφθαρμένου σώματος;

ΚΡ. Οὐδαμῶς.

ΣΩ. Ἀλλὰ μετ' ἐκείνου ἄρ' ἡμῖν βιωτὸν διεφθαρμένου, ᾧ τὸ ἄδικον μὲν λωβᾶται, τὸ δὲ δίκαιον ὀνίνησιν; ἢ φαυλότερον ἡγούμεθα εἶναι τοῦ σώματος ἐκεῖνο, ὅτι
48 ποτ' ἐστὶ τῶν ἡμετέρων, περὶ ὃ ἥ τε ἀδικία καὶ ἡ δικαιοσύνη ἐστίν;

ΚΡ. Οὐδαμῶς.

ΣΩ. Ἀλλὰ τιμιώτερον;

ΚΡ. Πολύ γε.

ΣΩ. Οὐκ ἄρα, ὦ βέλτιστε, πάνυ ἡμῖν οὕτω φροντιστέον, τί ἐροῦσιν οἱ πολλοὶ ἡμᾶς, ἀλλ' ὅτι ὁ ἐπαΐων περὶ τῶν δικαίων καὶ ἀδίκων, ὁ εἷς, καὶ αὐτὴ ἡ ἀλήθεια. ὥστε πρῶτον μὲν ταύτῃ οὐκ ὀρθῶς εἰσηγεῖ, εἰσηγούμενος τῆς τῶν πολλῶν δόξης δεῖν ἡμᾶς φροντίζειν περὶ τῶν δικαίων καὶ καλῶν καὶ ἀγαθῶν καὶ τῶν ἐναντίων.

ἀλλὰ μὲν δή, φαίη γ' ἄν τις, οἷοί τέ εἰσιν ἡμᾶς οἱ πολλοὶ ἀποκτιννύναι.

ΚΡ. Δῆλα δὴ καὶ ταῦτα· φαίη γὰρ ἄν, ὦ Σώκρατες. B

ΣΩ. Ἀληθῆ λέγεις. ἀλλ', ὦ θαυμάσιε, οὗτός τε ὁ λόγος ὃν διεληλύθαμεν ἔμοιγε δοκεῖ ἔτι ὅμοιος εἶναι [τῷ] καὶ πρότερον· καὶ τόνδε αὖ σκόπει εἰ ἔτι μένει ἡμῖν ἢ οὔ, ὅτι οὐ τὸ ζῆν περὶ πλείστου ποιητέον, ἀλλὰ τὸ εὖ ζῆν.

ΚΡ. Ἀλλὰ μένει.

ΣΩ. Τὸ δὲ εὖ καὶ καλῶς καὶ δικαίως ὅτι ταὐτόν ἐστι, μένει ἢ οὐ μένει;

ΚΡ. Μένει.

IX. ΣΩ. Οὐκοῦν ἐκ τῶν ὁμολογουμένων τοῦτο σκεπτέον, πότερον δίκαιον ἐμὲ ἐνθένθε πειρᾶσθαι ἐξιέναι μὴ ἀφιέντων Ἀθηναίων, ἢ οὐ δίκαιον; καὶ ἐὰν μὲν C φαίνηται δίκαιον, πειρώμεθα, εἰ δὲ μή, ἐῶμεν. ἃς δὲ σὺ λέγεις τὰς σκέψεις περί τε ἀναλώσεως χρημάτων καὶ δόξης καὶ παίδων τροφῆς, μὴ ὡς ἀληθῶς ταῦτα, ὦ Κρίτων, σκέμματα ᾖ τῶν ῥᾳδίως ἀποκτιννύντων καὶ ἀναβιωσκομένων γ' ἄν, εἰ οἷοί τ' ἦσαν, οὐδενὶ ξὺν νῷ, τούτων τῶν πολλῶν. ἡμῖν δ' ἐπειδὴ ὁ λόγος οὕτως αἱρεῖ μὴ οὐδὲν ἄλλο σκεπτέον ᾖ ἢ ὅπερ νῦν δὴ ἐλέγομεν, πότερον δίκαια πράξομεν καὶ χρήματα τελοῦντες τούτοις τοῖς ἐμὲ ἐνθένδε ἐξάξουσι καὶ χάριτας καὶ αὐτοὶ D ἐξάγοντές τε καὶ ἐξαγόμενοι, ἢ τῇ ἀληθείᾳ ἀδικήσομεν πάντα ταῦτα ποιοῦντες· κἂν φαινώμεθα ἄδικα αὐτὰ ἐργαζόμενοι, μὴ οὐ δέῃ ὑπολογίζεσθαι οὔτ' εἰ ἀπο-

θνῄσκειν δεῖ παραμένοντας καὶ ἡσυχίαν ἄγοντας οὔτε
ἄλλο ὁτιοῦν πάσχειν πρὸ τοῦ ἀδικεῖν.

ΚΡ. Καλῶς μέν μοι δοκεῖς λέγειν, ὦ Σώκρατες·
ὅρα δὲ τί δρῶμεν.

ΣΩ. Σκοπῶμεν, ὦ ἀγαθέ, κοινῇ, καὶ εἴ πῃ ἔχεις
ἀντιλέγειν ἐμοῦ λέγοντος, ἀντίλεγε, καί σοι πείσομαι·
E εἰ δὲ μή, παῦσαι ἤδη, ὦ μακάριε, πολλάκις μοι λέγων
τὸν αὐτὸν λόγον, ὡς χρὴ ἐνθένδε ἀκόντων Ἀθηναίων
ἐμὲ ἀπιέναι· ὡς ἐγὼ περὶ πολλοῦ ποιοῦμαι πείσας σε
ταῦτα πράττειν, ἀλλὰ μὴ ἄκοντος. ὅρα δὲ δὴ τῆς
σκέψεως τὴν ἀρχήν, ἐάν σοι ἱκανῶς λέγηται, καὶ πειρῶ
49 ἀποκρίνεσθαι τὸ ἐρωτώμενον ᾗ ἂν μάλιστα οἴῃ.

ΚΡ. Ἀλλὰ πειράσομαι.

X. ΣΩ. Οὐδενὶ τρόπῳ φαμὲν ἑκόντας ἀδικητέον
εἶναι, ἢ τινὶ μὲν ἀδικητέον τρόπῳ, τινὶ δὲ οὔ; ἢ οὐδα-
μῶς τό γε ἀδικεῖν οὔτε ἀγαθὸν οὔτε καλόν, ὡς πολλάκις
ἡμῖν καὶ ἐν τῷ ἔμπροσθεν χρόνῳ ὡμολογήθη; [ὅπερ
καὶ ἄρτι ἐλέγετο·] ἢ πᾶσαι ἡμῖν ἐκεῖναι αἱ πρόσθεν
ὁμολογίαι ἐν ταῖσδε ταῖς ὀλίγαις ἡμέραις ἐκκεχυμέναι
εἰσίν, καὶ πάλαι, ὦ Κρίτων, ἄρα τηλικοίδε [γέροντες]
B ἄνδρες πρὸς ἀλλήλους σπουδῇ διαλεγόμενοι ἐλάθομεν
ἡμᾶς αὐτοὺς παίδων οὐδὲν διαφέροντες; ἢ παντὸς
μᾶλλον οὕτως ἔχει ὥσπερ τότε ἐλέγετο ἡμῖν, εἴτε
φασὶν οἱ πολλοὶ εἴτε μή, καὶ εἴτε δεῖ ἡμᾶς ἔτι τῶνδε
χαλεπώτερα πάσχειν εἴτε καὶ πρᾳότερα, ὅμως τό γε
ἀδικεῖν τῷ ἀδικοῦντι καὶ κακὸν καὶ αἰσχρὸν τυγχάνει
ὂν παντὶ τρόπῳ; φαμὲν ἢ οὔ;

ΚΡ. Φαμέν.

ΣΩ. Οὐδαμῶς ἄρα δεῖ ἀδικεῖν;

ΚΡ. Οὐ δῆτα.

ΣΩ. Οὐδὲ ἀδικούμενον ἄρα ἀνταδικεῖν, ὡς οἱ πολλοὶ οἴονται, ἐπειδή γε οὐδαμῶς δεῖ ἀδικεῖν; C

ΚΡ. Οὐ φαίνεται.

ΣΩ. Τί δὲ δή; κακουργεῖν δεῖ, ὦ Κρίτων, ἢ οὔ;

ΚΡ. Οὐ δεῖ δήπου, ὦ Σώκρατες.

ΣΩ. Τί δέ; ἀντικακουργεῖν κακῶς πάσχοντα, ὡς οἱ πολλοί φασι, δίκαιον ἢ οὐ δίκαιον;

ΚΡ. Οὐδαμῶς.

ΣΩ. Τὸ γάρ που κακῶς ποιεῖν ἀνθρώπους τοῦ ἀδικεῖν οὐδὲν διαφέρει.

ΚΡ. Ἀληθῆ λέγεις.

ΣΩ. Οὔτε ἄρα ἀνταδικεῖν δεῖ οὔτε κακῶς ποιεῖν οὐδένα ἀνθρώπων, οὐδ' ἂν ὁτιοῦν πάσχῃ ὑπ' αὐτῶν. καὶ ὅρα, ὦ Κρίτων, ταῦτα καθομολογῶν ὅπως μὴ παρὰ D δόξαν ὁμολογῇς. οἶδα γὰρ ὅτι ὀλίγοις τισὶ ταῦτα καὶ δοκεῖ καὶ δόξει. οἷς οὖν οὕτω δέδοκται καὶ οἷς μή, τούτοις οὐκ ἔστι κοινὴ βουλή, ἀλλὰ ἀνάγκη τούτους ἀλλήλων καταφρονεῖν, ὁρῶντας τὰ ἀλλήλων βουλεύματα. σκόπει δὴ οὖν καὶ σὺ εὖ μάλα, πότερον κοινωνεῖς καὶ ξυνδοκεῖ σοι καὶ ἀρχώμεθα ἐντεῦθεν βουλευόμενοι, ὡς οὐδέποτε ὀρθῶς ἔχοντος οὔτε τοῦ ἀδικεῖν οὔτε τοῦ ἀνταδικεῖν οὔτε κακῶς πάσχοντα ἀμύνεσθαι ἀντιδρῶντα κακῶς· ἢ ἀφίστασαι καὶ οὐ κοινωνεῖς τῆς ἀρχῆς; ἐμοὶ μὲν γὰρ καὶ πάλαι οὕτω καὶ νῦν ἔτι δοκεῖ, E σοὶ δ' εἴ πῃ ἄλλῃ δέδοκται, λέγε καὶ δίδασκε. εἰ δὲ ἐμμένεις τοῖς πρόσθε, τὸ μετὰ τοῦτο ἄκουε.

ΚΡ. Ἀλλ' ἐμμένω τε καὶ ξυνδοκεῖ μοι· ἀλλὰ λέγε.

ΣΩ. Λέγω δὴ αὖ τὸ μετὰ τοῦτο, μᾶλλον δ' ἐρωτῶ· πότερον ἃ ἄν τις ὁμολογήσῃ τῳ δίκαια ὄντα ποιητέον ἢ ἐξαπατητέον;

ΚΡ. Ποιητέον.

XI. ΣΩ. Ἐκ τούτων δὴ ἄθρει. ἀπιόντες ἐνθένδε
50 ἡμεῖς μὴ πείσαντες τὴν πόλιν πότερον κακῶς τινας ποιοῦμεν, καὶ ταῦτα οὓς ἥκιστα δεῖ, ἢ οὔ; καὶ ἐμμένομεν οἷς ὡμολογήσαμεν δικαίοις οὖσιν ἢ οὔ;

ΚΡ. Οὐκ ἔχω, ὦ Σώκρατες, ἀποκρίνασθαι πρὸς ὃ ἐρωτᾷς· οὐ γὰρ ἐννοῶ.

ΣΩ. Ἀλλ' ὧδε σκόπει. εἰ μέλλουσιν ἡμῖν ἐνθένδε εἴτε ἀποδιδράσκειν, εἴθ' ὅπως δεῖ ὀνομάσαι τοῦτο, ἐλθόντες οἱ νόμοι καὶ τὸ κοινὸν τῆς πόλεως ἐπιστάντες ἔροιντο· εἰπέ μοι, ὦ Σώκρατες, τί ἐν νῷ ἔχεις ποιεῖν; ἄλλο τι ἢ τούτῳ τῷ ἔργῳ ᾧ ἐπιχειρεῖς διανοεῖ τούς τε
B νόμους ἡμᾶς ἀπολέσαι καὶ ξύμπασαν τὴν πόλιν τὸ σὸν μέρος; ἢ δοκεῖ σοι οἷόν τε ἔτι ἐκείνην τὴν πόλιν εἶναι καὶ μὴ ἀνατετράφθαι, ἐν ᾗ αἱ γενόμεναι δίκαι μηδὲν ἰσχύουσιν, ἀλλ' ὑπὸ ἰδιωτῶν ἄκυροί τε γίγνονται καὶ διαφθείρονται; τί ἐροῦμεν, ὦ Κρίτων, πρὸς ταῦτα καὶ ἄλλα τοιαῦτα; πολλὰ γὰρ ἄν τις ἔχοι ἄλλως τε καὶ ῥήτωρ εἰπεῖν ὑπὲρ τούτου τοῦ νόμου ἀπολλυμένου, ὃς τὰς δίκας τὰς δικασθείσας προστάττει κυρίας εἶναι. ἢ ἐροῦμεν πρὸς αὐτοὺς ὅτι ἠδίκει γὰρ ἡμᾶς ἡ πόλις
C καὶ οὐκ ὀρθῶς τὴν δίκην ἔκρινεν; ταῦτα ἢ τί ἐροῦμεν;

ΚΡ. Ταῦτα νὴ Δία, ὦ Σώκρατες.

XII. ΣΩ. Τί οὖν, ἂν εἴπωσιν οἱ νόμοι· ὦ Σώκρατες, ἦ καὶ ταῦτα ὡμολόγητο ἡμῖν τε καὶ σοί, ἢ ἐμμένειν ταῖς δίκαις αἷς ἂν ἡ πόλις δικάζῃ; εἰ οὖν αὐτῶν θαυμάζοιμεν λεγόντων, ἴσως ἂν εἴποιεν ὅτι, ὦ Σώκρατες, μὴ θαύμαζε τὰ λεγόμενα, ἀλλ' ἀποκρίνου, ἐπειδὴ καὶ εἴωθας χρῆσθαι τῷ ἐρωτᾶν τε καὶ ἀποκρίνεσθαι. φέρε γάρ, τί ἐγκαλῶν ἡμῖν καὶ τῇ πόλει ἐπιχειρεῖς D ἡμᾶς ἀπολλύναι; οὐ πρῶτον μέν σε ἐγεννήσαμεν ἡμεῖς καὶ δι' ἡμῶν ἐλάμβανεν τὴν μητέρα σου ὁ πατὴρ καὶ ἐφύτευσέν σε; φράσον οὖν, τούτοις ἡμῶν, τοῖς νόμοις τοῖς περὶ τοὺς γάμους, μέμφει τι ὡς οὐ καλῶς ἔχουσιν; οὐ μέμφομαι, φαίην ἄν. ἀλλὰ τοῖς περὶ τὴν τοῦ γενομένου τροφήν τε καὶ παιδείαν ἐν ᾗ καὶ σὺ ἐπαιδεύθης; ἢ οὐ καλῶς προσέταττον ἡμῶν οἱ ἐπὶ τούτοις τεταγμένοι νόμοι, παραγγέλλοντες τῷ πατρὶ τῷ σῷ σε ἐν μουσικῇ καὶ γυμναστικῇ παιδεύειν; καλῶς, E φαίην ἄν. εἶεν. ἐπειδὴ δὲ ἐγένου καὶ ἐξετράφης καὶ ἐπαιδεύθης, ἔχοις ἂν εἰπεῖν πρῶτον μὲν ὡς οὐχὶ ἡμέτερος ἦσθα καὶ ἔκγονος καὶ δοῦλος, αὐτός τε καὶ οἱ σοὶ πρόγονοι; καὶ εἰ τοῦθ' οὕτως ἔχει, ἆρ' ἐξ ἴσου οἴει εἶναι σοὶ τὸ δίκαιον καὶ ἡμῖν, καὶ ἅττ' ἂν ἡμεῖς σε ἐπιχειρῶμεν ποιεῖν, καὶ σοὶ ταῦτα ἀντιποιεῖν οἴει δίκαιον εἶναι; ἢ πρὸς μὲν ἄρα σοι τὸν πατέρα οὐκ ἐξ ἴσου ἦν τὸ δίκαιον καὶ πρὸς τὸν δεσπότην, εἴ σοι ὢν ἐτύγχανεν, ὥστε, ἅπερ πάσχοις, ταῦτα καὶ ἀντιποιεῖν, οὔτε κακῶς ἀκούοντα ἀντιλέγειν οὔτε τυπτόμενον ἀντιτύπτειν οὔτε ἄλλα τοιαῦτα πολλά· πρὸς δὲ τὴν 51 πατρίδα ἄρα καὶ τοὺς νόμους ἔσται σοι, ὥστε, ἐάν σε ἐπιχειρῶμεν ἡμεῖς ἀπολλύναι δίκαιον ἡγούμενοι εἶναι, καὶ σὺ δὲ ἡμᾶς τοὺς νόμους καὶ τὴν πατρίδα καθ' ὅσον δύνασαι ἐπιχειρήσεις ἀνταπολλύναι, καὶ φήσεις ταῦτα ποιῶν δίκαια πράττειν, ὁ τῇ ἀληθείᾳ τῆς ἀρετῆς ἐπιμελόμενος; ἢ οὕτως εἶ σοφός, ὥστε λέληθέν σε ὅτι μητρός τε καὶ πατρὸς καὶ τῶν ἄλλων προγόνων ἁπάντων τιμιώτερόν ἐστιν ἡ πατρὶς καὶ σεμνότερον καὶ B ἁγιώτερον καὶ ἐν μείζονι μοίρᾳ καὶ παρὰ θεοῖς καὶ παρ' ἀνθρώποις τοῖς νοῦν ἔχουσι, καὶ σέβεσθαι δεῖ καὶ μᾶλλον ὑπείκειν καὶ θωπεύειν πατρίδα χαλεπαίνουσαν ἢ πατέρα, καὶ ἢ πείθειν ἢ ποιεῖν ἃ ἂν κελεύῃ, καὶ πάσχειν, ἐάν τι προστάττῃ παθεῖν, ἡσυχίαν ἄγοντα, ἐάν τε τύπτεσθαι ἐάν τε δεῖσθαι, ἐάν τε εἰς πόλεμον ἄγῃ τρωθησόμενον ἢ ἀποθανούμενον, ποιητέον ταῦτα, καὶ τὸ δίκαιον οὕτως ἔχει, καὶ οὐχὶ ὑπεικτέον οὐδὲ ἀναχωρητέον οὐδὲ λειπτέον τὴν τάξιν, ἀλλὰ καὶ ἐν πολέμῳ καὶ ἐν δικαστηρίῳ καὶ πανταχοῦ ποιητέον ἃ C ἂν κελεύῃ ἡ πόλις καὶ ἡ πατρίς, ἢ πείθειν αὐτὴν ᾗ τὸ δίκαιον πέφυκε, βιάζεσθαι δ' οὐχ ὅσιον οὔτε μητέρα οὔτε πατέρα, πολὺ δὲ τούτων ἔτι ἧττον τὴν πατρίδα; τί φήσομεν πρὸς ταῦτα, ὦ Κρίτων; ἀληθῆ λέγειν τοὺς νόμους ἢ οὔ;

ΚΡ. Ἔμοιγε δοκεῖ.

XIII. ΣΩ. Σκόπει τοίνυν, ὦ Σώκρατες, φαῖεν ἂν ἴσως οἱ νόμοι, εἰ ἡμεῖς ταῦτα ἀληθῆ λέγομεν, ὅτι οὐ δίκαια ἡμᾶς ἐπιχειρεῖς δρᾶν ἃ νῦν ἐπιχειρεῖς. ἡμεῖς γάρ σε γεννήσαντες, ἐκθρέψαντες, παιδεύσαντες, μεταδόντες ἁπάντων ὧν οἷοί τε ἦμεν καλῶν σοὶ καὶ τοῖς

ἄλλοις πᾶσι πολίταις, ὅμως προαγορεύομεν τῷ ἐξουσίαν D
πεποιηκέναι Ἀθηναίων τῷ βουλομένῳ, ἐπειδὰν δοκι-
μασθῇ καὶ ἴδῃ τὰ ἐν τῇ πόλει πράγματα καὶ ἡμᾶς
τοὺς νόμους, ᾧ ἂν μὴ ἀρέσκωμεν ἡμεῖς, ἐξεῖναι λαβόντα
τὰ αὑτοῦ ἀπιέναι ὅποι ἂν βούληται. καὶ οὐδεὶς ἡμῶν
τῶν νόμων ἐμποδών ἐστιν οὐδ' ἀπαγορεύει, ἐάν τέ τις
βούληται ὑμῶν εἰς ἀποικίαν ἰέναι, εἰ μὴ ἀρέσκοιμεν
ἡμεῖς τε καὶ ἡ πόλις, ἐάν τε μετοικεῖν ἄλλοσέ ποι
ἐλθών, ἰέναι ἐκεῖσε ὅποι ἂν βούληται ἔχοντα τὰ αὑ-
τοῦ. ὃς δ' ἂν ὑμῶν παραμείνῃ, ὁρῶν ὃν τρόπον ἡμεῖς E
τάς τε δίκας δικάζομεν καὶ τἆλλα τὴν πόλιν διοικοῦμεν,
ἤδη φαμὲν τοῦτον ὡμολογηκέναι ἔργῳ ἡμῖν ἃ ἂν ἡμεῖς
κελεύωμεν ποιήσειν ταῦτα, καὶ τὸν μὴ πειθόμενον τριχῇ
φαμεν ἀδικεῖν, ὅτι τε γεννηταῖς οὖσιν ἡμῖν οὐ πείθεται,
καὶ ὅτι τροφεῦσι, καὶ ὅτι ὁμολογήσας ἡμῖν πείθεσθαι
οὔτε πείθεται οὔτε πείθει ἡμᾶς, εἰ μὴ καλῶς τι ποιοῦ-
μεν, προτιθέντων ἡμῶν καὶ οὐκ ἀγρίως ἐπιταττόντων 52
ποιεῖν ἃ ἂν κελεύωμεν, ἀλλὰ ἐφιέντων δυοῖν θάτερα, ἢ
πείθειν ἡμᾶς ἢ ποιεῖν, τούτων οὐδέτερα ποιεῖ.

XIV. Ταύταις δή φαμεν καὶ σέ, Σώκρατες, ταῖς
αἰτίαις ἐνέξεσθαι, εἴπερ ποιήσεις ἃ ἐπινοεῖς, καὶ οὐχ
ἥκιστα Ἀθηναίων σέ, ἀλλ' ἐν τοῖς μάλιστα. εἰ οὖν
ἐγὼ εἴποιμι· διὰ τί δή; ἴσως ἄν μου δικαίως καθάπ-
τοιντο λέγοντες, ὅτι ἐν τοῖς μάλιστα Ἀθηναίων ἐγὼ
αὐτοῖς ὡμολογηκὼς τυγχάνω ταύτην τὴν ὁμολογίαν.
φαῖεν γὰρ ἂν ὅτι ὦ Σώκρατες, μεγάλα ἡμῖν τούτων B
τεκμήριά ἐστιν, ὅτι σοι καὶ ἡμεῖς ἠρέσκομεν καὶ ἡ
πόλις· οὐ γὰρ ἄν ποτε τῶν ἄλλων Ἀθηναίων ἁπάντων

διαφερόντως ἐν αὐτῇ ἐπεδήμεις, εἰ μή σοι διαφερόντως ἤρεσκε, καὶ οὔτ' ἐπὶ θεωρίαν πώποτ' ἐκ τῆς πόλεως ἐξῆλθες, [ὅτι μὴ ἅπαξ εἰς Ἰσθμόν,] οὔτε ἄλλοσε οὐδαμόσε, εἰ μή ποι στρατευσόμενος, οὔτε C ἄλλην ἀποδημίαν ἐποιήσω πώποτε ὥσπερ οἱ ἄλλοι ἄνθρωποι, οὐδ' ἐπιθυμία σε ἄλλης πόλεως οὐδὲ ἄλλων νόμων ἔλαβεν εἰδέναι, ἀλλὰ ἡμεῖς σοι ἱκανοὶ ἦμεν καὶ ἡ ἡμετέρα πόλις· οὕτω σφόδρα ἡμᾶς ᾑροῦ καὶ ὡμολόγεις καθ' ἡμᾶς πολιτεύσεσθαι τά τε ἄλλα καὶ παῖδας ἐν αὐτῇ ἐποιήσω ὡς ἀρεσκούσης σοι τῆς πόλεως. ἔτι τοίνυν ἐν αὐτῇ τῇ δίκῃ ἐξῆν σοι φυγῆς τιμήσασθαι, εἰ ἐβούλου, καὶ ὅπερ νῦν ἀκούσης τῆς πόλεως ἐπιχειρεῖς, τότε ἑκούσης ποιῆσαι. σὺ δὲ τότε μὲν ἐκαλλωπίζου ὡς οὐκ ἀγανακτῶν, εἰ δέοι τεθνάναι σε, ἀλλὰ ᾑροῦ, ὡς D ἔφησθα, πρὸ τῆς φυγῆς θάνατον· νῦν δὲ οὔτ' ἐκείνους τοὺς λόγους αἰσχύνει, οὔτε ἡμῶν τῶν νόμων ἐντρέπει, ἐπιχειρῶν διαφθεῖραι, πράττεις τε ἅπερ ἂν δοῦλος φαυλότατος πράξειεν, ἀποδιδράσκειν ἐπιχειρῶν παρὰ τὰς ξυνθήκας τε καὶ τὰς ὁμολογίας, καθ' ἃς ἡμῖν ξυνέθου πολιτεύεσθαι. πρῶτον μὲν οὖν ἡμῖν τοῦτο αὐτὸ ἀπόκριναι, εἰ ἀληθῆ λέγομεν φάσκοντές σε ὡμολογηκέναι πολιτεύεσθαι καθ' ἡμᾶς ἔργῳ, ἀλλ' οὐ λόγῳ, ἢ οὐκ ἀληθῆ. τί φῶμεν πρὸς ταῦτα, ὦ Κρίτων; ἄλλο τι ἢ ὁμολογῶμεν;

ΚΡ. Ἀνάγκη, ὦ Σώκρατες.

E ΣΩ. Ἄλλο τι οὖν ἂν φαῖεν ἢ ξυνθήκας τὰς πρὸς ἡμᾶς αὐτοὺς καὶ ὁμολογίας παραβαίνεις, οὐχ ὑπὸ ἀνάγκης ὁμολογήσας οὐδὲ ἀπατηθεὶς οὐδὲ ἐν ὀλίγῳ χρόνῳ ἀναγκασθεὶς βουλεύσασθαι, ἀλλ' ἐν ἔτεσιν ἑβδομήκοντα, ἐν οἷς ἐξῆν σοι ἀπιέναι, εἰ μὴ ἠρέσκομεν ἡμεῖς μηδὲ δίκαιαι ἐφαίνοντό σοι αἱ ὁμολογίαι εἶναι. σὺ δὲ οὔτε Λακεδαίμονα προῃροῦ οὔτε Κρήτην, ἃς δὴ ἑκάστοτε φῂς εὐνομεῖσθαι, οὔτε ἄλλην οὐδεμίαν τῶν Ἑλληνίδων πόλεων οὐδὲ τῶν βαρβαρικῶν, ἀλλὰ ἐλάττω 53 ἐξ αὐτῆς ἀπεδήμησας ἢ οἱ χωλοί τε καὶ τυφλοὶ καὶ οἱ ἄλλοι ἀνάπηροι· οὕτω σοι διαφερόντως τῶν ἄλλων Ἀθηναίων ἤρεσκεν ἡ πόλις τε καὶ ἡμεῖς οἱ νόμοι δῆλον ὅτι· τίνι γὰρ ἂν πόλις ἀρέσκοι ἄνευ νόμων; νῦν δὲ δὴ οὐκ ἐμμένεις τοῖς ὡμολογημένοις; ἐὰν ἡμῖν γε πείθῃ, ὦ Σώκρατες· καὶ οὐ καταγέλαστός γε ἔσει ἐκ τῆς πόλεως ἐξελθών.

XV. Σκόπει γὰρ δή, ταῦτα παραβὰς καὶ ἐξαμαρτάνων B τι τούτων τί ἀγαθὸν ἐργάσει σαυτὸν ἢ τοὺς ἐπιτηδείους τοὺς σαυτοῦ; ὅτι μὲν γὰρ κινδυνεύσουσί γέ σου οἱ ἐπιτήδειοι καὶ αὐτοὶ φεύγειν καὶ στερηθῆναι τῆς πόλεως ἢ τὴν οὐσίαν ἀπολέσαι, σχεδόν τι δῆλον· αὐτὸς δὲ πρῶτον μὲν ἐὰν εἰς τῶν ἐγγύτατά τινα πόλεων ἔλθῃς, ἢ Θήβαζε ἢ Μέγαράδε — εὐνομοῦνται γὰρ ἀμφότεραι — πολέμιος ἥξεις, ὦ Σώκρατες, τῇ τούτων πολιτείᾳ, καὶ ὅσοιπερ κήδονται τῶν αὑτῶν πόλεων, ὑποβλέψονταί σε διαφθορέα ἡγούμενοι τῶν νόμων, καὶ βεβαιώσεις τοῖς δικασταῖς τὴν δόξαν ὥστε δοκεῖν C ὀρθῶς τὴν δίκην δικάσαι· ὅστις γὰρ νόμων διαφθορεύς ἐστι, σφόδρα που δόξειεν ἂν νέων γε καὶ ἀνοήτων ἀνθρώπων διαφθορεὺς εἶναι. πότερον οὖν φεύξει τάς τε εὐνομουμένας πόλεις καὶ τῶν ἀνδρῶν τοὺς κοσμιωτά-

τους; καὶ τοῦτο ποιοῦντι ἆρα ἄξιόν σοι ζῆν ἔσται; ἢ πλησιάσεις τούτοις καὶ ἀναισχυντήσεις διαλεγόμενος —τίνας λόγους, ὦ Σώκρατες; ἢ οὕσπερ ἐνθάδε, ὡς ἡ ἀρετὴ καὶ ἡ δικαιοσύνη πλείστου ἄξιον τοῖς ἀνθρώποις καὶ τὰ νόμιμα καὶ οἱ νόμοι; καὶ οὐκ οἴει ἄσχημον ἂν
D φανεῖσθαι τὸ τοῦ Σωκράτους πρᾶγμα; οἴεσθαί γε χρή. ἀλλ' ἐκ μὲν τούτων τῶν τόπων ἀπαρεῖς, ἥξεις δὲ εἰς Θετταλίαν παρὰ τοὺς ξένους τοὺς Κρίτωνος· ἐκεῖ γὰρ δὴ πλείστη ἀταξία καὶ ἀκολασία, καὶ ἴσως ἂν ἡδέως σου ἀκούοιεν ὡς γελοίως ἐκ τοῦ δεσμωτηρίου ἀπεδίδρασκες σκευήν τέ τινα περιθέμενος, ἢ διφθέραν λαβὼν ἢ ἄλλα οἷα δὴ εἰώθασιν ἐνσκευάζεσθαι οἱ ἀποδιδράσκοντες, καὶ τὸ σχῆμα τὸ σαυτοῦ μεταλλάξας· ὅτι δὲ γέρων ἀνήρ, σμικροῦ χρόνου τῷ βίῳ λοιποῦ ὄντος ὡς
E τὸ εἰκός, ἐτόλμησας οὕτως αἰσχρῶς ἐπιθυμεῖν ζῆν, νόμους τοὺς μεγίστους παραβάς, οὐδεὶς ὃς ἐρεῖ; ἴσως, ἂν μή τινα λυπῇς· εἰ δὲ μή, ἀκούσει, ὦ Σώκρατης, πολλὰ καὶ ἀνάξια σαυτοῦ. ὑπερχόμενος δὴ βιώσει πάντας ἀνθρώπους καὶ δουλεύων· τί ποιῶν ἢ εὐωχούμενος ἐν Θετταλίᾳ, ὥσπερ ἐπὶ δεῖπνον ἀποδεδημηκὼς εἰς Θετταλίαν; λόγοι δὲ ἐκεῖνοι οἱ περὶ δικαιοσύνης τε
54 καὶ τῆς ἄλλης ἀρετῆς ποῦ ἡμῖν ἔσονται; ἀλλὰ δὴ τῶν παίδων ἕνεκα βούλει ζῆν, ἵνα αὐτοὺς ἐκθρέψῃς καὶ παιδεύσῃς; τί δέ; εἰς Θετταλίαν αὐτοὺς ἀγαγὼν θρέψεις τε καὶ παιδεύσεις, ξένους ποιήσας, ἵνα καὶ τοῦτο ἀπολαύσωσιν, ἢ τοῦτο μὲν οὔ, αὐτοῦ δὲ τρεφόμενοι σοῦ ζῶντος βέλτιον θρέψονται καὶ παιδεύσονται, μὴ ξυνόντος σοῦ αὐτοῖς; οἱ γὰρ ἐπιτήδειοι οἱ σοὶ ἐπι-

μελήσονται αὐτῶν. πότερον ἐὰν εἰς Θετταλίαν ἀποδημήσῃς ἐπιμελήσονται, ἐὰν δὲ εἰς Ἅιδου ἀποδημήσῃς οὐχὶ ἐπιμελήσονται; εἴπερ γέ τι ὄφελος αὐτῶν B ἔστι τῶν σοι φασκόντων ἐπιτηδείων εἶναι, οἴεσθαί γε χρή.

XVI. Ἀλλ', ὦ Σώκρατες, πειθόμενος ἡμῖν τοῖς σοῖς τροφεῦσι μήτε παῖδας περὶ πλείονος ποιοῦ μήτε τὸ ζῆν μήτε ἄλλο μηδὲν πρὸ τοῦ δικαίου, ἵνα εἰς Ἅιδου ἐλθὼν ἔχῃς πάντα ταῦτα ἀπολογήσασθαι τοῖς ἐκεῖ ἄρχουσιν· οὔτε γὰρ ἐνθάδε σοι φαίνεται ταῦτα πράττοντι ἄμεινον εἶναι οὐδὲ δικαιότερον οὐδὲ ὁσιώτερον, οὐδὲ ἄλλῳ τῶν σῶν οὐδενί, οὔτε ἐκεῖσε ἀφικομένῳ ἄμεινον ἔσται. ἀλλὰ νῦν μὲν ἠδικημένος ἄπει, ἐὰν ἀπίῃς, οὐχ ὑφ' ἡμῶν τῶν νόμων ἀλλὰ ὑπὸ C ἀνθρώπων· ἐὰν δὲ ἐξέλθῃς οὕτως αἰσχρῶς ἀνταδικήσας τε καὶ ἀντικακουργήσας, τὰς σαυτοῦ ὁμολογίας τε καὶ ξυνθήκας τας πρὸς ἡμᾶς παραβὰς καὶ κακὰ ἐργασάμενος τούτους οὓς ἥκιστα ἔδει, σαυτόν τε καὶ φίλους καὶ πατρίδα καὶ ἡμᾶς, ἡμεῖς τέ σοι χαλεπανοῦμεν ζῶντι, καὶ ἐκεῖ οἱ ἡμέτεροι ἀδελφοὶ οἱ ἐν Ἅιδου νόμοι οὐκ εὐμενῶς σε ὑποδέξονται, εἰδότες ὅτι καὶ D ἡμᾶς ἐπεχείρησας ἀπολέσαι τὸ σὸν μέρος. ἀλλὰ μή σε πείσῃ Κρίτων ποιεῖν ἃ λέγει μᾶλλον ἢ ἡμεῖς.

XVII. Ταῦτα, ὦ φίλε ἑταῖρε Κρίτων, εὖ ἴσθι ὅτι ἐγὼ δοκῶ ἀκούειν, ὥσπερ οἱ κορυβαντιῶντες τῶν αὐλῶν δοκοῦσιν ἀκούειν, καὶ ἐν ἐμοὶ αὕτη ἡ ἠχὴ τούτων τῶν λόγων βομβεῖ καὶ ποιεῖ μὴ δύνασθαι τῶν ἄλλων ἀκούειν. ἀλλὰ ἴσθι, ὅσα γε τὰ νῦν ἐμοὶ δοκοῦντα, ἐὰν λέγῃς παρὰ ταῦτα, μάτην ἐρεῖς. ὅμως μέντοι εἴ τι οἴει πλέον ποιήσειν, λέγε.

ΚΡ. Ἀλλ', ὦ Σώκρατες, οὐκ ἔχω λέγειν.

E ΣΩ. Ἔα τοίνυν, ὦ Κρίτων, καὶ πράττωμεν ταύτῃ, ἐπειδὴ ταύτῃ ὁ θεὸς ὑφηγεῖται.

NOTES.

NOTES.

APOLOGIA SOCRATIS.

Page 43

A. Line 1. Ὅ τι . . . κατηγόρων. *In what manner you* 17 *have been affected by my accusers*, i. e., by their harangues, which had immediately preceded the defense of Socrates. μέν following ὅ τι contrasts the clauses; following ὑμεῖς it would contrast the pronouns ὑμεῖς and ἐγώ. Since πεπόνθατε denotes the receiving of an action, it is followed by ὑπό, as if it were a passive verb. G. 165, N. 1; H. A. 820.* So ὑπ' αὐτῶν just below; and in like manner *ab* in Latin. The accusers or prosecutors of Socrates were three, Anytus, 18 B., Meletus, 19 B., and Lycon, 23 E. ὦ ἄνδρες Ἀθηναῖοι. The trial of Socrates took place before the Heliæa, the most numerous and popular, and, at that time, by far the most important court at Athens. It consisted in all of 6,000 Athenian citizens (though they usually administered justice in sections of 500 each), and being also often thronged by spectators from the populace, its members might well be addressed by the same honorable title as the members of the popular assembly, ὦ ἄνδρες Ἀθηναῖοι, instead of the more distinctive title ὦ ἄνδρες δικασταί. Socrates uses the latter in addressing those judges who voted for his acquittal in the concluding paragraph of his defense, capp. xxxi–xxxiii, and gives his reason for it at 40.

---

* G. stands for Goodwin's Grammar; H. A. for Hadley's revised by Allen; M. and T. for Goodwin's Moods and Tenses of Greek Verbs.

Page 43 The 6,000 Heliasts were a majority of the adult citizens of Athens. The name ἡλιαία is connected in root with ἁλία, which in the Dorian states was the common term for an assembly of the people, and these Attic juries, even in their judicial functions, represented the people. Cf. Wachsmuth's His. Ant., Sec. 47, Meier's Attic Process, Smith's Dict. of Antiqq., and Grote's Hist. of Greece, vol. iv., chap. 31; also Mahaffy's Primer of Old Greek Life, Secc. 96–101. On the compliment implied in the title Ἀθηναῖος, cf. 29 D. 2. δ' οὖν. *But then, at any rate*, affirming the truth of the following statement, notwithstanding his ignorance about that in the previous clause. 3. ὀλίγου, sc. δεῖν, literally, to want little = *almost*. G. 268; H. A. 743, b. Cf. ὀλίγου δεῖν, 22, A. ἐμαυτοῦ ἐπελαθόμην, *forgot myself*, i. e., my true character. 4. ὡς ἔπος εἰπεῖν limits οὐδὲν εἰρήκασι, and is designed to qualify, or apologize for, that otherwise absolute negation of all truth in his accusers: *they have said, so to speak, nothing that is true at least*. Cf. Stallbaum in loc., and Gorg. 450 B, also Woolsey, ibid. 5. αὐτῶν ἓν ἐθαύμασα, etc. *One thing of theirs I most wondered at of the many falsehoods which they stated*, viz., *this*. αὐτῶν relates to persons and is the gen. of the possessor, while τῶν πολλῶν is the partitive gen. after the same word ἕν. Cf. Stallbaum ad loc.

B. 6. χρή. χρῆν, impf., has the better MSS. authority, but χρή, pres., gives the better, not to say the only suitable meaning, and is adopted by Cron, Wagner, and other recent editors. 8. μὴ αἰσχυνθῆναι. μή rather than οὐ regularly accompanies the inf., because the inf., from its very nature, usually denotes a mere conception: *that they should not be ashamed*. ὅτι = *because*. 9. ἔργῳ, *by the fact*, the actual trial. 9. μηδ' ὁπωστιοῦν. Observe the emphasis: *not even in any way whatever*. 10. αὐτῶν, *of them*, or in them. Cf. note on αὐτῶν ἓν ἐθαύμασα above. 11. εἰ μὴ ἄρα = *nisi forte, unless perchance*. Often used ironically: *unless forsooth*. 12. λέγειν depends on δεινόν = *powerful* (literally, *terrible*) *to speak*. εἰ . . . λέγουσιν may be rendered, if they *mean* this. 13. οὐ κατὰ τούτους, *not after their example*. He would acknowledge, that he was an orator according to that definition, but not according to their exemplification of it, since *they*, as he proceeds to say, *had spoken little or nothing that was true*. 14. ἤ τι ἢ οὐδέν = *little or nothing, next to nothing*. Cf. Herod. III, 140, ἀναβέβηκε δὲ ἤ τις ἢ οὐδείς κω παρ᾽ ἡμέας αὐτῶν. 15. πᾶσαν τὴν ἀλήθειαν, *truth throughout*, differing slightly from τὴν πᾶσαν ἀλήθειαν. G. 142, 4, N. 5; H. A. 672. Cf. Xen. Mem. 4, 8, 9: τὴν δίκην ἀληθέστατα εἰπών. 16. οὐ μέντοι μὰ Δί', κ.τ.λ. *Not, however, by any means, Athenians, speeches rhetorically decked out as theirs were in choice words and phrases, nor carefully arranged in ornate periods, but you shall hear facts, stated without premeditation in the words which chance to occur to me.* There is the most perfect rhetoric in Plato's presentation of this defense of Socrates. The conversational style is everywhere admirably kept up. 17. ὥσπερ οἱ τούτων, sc. λόγοι ἦσαν. In such comparative clauses, the noun may take the case of the preceding noun, or may be put in the nominative. λόγους is the object of ἀκούσεσθε, which is expressed in the last instead of the first clause, in order to declare emphatically and affirmatively what they *shall* hear. According to Stallbaum, ὀνόματα = singula nomina, ῥήματα = nomina una cum predicato. In the technical language of Greek grammar, ὀνόματα = nouns, ῥήματα = verbs.

C. 19. πιστεύω γάρ, κ.τ.λ., in this connection implies, that just sentiments do not need rhetorical ornaments. 1. δήπου, as usual, is somewhat playful = *methinks, to be sure*. 2. τῇδε τῇ ἡλικίᾳ, est: *mihi homini id ætatis*—verbum abstractum loco verbi concreti positum. Stallb. Socrates was 70 years old at the time of his trial. Cf. D. πλάττοντι takes the gender of μειρακίῳ, or of ἐμοί, implied in τῇδε τῇ ἡλικίᾳ, and implies more or less of *fictitious* and false elaboration. It is to be remembered that at this time the successful speeches in the Athenian courts were usually prepared by rhetoricians, and delivered as if their own by the parties. Lysias prepared scores of such orations, and wrote one for Socrates, which he declined to use. εἰς ὑμᾶς εἰσιέναι, to come *into* your presence, your dicastery, or your assembly. 4. παρίεμαι. Ruhnken, as cited and approved by Stallbaum, says: παρίημι = admitto, παρίεμαι = ad me admitti volo, i. e., *precor, deprecor*. 6. Καὶ

Page 43 / Page 44 (margin notes)

Page 44 ἐν ἀγορᾷ, κ.τ.λ. *Both in the agora at the counters, and elsewhere.* Cf. Mat. 21, 12: τὰς τραπέζας τῶν κολλυβιστῶν. τράπεζα in modern Greek = bank.

D. 8. ἔχει γὰρ οὑτωσί. *For the fact is thus*, sc. as follows. Then follows the explanatory clause, which, as usual, is without any connective (asyndeton). 9. ἀναβέβηκα, sc. the βῆμα, or stand of the accused. The accuser also had his βῆμα or *elevated* stand in the court. 10. τῆς ἐνθάδε λέξεως. The language of judicial proceedings. For the gen. see G. 182, 1; H. A. 756. 11. ὥσπερ οὖν ἄν. This ἂν belongs to the apodosis with ξυνεγιγνώσκετε, where it is repeated (δήπου ἄν). It stands with ὥσπερ to intimate at the outset (by way of anticipation), that the example is a mere supposition, and then, after the intervening protasis with εἰ, it is repeated with the verb or some other important word of the apodosis. G. 212, 2; H. A. 864. τῷ ὄντι = *in fact.* So very often, especially in Plato. ξένος, not an Athenian but still a Greek, who might be understood in the Athenian courts, but would speak in the dialect, tone, and manner of his native country. Compare Schleiermacher's note ad loc. 13. οἷσπερ. G. 151, N. 2; H. A. 628.

18 A. 13. Καὶ δὴ καὶ νῦν, κ.τ.λ.,=*so also now*, i. e., in my case at present, *I make this request of you, a reasonable one as to me it certainly seems.* For the personal form δοκῶ, instead of the impersonal δοκεῖ, see H. A. 944. The γε emphasizes the clause, not the pronoun, which therefore takes the unemphatic form μοι. Al. ὥς γ' ἐμοί. 16. αὐτὸ τοῦτο, *this very thing*, i. e., *this single point*, viz., whether I speak what is just or not. Here the demonstrative (enforced by the intensive, of which combination Plato is particularly fond) prepares the way for a clause, as it does above for the infinitive. 18. ἀρετή = *the virtue*, being in the predicate, omits the article in Greek, but requires it in English. G. 141, N. 8; H. A. 669. 20. δίκαιός εἰμι instead of δίκαιόν ἐστι with the acc. and inf.; another example of the personal for the impersonal construction.

B. 24. πολλὰ ἤδη ἔτη explains πάλαι, which is altogether indefinite: *for some time, many years now.* πάλαι. The

Clouds of Aristophanes was put on the stage 27 years before Page 44 the time of this trial. Cf. note 19, C, p. 46, l. 15. 26. **τοὺς ἀμφὶ Ἄνυτον.** Anytus and his associates, sc. Meletus and Lycon. For this use of ἀμφί see Lexicon. Anytus is named, as being the most popular and at the same time the most hostile of the three prosecutors of Socrates. He was a man of large fortune but loose principles. He gained the favor of the people as a leader of the exiles at Phyle in the time of the Thirty Tyrants, and having taken offense at Socrates partly on personal and partly on professional grounds (cf. 23, E), induced Meletus and Lycon to join with him in a prosecution. According to Diogenes Laertius (2, 38, 39), the Athenians repented of their condemnation of Socrates and put Meletus to death, and sent Anytus and Lycon into banishment. Grote disbelieves and denies this. His. of Gr., vol. viii, chap. 68. Cf. Stallb. and Smith's Dic. of Biog. and Mythol., *Anytus*. 27. **οἱ . . . παραλαμβάνοντες,** *who taking the mass of you from your boyhood*, sc. as it were, under their instruction. 1. **ὡς ἔστι,** Page 45 **κ.τ.λ.,** *saying, there is one Socrates*, etc. The introductory particle appropriate to an indirect quotation is followed by a direct quotation, and must be omitted in English. **σοφὸς ἀνήρ,** *a philosopher.* Compare the Latin *sapiens*. σοφός, as well as σοφιστής and φιλόσοφος, was more or less a term of reproach with the ignorant multitude. Cf. Grote, His. Gr., vol. viii, chap. 67, Eng. ed. 2. **τά τε μετέωρα φροντιστής.** φροντιστής governs the acc. as retaining the active force of φροντίζων. G. 158, N. 3; H. A. 718. 3. **τὸν ἥττω . . . ποιῶν,** *making the weaker the stronger argument*, or, as it is often expressed, *making the worse appear the better reason.* Cf. Cic. Brut. 8: docere quemadmodum caussa inferior dicendo fieri superior possit. The Sophists were open to this charge, as the physical philosophers were to that of inquiring into everything in the heavens above and in the earth beneath; and the art of the enemies of Socrates consisted in arraying against *him* the prejudices which the public mind already cherished, with greater or less reason, against *them*—in short, in confounding him with them, though he was, in fact, diametrically opposed to them both in faith and

Page 18 in philosophy. Cf. below, 23, D: τὰ κατὰ πάντων τῶν φιλοσοφούντων πρόχειρα ταῦτα λέγουσιν.

C. 5. οἱ δεινοί as pred.; those before mentioned as δεινοί. G. 141, N. 8; H. A. 669, a. 6. οὐδὲ θεοὺς νομίζειν, *do not even believe in the existence of the gods.* This, it is well known, was one point in the indictment against Socrates. Cf. Xen. Mem. I, 1, 1; also below, 24 B. The physical philosophers of the age afforded a plausible, not to say just, occasion for this charge, since they, for the most part, dispensed with all efficient causes, and either failed to recognize the Deity, or else confounded him with his works. The systems, if not the men, were chargeable with atheism or pantheism. Cicero ascribes to Anaxagoras the first distinct recognition of the divine existence and agency, as an intelligent cause, in the universe. 7. ἔπειτα . . . ἔτι δὲ καί = *then . . . still further also;* or *in the second place . . . in the third place also.* 8. ταύτῃ τῇ ἡλικίᾳ. Explained by παῖδες ὄντες, κ.τ.λ. 9. ἂν . . . ἐπιστεύσατε. ἐν ᾗ, *where you would have been most likely to believe.* G. 226, 2, N. 2. 11. ἐρήμην κατηγοροῦντες, *accusing me in my absence.* The form of expression (ἐρήμη, sc. δίκη) is derived from a suit at law, in which one of the parties does not appear. ἀτεχνῶς = *absolutely, really,* used especially by Plato and comic writers to affirm the improbable or unreasonable. See below, 18 D. 12. ὃ δὲ πάντων ἀλογώτατον, *but what is most unreasonable of all* is the fact *that.* Sometimes the ὅτι also, as well as τοῦτό ἐστιν, is omitted, thus leaving the following clause in direct apposition, as we often do in English. 13. εἰ . . . τυγχάνει ὢν implies no uncertainty: εἰ = *in case,* or *when.* The allusion is particularly to Aristophanes, who is *named* below, 19, C; though Cratinus, Ameipsias, Eupolis, and other comic poets, ridiculed Socrates. Cf. Stallb. ad loc.

D. 14. ὅσοι δέ, another more inaccessible class. φθόνῳ καὶ διαβολῇ χρώμενοι = *with envy and calumny.* The part. denotes means or manner, and may often be rendered *with.* See Lex. It belongs properly to διαβολῇ, and is extended to φθόνῳ by a species of zeugma. ἀνέπειθον. The impf. expresses the persistence of the persuasion and the growth of the calumny. 15. οἱ δὲ introduces another class of persuaders,

as if οἱ μὲν had preceded with φθόνῳ . . . χρώμενοι, the one Page 45
being the envious and calumnious, the other those who were really persuaded in their own minds of the guilt of Socrates. 16. ἀπορώτατοι, *most inaccessible* (ἀ and πόρος), *most difficult to approach and convince.* Cf. Lysis, 223, B: ἄποροι προσφέρεσθαι. 17. ἀναβιβάσασθαι . . . ἐνταυθοῖ, *to make . . . come up hither*, i. e., summon him to appear in court. Observe the force of the middle voice: *for my benefit*, cf. ἐξελέσθαι, 19, A. αὐτῶν is partitive genitive = *any of them*, separated from οὐδένα for emphasis. 18. ὥσπερ . . . ἀποκρινομένου, *to fight with shadows, as it were, in defending myself, and also to cross-examine while no one replies.* The participle and the infinitive in each part form a complex idea, and then the two parts or ideas are connected together by τε καὶ. Thus is the apparent confusion of participles and infinitives explained by Fischer. See his note ad loc. 20. Ἀξιώσατε = existimate, *hold*, or *deem;* so Bekker, Ast, Stallbaum; or, as Wagner, *grant, assume.*

E. 23. ἐκείνους, *those*, sc. *earlier* and more *remote* accusers. ἐκεῖνος refers to the *more remote idea*, though, as in this instance, it be to the *latter word* or *clause*. 26. Εἶεν. *Well, be it so.* For the root and signification of this particle see Lex. Schleiermacher: *wohl.* It marks the establishment and completion of what goes before and the transition to another topic. 27. ἐξελέσθαι. Cf. note on ἀναβιβάσασθαι, 18, D. τὴν διαβολὴν . . . χρόνῳ. *The calumny* (misconception produced by calumny) *which you have entertained a long time, this* to eradicate *in so short a time.* τοῦτο οὕτω γενέσθαι, sc. the eradication of false impressions from the minds of his judges. It is still further explained by καὶ πλέον . . . ἀπολογούμενον, *and to accomplish something by my defense.* On πλέον τι ποιεῖν = *proficere aliquid*, to get on or forward with a thing, to gain something by it; see Lexicon. Page 46

A. 2. εἴ τι ἄμεινον, κ.τ.λ. The sequel shows that he not 19
only doubted whether it was best for him to be acquitted, but that he did not desire to live by any such means as were likely to influence his judges to acquit him. He makes his

Page 18 defense rather as a matter of form in obedience to the laws, than with the expectation or desire of success.

B. 7. Ἀναλάβωμεν ἐξ ἀρχῆς. *Let us take up anew, from the beginning.* He has adverted to the charge in general terms before (18, B); but here he would resume its examination from the first, as if he had not before mentioned it. 8. ἡ ἐμὴ διαβολή, *the false opinion of me.* ἐμή = objective gen. Cf. εὐνοίᾳ τῇ σῇ, *good will to you*, Gorg. 486, A; G. 147, N. 1; H. A. 694. 9. με ἐγράψατο τὴν γραφὴν ταύτην. For the force of the middle voice, see G. 199, N. 3; H. A. 816, 6. For the double acc. (of the cognate signification γραφήν, and the direct object με), see G. 159, N. 4; H. A. 725. Render: *has preferred against me this indictment.* γραφή is a public indictment for a criminal offense; δίκη is applicable either to public or private causes, but when used in contradistinction to γραφή, it denotes a private suit. 10. ὥσπερ οὖν, κ.τ.λ. *Therefore just as* it is customary to read the *bill of indictment* presented by *formal accusers*, so *must we read theirs.* ἀντωμοσία is primarily the oath of a party at law, and then the bill or form of indictment. 12. περιεργάζεται, *is overbusy, excessively curious, is a busy-body.*

C. 14. τοιαύτη τίς, *something like this.* He does not profess to give it exactly. Cf. Xen. Mem. I, 1, 1. 15. ἐν τῇ Ἀριστοφάνους κωμῳδίᾳ. The Clouds, perhaps the master-piece of Aristophanes, in which he introduces Socrates, as the principal character, sitting in a basket in the air, and uttering declamations as windy as his position. Very different explanations are given of the motives which induced the poet to treat the moral philosopher with such palpable injustice. Some have supposed that he was influenced by personal hostility, and further instigated and suborned by the enemies of Socrates. But this supposition does not accord either with the comparatively respectful tone in which Aristophanes elsewhere alludes to Socrates (cf. Birds, 1280, 1554; Frogs, 1487), or with the mild and even complimentary terms in which Plato speaks of Aristophanes here and elsewhere. Had Plato regarded Aristophanes as a bitter personal enemy of Socrates, or as having occasioned his master's death, he never would have introduced the poet and the philosopher conversing on such friendly terms as in the Symposium, still less furnished for the poet's tomb such an epitaph as the following: "Jupiter, wishing to find an asylum for all the graces, found the soul of Aristophanes." Others have thought that Aristophanes really mistook the true character of Socrates, confounded his teachings with those of the Sophists, whom he opposed, and so in sober earnest visited upon his head the storm of indignation which was merited by the class, and by him as its leader and ablest representative. But, to say nothing of the want of discernment which is thus imputed to Aristophanes, the matter was not viewed in so serious a light either by Plato (as the considerations just mentioned suffice to show), or by Socrates, who, if we may credit the traditions, was present when the piece was performed, and stood forth before the audience that he might be recognized as "a host who furnished a large company an *agreeable entertainment.*" There was enough of general resemblance between him and the Sophists in their talkative habits, the subjects on which they conversed, and the manner in which they reasoned (especially as he often met them on their own ground, and refuted them with their own weapons), to give plausibility to the representation of him as an arch-sophist. Doubtless also the ultra-conservative poet viewed the speculating and revolutionizing spirit of the Socratic philosophy with not a little of the same fear and aversion with which he regarded the demoralizing instructions of the Sophists. Moreover, Socrates stood in the most friendly relations to Alcibiades and Euripides, both of whom, as arch-innovators though in different spheres, were subjects of unsparing ridicule and reproach in the comedies of Aristophanes. So much of objective reality we may suppose lay at the basis of the representation which is made of Socrates in the Clouds. The rest is comic exaggeration and extravagance got up purposely, but not maliciously, for the amusement of the πολυγέλοι Ἀθηναῖοι. And surely never was comedian furnished with a more fruitful theme for inextinguishable laughter than the grotesque person, outlandish dress, and singular gait of Socrates, with which friend and foe, Athenian and stranger, all had become

Page 46

Page 46 familiar as he stood and stared, or started and ran through the streets, or fascinated some and bored and vexed others in the shops and the market-places. The intent of the piece and its author may have been misunderstood by some, and it may have had some effect in preparing the way for the prosecution, which it suggests. But it is referred to in the Apology as an illustration of popular prejudices of long standing, rather than as a cause of the present indictment. And the utter failure of the Clouds to make any serious impression on the popular mind against Socrates is seen, not only in its want of success at the time (for it gained no favor and won no prize), but also in the fact that a period of twenty-four years intervened between its exhibition and the condemnation of the Moral Philosopher. Cf. Stallb. ad loc.; Smith's Dic. of Biog. 16. *περιφερόμενον*, sc. in a basket (*κρεμάθρα*), cf. the Clouds, 225 seqq. 17. *ἀεροβατεῖν*. When asked what he is doing, Socrates replies in the play: *ἀεροβατῶ καὶ περιφρονῶ τὸν ἥλιον*. 18. *ὧν . . . πέρι ἐπαΐω*. Observe the anastrophe and the position of *πέρι*, as in English: which I know nothing *about*. Socrates, as represented in the Phædo, suggests that he had in early life been a student of physics, 96 A. Xenophon quotes him as disparaging such studies, Mem. I, 1, 11. 19. *λέγω*, sc. the foregoing = *I say this*. *ἀτιμάζων* governs *ἐπιστήμην*. The Socratic irony is manifest in this clause, and in the following, which is parenthetical: *let me not, by any means, be prosecuted by Meletus on so weighty a charge!* sc. as undervaluing this kind of knowledge.

D. 22. *ἀλλὰ γὰρ, κ.τ.λ.* *But* I must speak, *for*, etc. 23. *αὐτοὺς ὑμῶν τοὺς πολλούς*. *The greater part of yourselves.* 24. *διδάσκειν τε καὶ φράζειν*, hysteron proteron. With *φράζειν*, *ἀλλήλοις* is to be supplied from the accusative. 28. *ἐκ τούτων*, Al. *τούτου*. The Greeks very often employ the plural of the demonstrative in reference to a foregoing clause or single idea, where we should use the singular. Render: *from this*.
Page 47 H. A. 635. 1. *περὶ ἐμοῦ* is placed before *ἃ* for emphasis = *which the many say about me*. 3. *τούτων*, the charges in the foregoing context—inquiring into things above, making the

worse the better reason, etc. *οὐδέ γ' εἰ, κ.τ.λ.* We should Page 47
expect *οὔτε* answering to the *οὔτε* in the previous clause, but *οὐδέ γε* is more emphatic and therefore more appropriate to introduce a new topic of special importance. It is made still more emphatic by being repeated before *τοῦτο ἀληθές*. 5. *χρήματα πράττομαι.* This charge also confounded Socrates with the Sophists, who amassed large sums of money for tuition. It is denied by Xenophon, Mem. I, 2, 60.

E. 5. *ἐπεί καὶ τοῦτο, κ.τ.λ.* The Attics use *ἐπεί* often like *γάρ* = *for;* and sometimes, like *quum* in Latin, it may be well rendered *although.* Socrates treats this charge, just as he did the other, ironically, representing it as a very beautiful and honorable thing, if one were only wise and capable of doing it; and yet he feels constrained to deny it simply because it is not true. 7. *Γοργίας τε ὁ Λεοντῖνος, κ.τ.λ.* He enumerates several of the most popular Sophists and rhetoricians who had enriched themselves by teaching the sons of the wealthy at Athens. They were all foreigners. For Gorgias of Leontini, a city of Sicily, cf. Diog. Laer, 9, 52; Cic. de Orat. I, 22; Brut. 8; Plat. Gorg., Hip., and Protag. For Prodicus of Ceos, one of the Cyclades Islands, cf. Cic. Brut. 8; Xen. Mem. II, 1, 21 seqq.; Plat. Protag. and Cratyl. For Hippias of Elis, a city of the Peloponnesus, cf. Cic. de Orat. 32, Brut. 8; Plat. Hip. and Minos. See also Smith's Dic. Biog. and Mythol., and Grote's His. Gr., vol. viii, chap. 67. Grote defends the Sophists as a class with great learning and eloquence. Doubtless they have been condemned too much in the gross —with too indiscriminate severity. But they belonged to an age which was losing its faith, and had the misfortune to be the recognized teachers of the people, with no instruction to offer which could reach the real difficulty. So, though there were doubtless wise and good men among them, it was not unnatural that they were charged with exerting an influence hostile to morals and religion, nor that they received the censure which Plato everywhere attaches to them. 10. *τοὺς νέους* would regularly be the object of *πείθειν*, depending on *οἷός τ' ἐστίν*, instead of which, however, by a singular anacoluthon, we have *πείθουσι.* H. A. 1063. It should be ob-

Page 47 served, that Plato abounds in such irregular constructions and unexpected changes, doubtless to keep up the appearance of a colloquial style appropriate to the dialogue, and which is no less appropriate to the plain talk which Socrates promises to hold with his judges in this Apology. The plural verb with ἕκαστος is not unnatural. H. A. 609, a. πολιτῶν is partitive genitive after ᾧ: *who have the opportunity to associate gratuitously with whomsoever they please of their fellow-citizens.* 18. προσειδέναι: *and besides* (paying them money) *to feel under obligation to them.*

A. ἐπεὶ introduces an illustration = γάρ, *for*, cf. note,
20 19, E. Schleiermacher renders it by the German *ja*. 14. ὃν . . . ἐπιδημοῦντα, *of whose sojourning here I* lately *became aware.* The reference is to Evenus, the poet and Sophist, as appears below, B. He was a native of the island Paros. He is mentioned in the Phædo, 60, D, and Phædrus, 267, A. Callias, the son of Hipponicus, who informed Socrates of Evenus' stay in the city, was proverbially rich (ὁ πλούσιος, Plutarch), and his lavish expenditure upon the Sophists is often referred to. He in fact utterly squandered his vast property and died in poverty. Protag. 314, B, C; Xen. Symp. i, 5; Aristoph. Birds, 285. See also Boeckh's Pub. Econ. Athens, vol. ii, p. 242. 20. ἔμελλεν is assimilated to the tense on which it depends, the thought being still under the influence of the unfulfilled condition. H. A. 919, b.

B. 21. ἀρετήν. Acc. of specification, or more accurately a cognate acc. with the adjective: *in the virtue* (or excellence) *becoming* them. So, in a similar illustration, Xenophon makes Socrates use the word δίκαιος of a horse and an ox, that is obedient to his proper law and trained for his appropriate work. Socrates used such illustrations, drawn from the lower animals and the common affairs of life, till they were threadbare and almost offensive, at least to those who could not but feel their force as directed against themselves. The "Great Teacher" abounded in this method of instruction. 22. ἦν δ' ἂν οὗτος. *And this* (overseer) *would be*, etc. 24. τῆς ἀνθρωπίνης τε καὶ πολιτικῆς, *that which is appropriate to man and also to the state.* 1. πέντε μνῶν = some $83. This was a small sum in comparison with the tuition fees which Protagoras, Gorgias, and some others exacted, who received 100 minæ. With the Greek μνᾶ compare the Latin *mina* and our word *money*. 2. ἐμακάρισα: the aor. is used to express the momentary action as having just taken place, or perhaps it would be better to say, without reference to time. It is so employed especially in the vividness of the drama. M. and T., 19, N. 5; H. A. 842. Page 48

C. 3. ἐμμελῶς, according to Stallbaum, has a double application to the *style* of teaching and to the *price* of tuition = *so properly* (literally, *in tune*), *so excellently* in both respects. He says, there is great urbanity in the expression. If Socrates had said, οὕτως εὐτελῶς, he would have too clearly ridiculed Evenus and so Callias. He used, therefore, a word by which, while he seemed to praise Evenus, he yet severely censured both his levity and the avarice of the other Sophists. It is used of a moderate or reasonable price in the Laws, 776, B, 760, A. 5. ἀλλ' οὐ γάρ, κ.τ.λ. The ellipsis is obvious: *but* I can not thus pride myself, *for*, etc. γάρ in such connection may be rendered *really*, *certainly*: *but I really do not* know. Cf. H. A. 1050, d. 6. ὑπολάβοι. Compare our *take up*. 7. τὸ σὸν τί ἐστι πρᾶγμα, *your* business, what is it? The emphasis is on *your*: you deny any acquaintance with the profession of the naturalist who inquires into the secrets of the universe, or of the Sophist who teaches, and is well paid for teaching, the art of persuasion; what then, Socrates, is *your* business, profession, or pursuit? 9. οὐδὲν περιττότερον, *nothing more or other*, *nihil aliud*. Stallbaum renders: *nihil curiosius*. ἔπειτα, *then, in that case, I suppose so much talk and discussion would not have arisen, as have arisen*. γέγονεν stands where ἂν ἐγένετο would regularly have been used, to denote that this bruit has actually arisen. Cron suggests that the conditional idea can not be contained in σοῦ . . . πραγματευομένου, for we should not then have οὐδέν. He translates: *It is inconceivable that such a report should have arisen about you alone who are no more busy than others.*

D. 13. τί ποτ', *quid tandem*. In questions, ποτέ, like

Page 48 *tandem*, indicates surprise, wonder, impatience, or some other lively emotion. It is here retained in the indirect question, just as it would have been used in the direct, as expressive of the wonder of the inquirer. 14. τό τε ὄνομα καὶ τὴν διαβολήν, *both the name*, sc. of a wise man, *and the calumny* connected with it. 16. εὖ μέντοι ἴστε, κ.τ.λ. *Be assured, however, I will tell you the whole truth.* Observe the omission of ὅτι. So in Crit. 54, D, ἀλλὰ ἴσθι, ὅσα γε, κ.τ.λ., and elsewhere after εὖ ἴστε. 17. ἀλλ' ἤ. H. A. 1046, 2 c; cf. also Jelf, 773, ob. 1. 18. ποίαν δὴ σοφίαν ταύτην, *pray what sort of wisdom this.* Cf. Laches, 194 D. Σω. Καί μοι δοκεῖ ἀνὴρ σοφίαν τινὰ τὴν ἀνδρείαν λέγειν. Λα. Ποίαν, ὦ Σώκρατες, σοφίαν; the clause takes the construction of σοφίαν in the preceding (acc. after διά). The omission of the preposition is especially frequent in questions and answers, and serves to give a more familiar form to the dialogue. This effect is illustrated by the fact that the usage belongs to comedy but not to tragedy; cf. Jelf, 650, 5. 19. ἥπερ ἐστὶν ἴσως, κ.τ.λ. *Just that, perhaps, which is*, etc. 20. τῷ ὄντι, *in reality.* ταύτην, *in this*, acc. of specification. So σοφίαν in the next clause.

E. 21. ἢ κατ' ἄνθρωπον, *than pertains to man, quam pro homine*, H. A. 646. 22. ἢ οὐκ ἔχω, τί λέγω, *or else I know not what to call it*—certainly it is not human wisdom—it is not any such wisdom as I possess. The irony of the passage is evident. λέγω is subjunctive. 24. ἐπὶ διαβολῇ τῇ ἐμῇ, *for the sake of calumniating me.* For the sense of ἐπί, cf. H. A. 799, 2, c; also Jelf, 634, 3, a. For τῇ ἐμῇ, instead of the objective gen., ἐμοῦ, cf. note, 19, A. 25. μὴ θορυβήσητε. *Do not raise a tumult against me*, or, as a speaker would say to a modern assembly, *do not hiss me* = *ne obstrepatis.* The reader will remember the popular constitution of the court, cf. note, 17, A. For the aor. subj. in prohibitions with μή and its compounds, cf. G. 254; H. A. 874. μηδὲ ἄν, *not even if.* μέγα λέγειν, properly denotes *boasting*, as μέγα φρονεῖν does *pride.* In the later Greek, it meant to *say something marvelous.* But it was the seeming *pride* and *arrogance* of what he said, which, he feared, would give offense, and which did actually give offense to the judges. Cf. Xen. Apol.

Soc. as cited below, 21, A; also Xen. Apol. Soc. 1, where he speaks of the μεγαληγορία, which all the Apologies ascribe to Socrates in his defense. 27. ἀξιόχρεων, *responsible*, primarily in regard to money, secondarily in regard to testimony. Cf. 38, B. τῆς γὰρ ἐμῆς, εἰ δή τίς ἐστι σοφία καὶ οἵα, *for of my wisdom, whether now I have any, and of what sort it is*, etc. By a somewhat peculiar *attraction*, σοφία is drawn from the principal into the subordinate clause. Page 48 Page 49

A. 2. ἐμός ἑταῖρος. Hence often attacked by Aristophanes in the Clouds and elsewhere. τῷ πλήθει. It is to be remembered that the word was used with frequent application to the Athenian democracy. 3. ξυνέφυγε . . . κατῆλθε, *he went with you in your recent exile and with you returned.* The allusion is to the exile of the principal men of the Athenian democracy under the Thirty Tyrants, which having taken place quite recently, is called τὴν φυγὴν ταύτην. This allusion was calculated to recommend Chærephon to popular favor. 5. ὡς σφοδρός. Cf. Aristoph. Clouds, 104, 503, seq., Birds, 1570; Xen. Mem. II, 3; Plat. Gorg., Charm., etc., pass. 6. καί, ὅπερ λέγω, μὴ θορυβεῖτε, *and, I repeat it, do not be raising a tumult.* It will be observed, that the aor. subj. is used in the first request (μὴ θορυβήσητε above), but in the repetition the pres. imp. The former is a general request *not to do it at all;* the latter is more definite, and means: *don't be doing it,* as you *are* doing and will be very *liable* to do while *I proceed,* especially with this to you most surprising and perhaps offensive part of my narrative. G. 202, 1; H. A. 874, a. The Apology, which bears the name of Xenophon, declares expressly, that this part of Socrates' Defense did call forth repeated expressions of displeasure from the judges. Xen. Apol. Soc. 15. 7. ἤρετο γὰρ δή. The Greeks use the particles, γάρ, δή, οὖν, in resuming a sentence after a parenthesis, where we use *I say.* 8. ἀνεῖλεν, *responded,* literally, *took up,* sc. her response. This famous response is worded differently in different authorities. Cf. Xen. Apol. Socr. 14; Diog. Laert. 2, 37; Schol. Aristoph. Clouds, 144. 9. ὁ ἀδελφός, sc. Chærecrates, Xen. Mem. II, 3. 10. οὑτοσὶ . . . ἐκεῖνος. Cf. note, 18, E.

Page 49 B. 13. *τί ποτε, what in the world.* Cf. note, 20, D. 15. *ξύνοιδα ἐμαυτῷ σοφὸς ὤν.* After *ξύνοιδα, συγγιγνώσκω*, etc., the participle expresses *that of which one is conscious*, and may either agree with the subject of the verb in the *nom.* or with the reflexive which follows the verb and refers to the same person, in the *dative*. Here we have the former construction; below, 22, D, we have the other: *ἐμαυτῷ ξυνῄδειν οὐδὲν ἐπισταμένῳ.* G. 280, N. 2; H. A. 982, a. *μέγα* and *σμικρόν* are adverbial accusatives. H. A. 719, b. 15. *τί οὖν ποτε λέγει, what in the world then, I say, does he mean?* *οὖν* is resumptive like *γάρ*, above, 21, A; and *λέγει* is best rendered, as it often is, by the English *mean*. Below the same form of expression follows *ἠπόρουν*, instead of the oratio obliqua, *ὅ τι . . . λέγοι.* G. 247; H. A. 932. 18. *ἔπειτα . . . ἐτραπόμην, but at length, with much labor, I betook myself to an examination of it* (sc. the oracle or the meaning of the god, *τί ποτε λέγει*) *somewhat as follows.* *τοιοῦτος* usually refers to the foregoing, *τοιόσδε* to the following (cf. note, 37, A), but not always. G. 148, N. 1; H. A. 696. Cf. *τοιαύτη τις*, 19, C, and note, ibid. 19. *ἦλθον* stands without a connective, because this clause is in *apposition* as it were with the preceding, being a fuller and more exact statement of the examination there mentioned. Cf. 17, D, and note, ibid. The reader will observe that such clauses or sentences are asyndetic; while, with the exception of such, each clause and sentence of connected discourse in Greek usually begins with some connective particle, *δέ, καί, γάρ, οὖν*, etc. Cf. H. A. 1039.

C. 20. *ὡς . . . ἐλέγξων, supposing, that there, if anywhere, I should confute*, etc. G. 277, N. 2; H. A. 978. 22. *ὅτι Οὑτοσί.* Cf. note on *ὡς ἔστι*, 18, B. *σὺ δ' ἐμὲ ἔφησθα, but you* (sc. the oracle) *said I* (sc. was wiser). 24. *πρὸς ὃν . . . ἔπαθον, in looking to whom I met with such an experience.* 25. *καὶ διαλεγόμενος.* *Καὶ* connects *διαλεγόμενος* to *διασκοπῶν* (the intervening clause being parenthetical), and the participle, belonging to the principal subject of the discourse (Socrates), is in the nominative, though, to agree with what follows, it should be in the dative with *μοι*. It is a species of anacoluthon. H. A. 1063.

D. 1. ἐντεῦθεν is both temporal and causal = *from that time and for that reason.* 3. πρὸς ἐμαυτὸν . . . ἐλογιζόμην, *I reasoned with myself.* τούτου μὲν τοῦ ἀνθρώπου. μέν = μήν, indeed. H. A. 1037, 12. The μέν after κινδυνεύει is correlative to ἀλλ', after which follows again the more usual correlation οὗτος μὲν . . . ἐγὼ δέ. After ὥσπερ οὖν οὐκ οἶδα, οὕτως is understood. 7. οὖν denotes not an inference but a correspondence with what he has before said of the ignorance of himself and others: *while I, just as in fact, and as I have already said, I do not know, so I do not even suppose that I know.* 8. σμικρῷ τινι denotes the *degree*, and αὐτῷ τούτῳ the *respect* in which he is wiser. αὐτῷ = alone, see Lex. I, 3. G. 188, 2; 188, 1, N. 1; H. A. 781, 780; cf. 18, A. The difference between μή and οὐδέ, the contingent and the absolute negative, is well illustrated in the clause ἃ μὴ οἶδα, κ.τ.λ.: *what I chance not to know, I do not even suppose that I know.* Page 50

E. 14. ὅτι ἀπηχθανόμην. Observe the imp. here and the aor. above. These words connect with each of the preceding participles, but in the different relations of the *fact* and the *cause*—with αἰσθανόμενος, ὅτι would strictly require to be rendered *that;* with λυπούμενος and δεδιώς, *because.* 15. τὸ τοῦ θεοῦ. G. 141, N. 4; H. A. 621, b. 16. ἰτέον οὖν σκοποῦντι. Socrates here passes suddenly from the indirect to the direct narration, and gives us the *very language* of his heart at the *time* when he made this examination: *I must go then* (thought I), *in investigating the oracle what it means, to all*, etc. σκοποῦντι agrees with μοι implied as the dative of the agent after ἰτέον. For χρησμόν, put as the object of σκοποῦντι instead of the subject of λέγει, see H. A. 878.

A. 18. νὴ τὸν κύνα. A very common oath in the mouth of Socrates. Cf. Gorg. 460, B; 482, B, and Prof. Woolsey's notes, ibid. In the last cited passage, Socrates adds: τὸν Αἰγυπτίων θεόν, which is probably to be regarded as a humorous addition. See Mitchell's note, D, App. to Aristoph. Wasps. Fischer, followed by Stallbaum, Cousin, etc., refers the origin of such oaths to Rhadamanthus, who is said, in order to avoid swearing always by the gods, to have invented several other formulæ as substitutes, such as by the dog, by 22

Page 50 the oak, by the goose, etc. In Xenophon, as well as Plato, Socrates is represented as swearing (somewhat singularly) by Juno, infra, 24, E; Gorg. 449, D; Hip. Maj. 291, 9; Xen. Mem. I, 5, 5; III, 10, 9; IV, 2, 9, et al. 20. *οἱ μὲν μάλιστα, κ.τ.λ.* An explanatory clause, hence without a connective. Cf. notes, 17, D; 21, B. 20. *ὀλίγου δεῖν.* Cf. note 17, A. 21. *τοῦ πλείστου* is governed by *ἐνδεεῖς.* The reader will observe the juxtaposition of the two contrasted words, *φαυλότεροι* and *ἐπιεικέστεροι.* 24. *πλάνην, wandering,* sc. to visit and examine the reputed wise men. *πονοῦντος* agrees with *μου* implied in *ἐμήν.* *πόνους* alludes to labors like those of Hercules. 25. *ἵνα . . . γένοιτο*: *that after all the oracle might in the end prove irrefutable,* i. e., in addition to all his labors, *also* (*καὶ*) to bring about a *result* the opposite of what he set out to accomplish, which was to show that the oracle must be false. Such seems to be the true interpretation of this much disputed passage. Cf. Fischer's Defense of Platonic Passages against the Amendments of Stephens; also the notes of Schleiermacher and Stallbaum ad loc. The opt. is used in *γένοιτο* because *πονοῦντος* is imperfect in sense. G. 204, N. 1; H. A. 856, a.

B. 28. *ὡς . . . καταληψόμενος.* Cf. note 21, C. *ἐπ' αὐτοφώρῳ καταληψόμενος* contains an allusion to the *detection* of
Page 51 a criminal *in the very act.* 2. *μάλιστα πεπραγματεῦσθαι*: *to have been most carefully composed.* 3. *διηρώτων ἄν.* The imperfect with *ἄν* denotes repetition according to the circumstances in each case: *I would ask them in each instance, what they meant to say.* G. 206; H. A. 835. So below, *ἂν βέλτιον ἔλεγον*: *almost all who were present would speak better* (i. e, give a better account) *than they* (the poets) *of the poems which they themselves had composed.*

C. 8. *οὐ σοφίᾳ, κ.τ.λ.* So in Ion 533, E, Socrates says, that poets and musicians, like prophets and soothsayers, compose their productions, not by *art,* but by an inspiration which displaces *reason.* The fundamental difference between real *science* or *art,* as based on established rules and understood reasons, and mere unintelligent knack, or unconscious instinct or inspiration, is an idea, on which Socrates often and earnestly insists. Cf. Gorgias pass.; Grote's His. Gr., vol. viii, chap. lxviii. 14. *οἰομένων*. G. 280; H. A. 982. *εἶναι ἀνθρώπων*. G. 136, N. 3; H. A. 941. *ἅ*, like its antecedent *τἆλλα*, is acc. of specification, and *σοφώτατοι* is understood in the predicate after *ἦσαν*: *in which they were not*, sc. the wisest. 15. *τῷ αὐτῷ οἰόμενος περιγεγονέναι*: *supposing that I surpassed them in the same respect in which* I surpassed *also the politicians*. Cf. 21, D. 17. *τελευτῶν*, *lastly*. H. A. 968, a. Page 51

D. 18. *ἐμαυτῷ . . . ἐπισταμένῳ*. Cf. note, 21, B. *ὡς ἔπος εἰπεῖν*. Cf. note, 17, A. 20. *τούτου*: *in this*. G. 171, 1; H. A. 748. 24. *δημιουργοί* is subject of *ἔδοξαν*. Besides its emphatic position, it is also made emphatic by *καί*, which is likewise repeated before the other subject of comparison *οἱ ποιηταί*, where it is superfluous in English, though very often so used in Greek. See above, C: *καὶ ἐντεῦθεν . . . ὥσπερ καὶ τῶν πολιτικῶν*. Cf. also Gorg. 479, B: *κινδυνεύουσι γὰρ ἐκ τῶν νῦν ὑμῖν ὡμολογημένων τοιοῦτόν τι ποιεῖν καὶ οἱ τὴν δίκην φεύγοντες*. 25. *τἆλλα τὰ μέγιστα*, e. g., the administration of the government, to which Socrates particularly refers. 27. *ἀνερωτᾶν*, to ask *again*, as in the case of the poets and the politicians. *ὑπὲρ τοῦ χρησμοῦ*: *nomine oraculi*. Stallb.

E. 28. *δεξαίμην*, in the sense of *prefer*, is very frequent in Plato. Cf. Gorg. 468, E; 471, C, et passim. 2. *ἀμφότερα* Page 52 is neuter, though it refers to the feminine nouns *σοφίαν* and *ἀμαθίαν* = *both the things*. G. 138, N. 2, a; H. A. 615 (2).

A. 8. *σοφὸς εἶναι* explains *ὄνομα τοῦτο* = *called this name*, 23 sc. *to be wise*. *To be* is superfluous in English, but *εἶναι* often follows verbs of calling. Cf. Protagoras, 311, E: *σοφιστὴν ὀνομάζουσι τὸν ἄνδρα εἶναι*. *σοφός* is nom. instead of acc., because, in the mind of the speaker, *himself* is the main subject of the sentence, as having become odious—as if he had said *ἀπεχθὴς γέγονα* instead of *ἀπέχθειαί μοι γεγόνασι*. On the popular prejudice against this name, see note 18, B, and Grote as there cited. 10. *ἃ ἂν ἄλλον ἐξελέγξω*: *in which I may chance to confute another*, or *in whatsoever I may confute another*. G. 233; H. A. 913. *τὸ δέ*: *but as to the matter of fact*. It is strengthened by *τῷ ὄντι* = in *reality*. The fuller

Page 52 formula, τὸ δὲ ἀληθές, is often used in the same way. 11. κινδυνεύει: *seems likely*, lit., runs the risk, has a chance. The use of this verb with this signification is especially common in Plato. It was suited to express his view of the uncertainty, or the probability only of all human knowledge. 13. ὀλίγου τινὸς . . . καὶ οὐδενός: *a little and indeed nothing*. So often μικρὰ καὶ οὐδέν = little or nothing. So *atque* in Latin sometimes adds a clause, which corrects, and at the same time increases the force of, the foregoing. For the force of τινὸς, cf. ἤ τι ἢ οὐδέν, 17, B, and note ibid. καὶ φαίνεται . . . Σωκράτη: *and he appears to mean this of Socrates*, sc. that human wisdom is of no account. For two acc. after a verb of *saying*, cf. G. 165; H. A. 725, a. 14. προσκεχρῆσθαι: made use of my name *besides*, i. e., *incidentally*, for another purpose. 15. ὥσπερ ἂν εἰ εἴποι: *as if he would say*. There is an ellipsis of ποιοῖτο or some such verb, constituting an implied apodosis, with which the ἄν belongs. Cf. note, 17, D, ὥσπερ οὖν ἄν. ἄν not infrequently leaves its verb to be supplied from the connection. So especially with ὥσπερ ἄν, also with πῶς γὰρ ἄν, and similar phrases.

B. 19. κατὰ τὸν θεόν: according to the god, i. e., in accordance with his oracle, or out of regard to his authority. So in Rom. viii, 27, and elsewhere in the New Testament. καὶ τῶν ἀστῶν καὶ τῶν ξένων, κ.τ.λ.: *both of the citizens and of the foreigners if I suppose any to be wise*. Partitive gen. after τινά. 22. τι τῶν τῆς πόλεως. Socrates apologizes elsewhere in Plato (e. g., below, 31, 32) and in Xenophon (e. g., Mem. I, 6, 15) for not participating in the affairs of the state. His was a higher mission, viz., to educate the individual citizens. 24. πενίᾳ μυρίᾳ: *the greatest poverty*. μυρίᾳ, Riddell compares Legg. 677, C, μυρίαν τινὰ φοβερὰν ἐρημίαν. πενία = paupertas, poverty; πτωχεία = egestas, destitution. The former is the usual condition of the poorer and laboring classes; the latter, of mendicants. As to the pecuniary circumstances of Socrates, cf. Xen. Œcon. 2, 3, where it appears he was commonly called πένης, and where it is said his house and all his property were worth five minæ; cf. also 38, B.

C. 27. οἱ τῶν πλουσιωτάτων. For omission of substantive,

see G. 141, N. 4; H. A. 621, c. This is no unimportant circumstance to show how the prejudices and passions of the *multitude* were awakened against him. 27. *αὐτόματοι*. Socrates, as not being a professional teacher, will not be responsible for his associates, who are entirely free. 1. *εἶτα* instead of *καὶ εἶτα*, as we often use *then* for *and then* between two verbs. 5. *ἀλλ' οὐχ αὑτοῖς*, *but not with themselves*, as they might well be angry with themselves for their own ignorance, instead of being angry with him who exposed it. Al. *αὐτοῖς*, sc. the young men, but this would require *ἐκείνοις*.

(Margin: Page 52 — beside "circumstance"; Page 53 — beside "καὶ")

D. 9. *τὰ κατὰ πάντων τῶν φιλοσοφούντων, κ.τ.λ.* Cf. notes, 18, B. 10. *ὅτι τὰ μετέωρα, κ.τ.λ.*, sc. *διαφθείρει τοὺς νέους διδάσκων*; *that* he corrupts the young by teaching *things in heaven and things under the earth, and not to believe in the gods*, etc.

E. 18. *ἐκ τούτων*, *as the outcome of these.* *Μέλητος μὲν ὑπὲρ τῶν ποιητῶν*. Al. *Μέλιτος*. This man is ridiculed by Aristophanes as well as Plato for his person, his character, and his bad *tragic poetry*. We learn from the Euthyphron (2, B, C), that his share in the prosecution of Socrates was to bring the indictment before the Archon Basileus, at which time he is described as still young and obscure, but vain and conceited. Besides his professional resentment in common with his brother poets, he had a personal grudge against Socrates for having refused to participate in, and severely animadverted upon, the arrest and "rendition" of Leon of Salamis by Meletus and three others at the command of the Thirty Tyrants. Xen. Mem. IV, 4, 3; Andoc. De Myster. 20. *Ἄνυτος ὑπὲρ τῶν δημιουργῶν*. He was a leather-dresser, and, besides sharing with other "*mechanics*" in the resentment provoked by Socrates' exposure of their ignorance as above described, he had, very likely, taken offense at his constant reference to shoemakers and other mechanics in the familiar illustration of his sentiments. He was also a popular demagogue, and had received the highest honors of the Athenian democracy. Hence in the text, *ὑπὲρ τῶν πολιτικῶν*. See note, 18, B. In Plato's Men. (91, A–C), we find him warning Socrates against a too free use of his tongue, lest he

Page 53 should get himself into trouble. 21. Λύκων ὑπὲρ τῶν ῥητόρων. Lycon was an orator and demagogue, probably the same who is held up as a drunken brawler by Aristophanes, Wasps, 1301. It was his part to prepare the accusation against Socrates. On all these accusers, see further in Stallbaum ad loc., and Smith's Dict. Ant.

24 A. 21. ἀρχόμενος. G. 277, 1; H. A. 968, a. 24. ταῦτ' ἔστιν ὑμῖν . . . τἀληθῆ. *This is the truth for you*, sc. which I promised to tell you, cf. 17, B. 27. τοῖς αὐτοῖς ἀπεχθάνομαι. I incur hatred *by the same*, sc. τἀληθῆ. On the sentiments of this and the following clause, cf. John, viii, 46, v. 48; Gal. iv, 16.

Page 54 B. 5. τὸν ἀγαθόν τε καὶ φιλόπολιν. These epithets are applied in accordance with polite usage, and yet not without irony. φιλόπολις differs from φιλόπατρις, according to Stallb., as *friend of Athens* from *friend of Greece*. 7. αὖθις γὰρ δὴ . . . λάβωμεν αὖ: *for now again let us take up on the other hand.* The language implies some formality and gravity in the examination of this, as also of the former accusation. ὥσπερ ἑτέρων τούτων ὄντων κατηγόρων: *inasmuch as these are different accusers*, i. e., another class, a *second*, in contradistinction to the *first*, whom he has just disposed of. 8. ἀντωμοσίαν. Cf. note, 19, B. 9. πως ὧδε, *nearly as follows.* Cf. τοιαύτη τίς, 19, C, and note ibid. The order of the points in the indictment is inverted, as it is given by Xenophon, Mem. I, 1, 1. Diogenes Laertius gives it on the authority of Phavorinus, as still existing in due form in the second century, in these words: "Socrates is guilty in not recognizing the gods that the state recognizes, but introducing other new divinities; and he is guilty also of corrupting the youth. Penalty, death." φησίν, sc. Meletus. 11. δαιμόνια, not = δαίμονες, divinities, but divine things, or things pertaining to gods.

C. 14. ἐγὼ δέ γε, *but I for my part.* The γε is omitted in the earlier editions, but inserted by Bekker, Ast, Stallbaum, etc., on the authority of the best MSS. 15. σπουδῇ χαριεντίζεται, *serio ludit;* literally, *jokes in earnest.* It is an example of the figure called *oxymoron.* It is explained by the following participial clauses. Meletus seemed as if he must

be merely *joking, playing a part*, when he *pretended to feel* Page 54
so much concern about matters (such as the education of the youth and the worship of the gods) *on which he never had bestowed an anxious thought;* and yet he made a *serious business* of it when he *rashly* (ῥᾳδίως) *brought men to trial* (εἰς ἀγῶνας καθιστὰς ἀνθρώπους). 17. ὧν τούτῳ ἐμέλησεν. G. 184, N. 1.

D. 20. δεῦρο, *hither*, ἄγε being understood, or instead of ἔρχου. The law allowed the parties in a suit to *question* each other, and obliged the party questioned to answer. Cf. below, note, 25, D. Few probably ever turned the law to so good account, as Socrates knew how to do by his method of question and answer. ἄλλο τι ἤ. This formula, frequently with ἤ omitted, is often used, especially in Plato's Dialogues, simply to ask a question, implying an affirmative answer, like οὐκοῦν, or nonne, only with perhaps still stronger affirmative implication. G. 282, 3; H. A. 1015, b. Render: *do you not*, etc. 21. ὅπως . . . ἔσονται. ὅπως, with the fut. ind., emphasizes the *future fact;* with the aor. subj. the *present purpose*. The former = *how they shall be;* the latter = how they may be. Render: *Do you not make it a question of much importance how the young shall be of the best character* possible? G. 217; H. A. 885; M. and T. 45. 23. μέλον γέ σοι, *especially* (γε) *since it so concerns you*, or even more vague, *since you are so careful*. The participle is used in acc. absolute, with its subject the suggested thought of the previous clause. G. 278, 2; H. A. 973, a. 24. τὸν μὲν . . . διαφθείροντα, *the one who is corrupting them*. It is in emphatic contrast to τὸν δὲ ποιοῦντα, which is also made emphatic by prolepsis. H. A. 878. ἐμέ is appositive and explanatory of τὸν διαφθείροντα, and together with that is the object both of εὑρών and εἰσάγεις. εἰσάγεις, literally, *bring in*, sc. to court, cf. 29, A: εἰσάγοι . . . εἰς δικαστήριον. Here, however, it is followed by a *dative* of the *persons*, *before* whom he is brought, sc. the judges (τουτοισί). Either the magistrate or the prosecutor might be said εἰσάγειν, though more properly the former. It may usually be rendered *impeach*, or *prosecute*.

E. 4. οὗτοι, κ.τ.λ., *these the judges*. 8. νὴ τὴν Ἥραν. Page 55
Cf. note, 22, A. 9. ἀκροαταί. The spectators, at trials of

Page 55 any interest before the Heliaea, were very numerous, thus bringing that court still more under popular influence.

25 A. 10. *οἱ βουλευταί.* The members of the βουλή, or senate, of which there were two, the Senate of the Areopagus and the Senate of Five Hundred. Both kinds of *senators* are perhaps here intended. 11. Ἀλλ' ἄρα, κ.τ.λ. *But then, Meletus, do those in the assembly, the assemblymen, corrupt the young?* The μή implies a negative answer, and here suggests some fear or anxiety, lest it may be so. ἄρα (not ἆρα) is used as suggesting that this is the only class left. 17. ἐμοῦ. G. 173, 2, N.; H. A. 752. The κατά in comp. gives disadvantageous or hostile sense to the verb.

B. 18. *οἱ μὲν βελτίους ποιοῦντες αὐτούς*, sc. δοκοῦσι, supplied from the preceding clause, of which this is explanatory, and therefore without a connective. 20. *τοὐναντίον τούτου πᾶν.* τοὐναντίον is to be taken as an appositive of the previous sentence, or a resumption of its thought, independent of construction. It may be considered as either nom. or acc. G. 137, N. 3; H. A. 626, b. 24. *πάντως δήπου, altogether so no doubt, whether you and Anytus deny it or not.* οὐ, instead of μή, follows the conditional particle (ἐάν), because it unites with φῆτε to convey one idea, οὐ φῆτε = *deny*. 27. εἰ . . . διαφθείρει. The use of the ind. pres. implies a kind of ironical assent to the truth of the supposition: *if* (really, as you affirm) *only one corrupts them.* G. 227, 1; H. A. 901, b. *οἱ ἄλλοι, the rest, all others.*

C. 27. *ἀλλὰ γάρ, but* it is not so, *for;* or *but really*, cf. note, 20, C. 28. ὦ Μέλητε . . . ἀμέλειαν . . . μεμέληκε. A play upon the name: *Careful* One, you show your *want of care*,

Page 56 that you have *never cared*, etc. 3. *εἰσάγεις*, cf. note, 24, D. 4. ὦ πρὸς Διὸς Μέλητε. The πρὸς Διός seems to be placed between ὦ and Μέλητε to carry out the play on the name in the foregoing sentence: *Thou before Zeus, Careful One.* Notice, however, Mem. 71, D: ὦ πρὸς θεῶν Μένων. Cases are more numerous where we have ὦ πρὸς Διός with the voc. omitted. 7. τοὺς ἀεὶ . . . ὄντας. ἀεί, preceded by the art. and followed by a part. means, *in every case*, i. e., *in every instance*, in which the supposition holds.

D. 11. *ὁ νόμος κελεύει ἀποκρίνεσθαι.* The very words of Page 56
the law are cited by Demosthenes in his Second Oration against Stephanus: Νόμος. *Τοῖν ἀντιδίκοιν ἐπάναγκες εἶναι ἀποκρίνασθαι ἀλλήλοις τὸ ἐρωτώμενον, μαρτυρεῖν δὲ μή.* 16. *τηλικούτου, at my time of life,* sc. so old, i. e., 70, cf. 17, D. *τηλικόσδε, at your time of time,* sc. so young, cf. note, 23, E. The words both mean the same, viz., either *so old* or *so young,* according to the connection.

E. 22. *ταῦτα,* the active of *πείθω* takes two accusatives, and one is retained with pass. H. A. 724. 23. *οἶμαι . . . οὐδένα,* sc. *πείσεσθαί σοι.* So in the next clause, there is an ellipsis of *διαφθείρω* with *ἄκων,* and still further on of *ποιῶν* with *παύσομαι.* Throughout this passage Socrates manifestly takes the ground that virtue is coextensive with knowledge. It is impossible for any man to injure others without injuring himself; and no man who really *knows* this, will wrong another any sooner than he would injure himself, which no one ever does intentionally. Such is his argument here. So in Xen. Mem. III, 9, 5, he reasons, that no man who *knows* temperance, justice, and moral excellence, would prefer anything else to these virtues. These virtues, therefore, are all resolvable into knowledge or wisdom. Every man *does* what seems to him best, and if he *knows* what is best, he will *do* it, and therefore do right. See also Xen. Mem. IV, 2, 20; Arist. Ethic. Eudem. 1, 5; Protag. 345; Gorg. 460; and Prof. Woolsey's remarks upon it in his Introduction. Page 57

B. 9. *ὅτι κατὰ τὴν γραφήν, ἣν ἐγράψω,* sc. *με φῂς διαφθείρειν* 26
τοὺς νεωτέρους, repeated from above. 11. *οὐ ταῦτα, κ.τ.λ. ταῦτα* is the obj. of *διδάσκων* placed where it is for emphasis. 13. *ὧν νῦν ὁ λόγος ἐστίν, of whom our discussion now is.* *ὧν* is objective genitive, = *οὓς λέγομεν.*

C. 16. *Καὶ αὐτὸς ἄρα, and I myself accordingly.* 18. *οὐ μέντοι, κ.τ.λ., not however the same as the city indeed recognizes,* but *others, and this is what you accuse me of, that* (I teach them to believe that there are) *others; or do you say that I both do not believe in any gods at all myself, and that I teach others this doctrine.* Observe the correlation of *οὔτε —τε,* in the last member of this somewhat complicated and

Page 57 irregular sentence. *θεούς* usually omits the article after *νομίζειν*, *ἡγεῖσθαι*, etc., = believe in gods.

D. 22. *ἵνα τι*, with verb omitted, cf. Lex.; also H. A. 612. The idiom was, however, so established that a Greek would probably be unconscious of the ellipsis. 23. *οὐδὲ . . . οὐδέ*, not simply correlative, like *οὔτε . . . οὔτε* = *neither . . . nor*, but emphatic = *not even . . . nor yet*. Cf. note, 18, C. The language implies that it was quite incredible that Socrates should not believe even in gods so universally recognized as the sun and the moon. For the omission of the article with *ἥλιον* and *σελήνην*, cf. H. A. 663. 24. *Μὰ Δί'*, sc. *οὐ νομίζει*, which is understood from the foregoing question. *Μά* is not of itself negative; hence it may be used with either *ναί* or *οὔ*; but when preceded by neither of these particles, a negative clause precedes or follows, or it is clear from the context and from an accompanying adversative particle, that the sentence is to be understood as negative. Cf. G. 163; H. A. 723; see also Lex. 26. *Ἀναξαγόρου*. Anaxagoras of Clazomene taught (according to Diog. Laert. II, 8) that the sun was a mass of hot *iron*, as some understand it, or *stone*, as Socrates takes it here and Xen. Mem. IV, 7, 7, and the moon an earthy body, like our own planet. There was the more plausibility in imputing to Socrates the doctrines of Anaxagoras, since Socrates was a disciple of Archelaus Physicus, who was a disciple of Anaxagoras. 28. *οὐκ εἰδέναι*. For *οὐκ*, instead of *μή*, see
Page 58 note on *οὐ φῆτε*, 25, B. 2. *Καὶ δὴ καί*, *and so now*, etc. The sentence which follows is ironical, cf. *σοφὸς δή*, 27. 3. *ἃ* is the object of *πριαμένοις*.

E. *εἰ πάνυ πολλοῦ, δραχμῆς*, *for a drachma at the very highest*. *πολλοῦ*, like *δραχμῆς*, is gen. of price. This was the highest price which the managers could lawfully demand for a seat in the theatre. The common price was two oboli (Dem. de Cor. 28), which was paid out of the treasury. Cf. Boeckh's Pub. Econ. Ath. II, 13; Beck. Char. Ex. Sc. 10; and Smith's Dic. Antiqq. The doctrines of the philosophers were brought upon the stage, partly to be commended, as by Euripides in his tragedies, partly to be ridiculed, as by Aristophanes in his comedies. Some have thought that the

allusion is not to the performances on the stage, but to the sale Page 58
of the books of Anaxagoras at the orchestra. Cf. Schleier-
macher ad loc. But as Forster well remarks, we never read
of book sales there. See also Journal of Philology (English),
vol. x, pp. 37, 38. 5. ἄλλως τε καί, κ.τ.λ., *especially when
they are so absurd;* literally, *for other reasons and also* (in
particular) *they being so absurd.* 6. οὑτωσί, *thus* entirely and
absolutely. 8. Ἄπιστός γ' εἶ . . . δοκεῖς. Cf. note on δίκαιός
εἰμι, 18, A.

A. 13. ἔοικε . . . διαπειρωμένῳ, *for he seems like one hav-* 27
ing composed (i. e., he seems to have composed) *as it were an
enigma, testing the question, Whether will Socrates, the wise
man forsooth, know,* etc. In the earlier editions καί is in-
serted between the two participles. But Plato often uses
two or more participles without a connective, especially when,
as here, the action expressed by one participle is preliminary
to that expressed by the other—he seems to have composed
as it were an enigma *in order* to test. Cf. Gorg.: τέτραχα
ἑαυτὴν διανείμασα, ὑποδῦσα, κ.τ.λ. = having divided herself
into four parts *and thus* put on, or *in order to* put on, etc.
For the use of the part. after ἔοικε, cf. G. 280; H. A. 981.
The nom. would be possible. Compare note on ξύνοιδα with
the part. 21, B. 14. ἐμοῦ χαριεντιζομένου. γιγνώσκω, though
usually followed by the acc., sometimes takes the gen. in
common with other verbs denoting mental state. Jelf, 485.
17. ὥσπερ ἄν. Cf. note, 17, D. 20. ᾗ . . . λέγειν, *how it is
clear to me that he is speaking thus,* sc. contradictions.

B. 23. ἐν τῷ εἰωθότι τρόπῳ, *in my usual method,* sc. of
question and answer, with common illustrations. 26. ἄλλα
καὶ ἄλλα, *one after another,* again and again. The acc. is
cognate. 3. τὸ ἐπὶ τούτῳ, *the question which follows,* i. e., in Page 59
order and thought.

C. 4. δαιμόνια μὲν νομίζει πράγματ' εἶναι. δαιμόνια is here
constructed as an adjective. So Cicero translates τὸ δαιμόνιον
by *divinum quiddam,* de Div. 1, 54. Schleiermacher and
Stallbaum (see their notes ad loc.) argue, that Xenophon,
Plato, and Aristotle understood it to be used in this sense in
the indictment. Certainly if he could have taken it as a noun

Page 59 (meaning divinities, instead of an adjective meaning divine things), it would have been far easier for Socrates to show the glaring inconsistency of his accuser, and he might have spared all his argumentation and illustration drawn from *ἱππικὰ πράγματα, ἀνθρώπεια πράγματα*, etc. The expression in the indictment had reference to those divine voices or monitions which Socrates professed to hear and obey as the guide of his life (cf. 31, D, and notes ibid.), and which would more properly be called *divine things*, than *divinities*. 5. *ὡς ὤνησας*: *what a service you have rendered—how obliging you are*—que tu m'oblige. Cousin. Al. *ὤνησας*. *μόγις* = tandem aliquando, Stallb. 8. *ἀλλ' οὖν δαιμόνιά γε νομίζω*, *but then I believe in divine things at all events*, sc. whether they be old or new, i. e., though they be new ones as charged in the indictment. 9. *ἀντιγραφῇ* = *ἀντωμοσίᾳ*, cf. note, 19, B, and Fischer's note ad loc.

D. 18. *ἤτοι θεούς γε ἡγούμεθα ἢ θεῶν παῖδας.* The word *δαίμονες*, in Homer and the early Greek poets, is synonymous with *θεοί*; in Plato and other writers of his day it denotes more especially the inferior deities constituting an intermediate and connecting link between the superior gods and men; and in Plutarch and some of the latest Greek classics, it sometimes signifies bad as well as good beings of a superhuman order, thus *approaching* to the New Testament sense of demons or evil spirits. Cf. Symp. 202, E: *πᾶν τὸ δαιμόνιον μεταξύ ἐστι θεοῦ τε καὶ θνητοῦ, κ.τ.λ.* 16. *τοῦτ' . . . χαριεντίζεσθαι*, *this would be wherein I say* (27, A) *that you speak riddles and joke, to say that I who do not believe in gods, on the other hand do again believe in gods; since at all events I believe in demons.* The last clause repeats the premise (already laid down at the beginning of the sentence) in closer connection with the main point in the conclusion—a practice not unfrequent with Plato, and one of many by which his style is made to resemble the language of conversation. 20. *ὧν δὴ καὶ λέγονται*, *from whom you know they are said to be.* The preposition (*ἐκ*) is often omitted before the relative after having been inserted before the antecedent. H. A. 1007. 23. *ἢ [καὶ] ὄνων.* Forsterus delendam censebat hanc particu-

lam (ἥ); sine caussa idonea; nam ἡμίονοι dici possunt, et Page 59
ἵππων παῖδες, et ὄνων παῖδες. Fischer. That is, mules may have horses *or also* asses for their *male* parents, for the case to be illustrated limits the comparison to *male* parents.

E. 25. οὐχί limits ἐγράψω; ἀποπειρώμενος denotes the end in view = *for the purpose of testing me*, and ἀπορῶν the cause = *because you were at a loss.* 27. ὅπως δὲ σύ, κ.τ.λ. *But that you should persuade any man possessed of the least understanding, that it is the part of the same man to believe in things pertaining both to demons and to gods, and the same man not to believe either in demons or gods or heroes, is beyond the scope of human ingenuity*, lit., *there is no means by which* (ὅπως) *you could persuade*, etc. I have inclosed οὐ in brackets (as does also Oron), because, though found in most of the MSS., and therefore inserted by Becker and Stallbaum, neither they nor any other editor has been able to explain or translate it, and it is omitted by Forster, Fischer, Ast, Schleiermacher, and Cousin. Page 60

4. Ἀλλὰ γάρ. Cf. note, 25, C. Socrates here brings the 28
direct defense to a close, saying that it does not require much argument, since what he has to fear is not the indictment or the prosecutors, but the multitude—not the evidence or the argument, but popular prejudice and passion. What follows is intended, not so much to avert the sentence which he anticipates from the judges or even to deprecate the displeasure of the people, as to vindicate his character, assert his mission, and bear witness to the truth, that more impartial judges may appreciate his merits—that a better age may honor him, as a missionary and a martyr. 9. καὶ τοῦτ᾽ . . . αἱρῇ, *and this it is which will convict me, if indeed it should lead to my conviction.* 10. ἀλλ᾽ . . . φθόνος. This clause is an emphatic repetition and explanation of the τοῦτ᾽ at the beginning. Such colloquial repetitions (cf. note, 27, D) are especially frequent in antithetic clauses. 12. οὐδὲν δὲ δεινὸν μὴ ἐν ἐμοὶ στῇ, *and there is no reason to fear lest it should* (that it will) *stop with me*, i. e., that I shall be the last victim.

B. 13. Εἶτ᾽ οὐκ αἰσχύνει. Εἶτα in questions implies astonishment or indignation, as ποτέ does surprise and wonder, cf.

Page 60 note, 20, D. 17. τοῦ ζῆν ἢ τεθνάναι are taken together as a limiting gen. with κίνδυνον, literally, the risk of living or dying, i. e., *the question of life or death.* 18. ἄνδρα, a *man* emphatically, not merely a human being, ἄνθρωπον. It is the subject of ὑπολογίζεσθαι. ὅτου . . . ὄφελός ἐστιν, *who is of any use, however little.* ὄφελος takes the person to whom it belongs, or of whom it is predicated, in the genitive. See examples in the Lexicon. With the sentiment of this passage compare Crito, 48.

C. 22. οἵ τε ἄλλοι καί = *especially;* literally, *both the others and* (in particular) *the son of Thetis.* For ἄλλως τε καί = especially, cf. note, 26, E. The allusion is to Achilles, Hom. Il. xviii, 90–125. 23. παρὰ τὸ αἰσχρόν τι ὑπομεῖναι, *in comparison with* (properly, *alongside of*) *submitting to anything dishonorable.* 25. θεὸς οὖσα, *being a goddess,* and therefore able to foretell the future. 26. τιμωρήσεις. G. 199, N. 8; H. A. 816, 12. Render: *if you shall avenge the murder of Patroclus your friend.* 28. αὐτίκα γάρ τοι, κ.τ.λ.; the very words of Thetis to her son, Il. xviii, 96. This quotation interrupts the sentence, and instead of a clause depending on ὥστε (l. 24), which should regularly have followed, it goes on Page 61 with an independent clause connected by δέ. 2. τοῦ θανάτου. The article is unusual with θανάτου as abstract.

D. 3. Κακὸς ὢν denotes the *state in which* to live were to be dreaded more than death: *to live being a bad* man, that is, an unfaithful friend and a cowardly soldier. 4. Αὐτίκα τεθναίην . . . ἄχθος ἀρούρης. Parts of two Homeric verses (Il. xviii, 98 and 104) brought together. 6. μὴ . . . οἴει, *you do not suppose, do you,* implies a neg. answer. G. 282, 2; H. A. 1015. 7. οὕτω γὰρ ἔχει. Cf. note, 17, D. 8. οὗ ἄν, *wherever.* 9. ἢ ὑπ' ἄρχοντος ταχθῇ. Anacoluthon for ἢ ὑπ' ἄρχοντος ταχθείς, which would correspond with ἢ ἡγησάμενος βέλτιον; instead of which we have ὑπ' ἄρχοντος ταχθῇ, corresponding to ἑαυτὸν τάξῃ, as if the first ἢ had preceded τάξῃ, instead of ἡγησάμενος. 11. πρὸ τοῦ αἰσχροῦ, *before,* i. e., *more than the dishonorable.*

E. 12. εἴην εἰργασμένος. Heindorf makes ἐργάζεσθαι here, as he says it often is, equivalent to ποιεῖν. But Stallbaum,

with good reason, renders *εἴην εἰργασμένος*, I should have Page 61
perpetrated (not merely *done*). 13. *εἰ, ὅτε μέν με . . . τότε μεν οὐ . . . τοῦ δὲ θεοῦ . . . ἐνταῦθα δέ*, *if, when on the one hand the commanders . . . then on the one hand I . . . but when on the other hand the god . . . then on the other hand I*, etc. *μέν . . . μέν* and *δέ . . . δέ*, with their clauses, seldom appear so regularly and formally balanced. Cf. Jelf, 765, 6. The clauses introduced by *δέ* contain the main point, which the clauses introduced by *μέν* only illustrate and enforce. 14. *ὑμεῖς εἵλεσθε*. The judges are taken as representing the entire people. 16. *ἔμενον* (past tense of the ind.) denotes an historical fact; *λίποιμι* (contingent) implies a mere supposition. The bravery and physical endurance of Socrates, as a soldier, were a prodigy and a proverb in that already somewhat degenerate age. In the battle at Delium, the Athenian general Laches declared, that if all the Athenians had fought as bravely as he, the Bœotians would have erected no trophies. It will be observed, that the preposition *ἐπί* is used to denote the locality of this battle, while *ἐν* is used with *Ποτιδαίᾳ* and *Ἀμφιπόλει*. Wherever this battle is referred to, it is thus designated *ἐπὶ Δηλίῳ* (cf. Xen. Mem. III, 5, 4), whereas in other battles *ἐν* is the usual preposition. The reason seems to be, that Delium was properly the name of the *temple* of Apollo, and, though the city received the same designation, the old association forbade its extension so as to embrace the surrounding country, where the battle was fought. 18. *δεῖν* is used as appropriate to *ᾠήθην* rather than to *τάττοντος*, to which it should belong. The style is conversational.

A. 20. *δεινὸν τἂν εἴη*, *a strange thing indeed it would be.* 29
It is a repetition or resumption of *δεινὰ ἂν εἴην εἰργασμένος* at the beginning of the section. 21. *ὡς ἀληθῶς*. *ὡς* gives emphasis to some adverbs and adjectives besides superlatives. There is an ellipsis of a corresponding demonstrative (*οὕτως*), and also of an appropriate verb: *εἰσάγοι οὕτως ὡς ἀληθῶς εἰσάγοι. εἰσάγοι εἰς δικαστήριον*. Cf. note, 24, D. 27. *τῷ ἀνθρώπῳ*, *to man*, i. e., mankind. H. A. 659. 27. *ὂν* is attracted into the gender of the predicate.

B. 1. *Καὶ τοῦτο, κ.τ.λ.*, *and this, how is not this ignorance* Page 62

Page 63 *which is to be censured, that of supposing that one knows what he does not know.* 3. τούτῳ καὶ ἐνταῦθα, *in this respect and here,* emphatic repetition in order to limit the superiority strictly to this single point. 4. τῳ, *in anything,* dat. of the respect. 5. τούτῳ ἄν, sc. φαίην εἶναι, *I should say that it was* (i. e., that I was wiser) *in this.* 6. οὕτω καὶ οἴομαι corresponds to οὐκ εἰδώς, which is equivalent to ὥσπερ οὐκ οἶδα. 7. τῷ βελτίονι, καὶ θεῷ καὶ ἀνθρώπῳ, *the better, whether god or man.* 8. πρὸ οὖν τῶν κακῶν ὧν, κ.τ.λ., *in comparison therefore with the evils which* (ὧν, gen. by attraction) *I know to be evils, I will never fear nor flee those which I know not if perchance they are good,* that is, I will never shun the latter *rather than* the former—the uncertain rather than the certain. Cf. πρὸ τοῦ αἰσχροῦ, 28, D.

C. 11. ἀπιστήσαντες = ἀπειθήσαντες, which Stephens substituted for it in his edition = disobeying, *disregarding.* τὴν ἀρχήν with a negative means, not in the first instance, i. e., *not at all.* 12. εἰσελθεῖν for εἰσάγεσθαι, *to be brought in hither for trial.* 13. ἀποκτεῖναι, to put me to death, i. e., *condemn me to death.* So Xen. Mem. IV, 8, 5. 14. εἰ διαφευξοίμην. G. 202, 4; H. A. 855, a. ἂν . . . ἐπιτηδεύοντες . . . διαφθαρήσονται. On the use of ἄν with the fut. ind., which is rare in the Attic Greek and entirely denied by some, see G. 208, 2, at end; H. A. 845. Stallbaum is inclined here to connect ἄν with ἐπιτηδεύοντες only = ἂν . . . ἐπιτηδεύοιεν . . . καὶ . . . διαφθαρήσονται. But it is more natural to suppose that ἄν gives a contingent sense to διαφθαρήσονται also. 18. ἐπὶ τούτῳ μέντοι, ἐφ' ᾧτε, *on this condition, however, that you no longer,* etc. ἐφ' ᾧτε is equivalent to ὥστε, and is accordingly followed by the inf. G. 267; H. A. 999, a.

D. 20. εἰ οὖν . . . ἀφιοῖτε. οὖν is here resumptive = *I say.* It will be observed that the same protasis is resumed twice—that is, the sentence is commenced with essentially the same condition, varied only in form, three times (εἴ με νῦν ὑμεῖς ἀφίετε . . . εἴ μοι πρὸς ταῦτα εἴποιτε . . . εἰ οὖν με, ὅπερ εἶπον, ἐπὶ τούτοις ἀφίοιτε), before the apodosis is subjoined. In the first instance, the ind. (ἀφίετε) is used, implying some probability of his release; in the other instances, the same condition is expressed as a mere contingency by the use of the opt. (εἴποιτε, ἀφίοιτε), corresponding to which we have the opt. with ἄν (εἴποιμ' ἂν ὑμῖν) in the apodosis. 22. ἀσπάζομαι μὲν καὶ φιλῶ. Ἀσπάζεσθαι *est aliquem salutare ita ut eum amplectaris;* φιλεῖν, *salutare aliquem ita, ut eum osculeris.* Hoc loco significant haec verba: *grato lætoque animo vestram humanitatem et clementiam amplector atque veneror.* Stallbaum. 22. πείσομαι μᾶλλον τῷ θεῷ ἢ ὑμῖν. Cf. Acts v, 29, and iv, 19. 24. οὐ μὴ παύσωμαι. οὐ μή, with the subj. instead of the fut., is used in strong denial. G. 257; H. A. 1032. 25. ἀεί, *continually, from time to time.* 26. Ἀθηναῖος ὤν, πόλεως, *being a citizen of Athens, the greatest city.* G. 187, N. 1. 28. ἰσχύν, *strength of mind, intellectual and moral power,* particularly *fortitude* and the kindred masculine virtues, as appears from what follows. Compare the glorification of Athens in the funeral oration of Pericles. Thuc. II, 35. Page 62

E. 5. ἄπειμι. The present of εἶμι and its compounds is generally used by the Attics in a future sense. So in English, I go or am going = I shall or will go. ἐρήσομαι, ἐξετάσω, ἐλέγξω. Notice the progressive meaning of the words as descriptive of the Socratic method. 7. φάναι δέ, *but to say that he does.* In Laches, 187, 188, Nicias gives a very similar though more minute account of the manner in which Socrates would *hold* every one he conversed with to the work of self-examination: "You do not seem to know, that whoever is nearest to Socrates in reasoning, just as in relationship, and whoever approaches him in conversation, even though he should begin to converse at first on some other subject, he will, with infallible certainty, be brought round in the discussion, till he is obliged to give an account of himself, in what manner he is now living, and how he has lived his past life; and once caught in it, Socrates will not let him go, till he has well and beautifully put all these things to the test . . . and I almost knew, long ago, that our discussion now, being in the presence of Socrates, would not be about the young men, but about ourselves." Page 63

A. 9. Καὶ νεωτέρῳ καὶ πρεσβυτέρῳ. Cf. καὶ θεῷ καὶ 30

Page 63 *ἀνθρώπῳ*, 29, C. Verbs of *doing* and *saying* more commonly take the indirect as well as the direct object in the acc. G. 165, N. 3. The dat. suggests *for the sake of*. 10. *ὅσῳ*, *by as much as*. The full construction would require a corresponding demonstrative (*τοσούτῳ*) with *μᾶλλον*, denoting the *degree of difference*. G. 188, 2; H. A. 781, a. 11. *ἐγγυτέρω* may be followed either by a gen. or a dat. denoting that *to which* there is a *nearness*. G. 182, 2, and 186. That *in which*, or *in respect to which*, the nearness exists, may also be either gen. or dat. But it is not according to usage to put both in the gen. or both in the dat. See Stallbaum's note on the proper reading of this passage, and compare ad rem, as well as ad verba, the passage above cited from Laches: *ὃς ἂν ἐγγυτάτω Σωκράτους ᾖ λόγῳ ὥσπερ γένει*. 13. *τὴν ἐμὴν τῷ θεῷ ὑπηρεσίαν*, *my service to the god*. The dat. *to* or *for* can follow substantives. G. 185; H. A. 765, a. 16. *μηδὲ οὕτω σφόδρα*, *no, nor so zealously*, cf. note on *μηδ' ὁπωστιοῦν*, 17, B.

B. 17. *λέγων*, *κ.τ.λ.* Observe the sentiment, that the higher good includes the lower, as the greater does the less. 20. *εἰ . . . διαφθείρω*. Cf. note, 25, B. 21. *ταῦτ' ἂν εἴη βλαβερά*, *these* instructions and persuasions *must be injurious*. Compare the argument of Xen. Mem. I, 2, 8: how then could such a man corrupt the young, unless the cultivation of virtue is corrupting. 22. *οὐδὲν λέγει*, *he says nothing*, that is, *he is utterly mistaken*. Cf. Laches, 195, B; N. 1: *ἀλλά μοι δοκεῖ, ὦ Σώκρατες, Λάχης ἐπιθυμεῖν κἀμὲ φανῆναι μηδὲν λέγοντα, ὅτι καὶ αὐτὸς ἄρτι τοιοῦτός τις ἐφάνη. ΛΑ. Πάνυ μὲν οὖν, ὦ Νικία· καὶ πειράσομαί γε ἀποφῆναι. οὐδὲν γὰρ λέγεις.* So *τὶ λέγειν* is to say something, i. e., to speak well and truly, cf. Crit. 46, D; Xen. Mem. II, 1, 12. *πρὸς ταῦτα*, *wherefore*, literally, in reference to these things, in *view* of them. 23. *ἢ πείθεσθε . . . ἢ μή*, that is, unconditionally—don't propose any conditional acquittal, like that suggested 29, C; *since I would not* on any condition (*ἂν* refers to an implied condition) *do differently*, *not even if I must die* (strictly and emphatically *be dead*) *many times over*. *ὡς* has its ordinary subjective effect. G. 277, N. 2; H. A. 978. Notice *ἂν* with future participle is a peculiar apodosis representing ποιήσω ἄν. Cf. 29, C; M. and T. 41, 4; p. 58, l. 3, and reference there. Page 63

C. 26. Μὴ θορυβεῖτε. Cf. note, 21, A. Socrates here enters upon another topic, and discourses upon it with such freedom and boldness, such a consciousness of his own innocence not merely, but such an assurance of his divine mission, and such compassion not for himself but for them if they should reject his instructions and condemn him to death, that they must either recognize his superior wisdom or take offense at his arrogance. Some modern critics even, Ast for example, regard the self-complacency of this and some other parts of the Apology as quite insufferable, quite un-Socratic. But is there not the Socratic irony here? Are there not at the same time Socratic truthfulness, fearlessness, and earnestness? It should be remembered that he presents himself throughout as vindicating, not so much himself as truth and justice, philosophy and religion, and God. 27. ἐμμείνατέ μοι οἷς ἐδεήθην ὑμῶν, *stand by what I asked of you.* Cf. 17, D. μοι is the ethical dat., and may be expressed by *pray*. 1. μέλλω Page 64
γὰρ οὖν, *for I am about now* (οὖν, accordingly, in accordance with that request) *to say also some other things at which perhaps you will cry out.* This clause is connected by γὰρ οὖν (more closely than it would be by γάρ alone), not to the clause which immediately precedes, but to the previous one (ἐμμείνατε, κ.τ.λ.). 6. οὐδὲ γὰρ ἂν δύναιντο, *for they would not even be able*, sc. if they wished. ἄν referring to an implied condition. G. 226, b; H. A. 903.

D. 6. οὐ . . . θεμιτόν = nefas, not in accordance with the law of nature and of God, and therefore not possible in the nature of things. Schleiermacher: *nicht in der Ordnung.* Cousin: *pas . . . au pouvoir.* Stallbaum: *neque legibus divinæ sapientiæ respondere.* 7. ἀμείνονι ἀνδρί, *for* a better man to be injured by *a worse*, instead of ἀμείνονα ἄνδρα, *that* a better man, etc., the design being to link it more closely with οὐ . . . θεμιτὸν εἶναι. This famous saying of Socrates has been widely quoted and commented on from the earliest times. Cf. Epic. Encheir. 52; Max. Tyr. Diss. 18, 8; Plut. de Tranq. 17; and not only by philosophers but by the Christian Fathers,

Page 31 as Origen, Theodoret, etc. The reason for the assertion, as explained by Plutarch, and illustrated by Crito, 44, D, is, that bad men, however numerous and powerful, can not make the good man bad or the wise man a fool, and that is the only real evil which can befall a man. ἀποκτείνειε. Cf. note, 29, C. Here the word not only refers to the condemnation rather than the execution of the sentence, but, like the two verbs which follow, it has a causative sense = *procure* my condemnation to death, to exile, or to disfranchisement. 8. ἀτιμώσειεν denotes (not dishonor in general, as some have understood it, but) *deprivation* of *civil rights*. This might deprive of *all* rights and privileges, or do so only in part. ἀλλὰ ταῦτα, κ.τ.λ., *but these this man* (viz., the prosecutor) *probably supposes, and many another man perchance, to be great evils*. τίς here gives an indefinite extension and application to ἄλλος, like *many a* in English. 10. ἀλλὰ πολὺ μᾶλλον, intell. οἴομαι μέγα κακόν. Stallb. 12. πολλοῦ δέω ἐγὼ ὑπὲρ ἐμαυτοῦ ἀπολογεῖσθαι, *I am very far from making a defense for my own sake*. Observe the emphatic insertion and juxtaposition of ἐγώ with ὑπὲρ ἐμαυτοῦ = *I for myself*. H. A. 1062. 14. ὑμῖν, dat. after δόσιν. Cf. note, 30, A. Socrates means that he was given or sent to the Athenians by Apollo to be their monitor and reprover.

E. 16. ἀτεχνῶς . . . προσκείμενον, *really, though the comparison may be too ridiculous, attached to*, etc. προσκείμενον, besides the passive sense of *being attached to*, involves also the active signification of *pressing upon* or *following up*, as a *gadfly* does a *horse*, to suit which the word was chosen. γελοιότερον. H. A. 649, b. The clause explains τοιοῦτον instead of the more regular construction with οἷος. 19. μύωπος may mean a *spur* or a *gadfly*. Ficinus, Schleiermacher, Ast, Cousin, and some others, take it here in the former sense. But the epithets προσκείμενον, προστεθεικέναι, and προσκαθίζων, apply better to a gadfly. Moreover, this makes the comparison more laughable (γελοιότερον), and is more in the spirit of the Socratic irony. So Forster, Stallbaum, Carey, etc. 20. οἷον δή, *as for instance now*, introduces the explanation or application of the simile of the gadfly. Such is the prevailing use of οἷον by Plato.

Page 64

A. 25. *ἴσως* is often strengthened by *τάχ' ἄν*, and is 31
equivalent to *mayhap*. *ἀχθόμενοι . . . πειθόμενοι*. The reader will observe the singular succession of participles. Some of them may be rendered into English by verbs; *ἄν* gives a potential sense to the participle (*κρούσαντες*), G. 207, 1; H. A. 987, a: *but you mayhap being offended, just like sleepers when they are roused out of sleep, would* (will) *dash at me, and hearkening to Anytus, rashly put me to death.* 26. *κρούσαντες* still keeps up the allusion to the gadfly. So does *ἐπιπέμψειε*, *send upon you.* 1. *ὅτι δ' ἐγὼ τυγχάνω, κ.τ.λ.*, *but that I am* Page 65
just (*τυγχάνω ὤν*) *such a person, as to have been given by the god to the city, you might discern from this fact.* The thing to be proved is that his character is such, that he might well be supposed to have a divine mission; and the proof is his self-forgetfulness and disinterested devotedness to the highest good of others, which, he argues, is something more than human (*οὐ γὰρ ἀνθρωπίνῳ ἔοικε*). Compare Cousin's translation and Stallbaum's note ad loc. *δεδόσθαι*. G. 261; H. A. 952.

B. 5. *ἀνέχεσθαι τῶν οἰκείων ἀμελουμένων*, *to suffer my private affairs to be neglected.* It will be seen, from the *τοσαῦτα ἤδη ἔτη*, that both *ἀνέχεσθαι* and *πράττειν* express *continued past* action, in other words, they are *imperfects.* 10. *εἶχον ἄν τινα λόγον*, *I should have some reason*, i. e., my conduct would be explicable on ordinary grounds without supposing a divine mission. 12. *τοῦτο . . . ἀπαναισχυντῆσαι*, *to reach this* (such a) *pitch of shamelessness.* G. 159, N. 2; H. A. 716, b. *ἀπό* in the verb is emphatic, *to be so utterly* shameless.

C. 14. *ἢ ἐπραξάμην . . . ἢ ᾔτησα*, *that I ever either exacted or asked pay of any one.* *πράττεσθαι* = exigere (ex-*agere*), aus*machen*, *make* money. *ἱκανον . . . πενίαν*, *for sufficient*, I think, *is the witness* (observe the article *τὸν μάρτυρα*) *I bring forward, that I speak the truth*, viz., *my* (well-known) *poverty: παρέχομαι μάρτυρα καὶ ὁ μάρτυς ὃν παρέχομαι ἱκανός ἐστιν*, pred. use of adj. Ad rem, cf. note, 23, B. 18. *ἀναβαίνων*, unemphatic. Socrates, like other citizens, was obliged to be present in the assembly.

Page 65 D. 21. θεῖόν τι καὶ δαιμόνιον, *something divine and demoniacal*, if we may be allowed to use the word demoniacal in its etymological sense of *superhuman*, or *proceeding from* δαίμονες. Cf. note, 27, D. 22. ἐπικωμῳδῶν, *calumniating* or *satirizing* after the manner of the ancient comedy. The reference is to the ἕτερα δαιμόνια καινά of the indictment, 24, B. 24. ἀεὶ ἀποτρέπει . . . προτρέπει δὲ οὔποτε. Ast makes this statement an argument against the Platonic authorship of the Apology, as being inconsistent with what Xenophon (Mem. IV, 8, 5) and others say of the positive as well as negative character of the divine influence. But the same declaration is made almost in the same words in the Theages, 128, D. So Cicero likewise understood it, de Div. 1, 54: nunquam impellenti, sæpe revocanti. And though Xenophon, and Plato himself in other passages (e. g., Phæd. 242, B, C; Theæt. 151. A), appear to ascribe to the voice a persuasive as well as dissuasive influence, that is only a general statement of the *fact*, whereas here we have a more definite and precise explanation of the *manner*; for, after all, the discrepancy is more apparent than real, since a dissuasive from all that he should not do, involved instruction in all that he should do. Cf. 40, A, B, C; also Schleiermacher's note ad loc. As to the nature of this voice, or sign or oracle, as he elsewhere calls it (ἡ μαντικὴ ἡ τοῦ δαιμονίου . . . τὸ τοῦ θεοῦ σημεῖον, 40, A), there has always been much discussion, and the question may still perhaps be said to be sub judice. Some have supposed that Socrates believed himself to be under the guidance of a particular δαίμων, guardian genius or tutelar divinity, whose special, if not sole office, was to lead and protect him. But no such idea would be gathered from this, nor indeed from any other passage in Plato or Xenophon, where this subject is mentioned. Others have gone to the opposite extreme and have come to the conclusion that the δαίμων of Socrates was nothing more than the voice of reason, considered as the voice of God, in his own soul. But this falls as far below the demands of the passage before us—of the appropriate significance of the language of Socrates—as the other goes beyond and superadds to it. After a diligent comparison of the language of Plato and Xenophon, together with such light as Plutarch, Cicero, and subsequent writers have shed on the subject, I find scarcely any room left for doubt that Socrates meant by his *φωνή*, and *θεῖόν τι καὶ δαιμόνιον*, very nearly that same divine teaching and guidance which good men in every age have believed to be communicated to themselves, and to all who seek it by prayer and in the use of proper means—partly within the soul, and yet not *from* within but from above—partly by outward signs, omens, oracles, dreams, and visions. Cf. below 33, C; *ἐκ μαντειῶν καὶ ἐξ ἐνυπνίων, κ.τ.λ.* Certainly the Apology gives us no intimation of a tutelary divinity peculiar to himself, and in the Memorabilia, Socrates explicitly declares, that the same divine teaching is within the reach of all men. Cf. below, 40, A, B, C; Xen. Mem. I, 1, 3, 4; I, 4, 15, 18; IV, 3, 13; IV, 8, 1. See also an interesting discussion of this question in Plutarch, De Genio Socratis. 24. *τοῦτο* is the object of *πράττειν*, which is transferred to the relative clause = *τοῦτο πράττειν ὃ ἂν μέλλω πράξειν*. Al. *τούτου* gen. after *ἀποτρέπει*. 28. *πάλαι*. He would be allowed to take part in public life from the age of 20. Page 65

E. 1. *ἀπολώλη . . . ὠφελήκη*. This form of the pluperfect is common in Plato, though not to the exclusion of the common form, cf. *ξυνῄδειν . . . ᾔδειν*, 22, D. G. 119, 4; H. A. 458, a. Observe the repetition of *ἂν* in each disjunctive clause (*πάλαι ἂν . . . οὔτ' ἂν ὑμᾶς . . . οὔτ' ἂν ἐμαυτόν*) and compare the examples in Stallb. here and at Gorg. 475, E. 3. *οὐ γάρ ἐστιν . . . οὔτε ὑμῖν οὔτε ἄλλῳ πλήθει οὐδενὶ . . . ἐναντιούμενος*. A striking repetition of the negative. Socrates shows himself no demagogue or even democrat. In this, he had the company and sympathy of most of the literary men and philosophers of Athens, who, as a class, cherished little respect or affection—and had little reason, in their personal relations to it, to cherish respect or affection—for the Athenian democracy. But more than this, the unbending integrity and firmness of Socrates placed him often in the attitude of *opposition* to the *existing* government, whether democratic or aristocratic, insomuch that he was deemed quite an impracti- Page 66

Page 63 cable. Compare his resistance to the popular assembly as described below, 32, B, with his refusal to obey the thirty tyrants in the arrest and "rendition" of a fugitive from oppression, 32, D; Xen. Mem. IV, 4, 2, 3.

32 A. 7. **Καὶ εἰ μέλλει.** Καὶ εἰ, *even if*, is to be distinguished from *εἰ καί*, *although*. *καὶ εἰ* concedes what is not true, or what is true only to a limited degree (the limit here being marked by ὀλίγον χρόνον); *εἰ καί* concedes what is true, simply and without degrees. Cf. Hermann ad Viger. 832; Stallb. ad loc.; and H. A. 1053, 2, a. 8. *μὴ δημοσιεύειν.* In Xen. Mem. I, 6, 15, Socrates gives as a reason for not engaging in public affairs, that he could do more to control and benefit the state by educating as many others as possible to be good citizens and able statesmen, than he could by undertaking the affairs of state in his own person. 13. *οὐδ' ἂν ἑνὶ ὑπεικάθοιμι*, *I would not yield in the least to any one whatever.* *οὐδ' . . . ἑνί* is more emphatic than *οὐδενί*. *ὑπεικάθοιμι*: for the form, cf. G. 119, 11; H. A. 494. The verbs of this form have been taken as intensive, but examples fail to prove that they differ in meaning from the simple forms. It remains also a matter of question whether they should be treated as presents or aorists, though this verb is now generally taken as the latter. 14. *μὴ ὑπείκων δέ, κ.τ.λ.*, *and as soon as I did not yield, just so soon I should perish.* The first ἅμα belongs with *ὑπείκων*, the second, strengthened by *καί*, with *ἀπολοίμην*. 15. *φορτικὰ μὲν καὶ δικανικά*, *displeasing and wearisome indeed.* *δικανικά* has reference primarily to *pleadings in the courts of law*, which are apt to be tediously minute and circumstantial. Some take it here in the sense of *boastful.* It is fair to say that the exact meaning of these words is not very well established.

B. 16. *ἄλλην μὲν . . . ἐβούλευσα δέ*, *I never held any other office, but I was made a member of the βουλή* (council of five hundred). See the same fact, and *βουλεύειν* used in the same sense, Xen. Mem. I, 1, 18. For the use of the aor. to signify entrance upon the office, cf. G. 200, N. 5, b; H. A. 841. 17. *ἡμῶν ἡ φυλὴ Ἀντιοχίς*, *the tribe* to which *Socrates* belonged, viz., *Antiochis.* 18. *πρυτανεύουσα*, *presiding*, i. e., *furnishing the prytanes*, who acted as presidents both of the council and Page 68 of the popular assembly. Each of the ten tribes chose by lot fifty representatives in the council, and these representatives, or the tribe through them, presided during about one tenth of the lunar year, or thirty-five days. Moreover, these fifty representatives of the tribe were subdivided into five bodies of ten men each, each of which presided during a fifth part of the presidency of the tribe, i. e., about one week. Out of these ten proedri (as they were called) for the week, an *ἐπιστάτης* or chief president was chosen by lot, who held the keys of the public treasury and archives, and presided as chairman in the council and also in the assembly for one day. Socrates was *ἐπιστάτης* on that day when the fate of the ten generals was to be decided, and refused to put the illegal proposition to vote in the assembly. Cf. Xen. Mem. IV, 4, 2: *ἐν ταῖς ἐκκλησίαις ἐπιστάτης γενόμενος.* *τοὺς δέκα στρατηγούς.* The Athenians chose ten generals, one for each tribe, at the commencement of a war. Sometimes they were all in the field together. More frequently, however, only three were sent out to carry on the war, while the others took charge of the war department at home. In the case before us, the battle at Arginusæ, only eight were actually present. For the details, see Xen. Hellen. I, 7. 19. *τοὺς οὐκ ἀνελομένους*, *who did not bring away for burial* the bodies of the slain. They were victorious in the battle (over the Lacedemonians at Arginusæ), and in order to pursue the enemy, they left the care of the dead to some of the inferior officers, instead of attending to it in person. For this they were accused before the assembly, and, in spite of the intervention of Socrates, condemned, and six of them actually put to death. The fact illustrates in a striking manner the sacred interest and importance which the Greeks attached to the rite of burial. Though they had gained the victory, the generals had not done their duty or *finished* their work, till the dead were buried. So the Iliad was not deemed complete till the burial rites of the heroes, Achilles and Hector, were narrated in the 23d and 24th Books; and the Ajax and Antigone of Sophocles are prolonged to considerable extent beyond the

Page 66 catastrophe for the same purpose—to put the minds of Grecian hearers and readers at rest from that pious horror which they entertained of remaining unburied. Had certain critics of the Homeric poems considered this matter duly, they would not have found in the last two books an argument against the unity of the Iliad. For the account of the feeling at Athens, cf. Grote, Part II, chap. lxiv. *τοὺς ἐκ τῆς ναυμαχίας.* Cf. G. 191, N. 6; H. A. 788 and a. 20. *ἀθρόους*, *together*, by one vote, cf. *μιᾷ ψήφῳ*, Xen. Mem. I, 1, 18. *παρανόμως.* The law required that the vote should be taken separately, cf. Xen. Hel. I, 7, 37: *κρίνεσθαι δίχα ἕκαστον.* *ὡς . . . ἔδοξε.* Xenophon says (Hel. I, 7, 39), they soon repented of it, and punished the authors of the measure as deceivers of the people. 21. *ἐγὼ μόνος, κ.τ.λ.* The prytanes all opposed at first, but when threatened with the vengeance of the people, they all gave in except Socrates, the son of Sophroniscus. Xen. Hel. I, 7, 15. 22. *μηδὲν ποιεῖν.* G. 283, 6; H. A. 1029. Compare, however, 31, D and E. It is to be noticed that *κωλύω* does not take *μή* with its inf. *ἐνδεικνύναι καὶ ἀπάγειν*, to *indict* me and *lead me away* to punishment. As Attic law terms, these verbs signify an especially summary proceeding without the formality or delay of a criminal prosecution. See Lex. under *ἔνδειξις* and *ἀπαγωγή*. 25. *βοώντων.* See in Xen. Hel. I, 7, 13, 14, the tumult and uproar of the meeting.

Page 67 C. 1. *Ἐπειδὴ δὲ ὀλιγαρχία . . . οἱ τριάκοντα.* There was always an oligarchic faction at Athens, who were aided and sustained by Lacedemonian influence; and when, at the close of the Peloponnesian war, the Lacedemonians triumphed, they placed thirty of this faction in the supreme power, who were afterward known as *the thirty* (or the thirty tyrants). The noun added to the numeral is a later expression. 2. *με πέμπτον αὐτόν*, myself *and four others*. H. A. 681, b. *εἰς τὴν θόλον.* The round building where the fifty prytanes held their sittings and dined together at public expense, used also by the thirty. Compare the round temple of Vesta in Rome, which was the *fireside* or hearthstone of the early Romans. 3. *Λέοντα τὸν Σαλαμίνιον.* A native of Salamis, but a citizen of Athens, who had withdrawn to Salamis to escape the power of the tyrants. 6. *ἀναπλῆσαι αἰτιῶν*, *to implicate in* their own *crimes*. Page 67

D. 7. *αὖ*, *again*, or *in turn*, sc. as in the case of the ten generals under the democracy. So *αὖ* above, l. 2. He resisted the democracy and the oligarchy *alike* in their wrong doings. 8. *εἰ μὴ ἀγροικότερον*, *if it were not too rude* (rustic) *an expression*, is an apology for the use of *οὐδ' ὁτιοῦν* in such a connection as would probably offend the polite ears of the Athenians. Cf. Euthyd. 283, E; Gorg. 509, A. 9. *τούτου δὲ τὸ πᾶν μέλει*, *for this*, *I say*, *I care everything*. *τὸ πᾶν* is an adverbial or synecdochial acc., the exact opposite of *οὐδ' ὁτιοῦν*. 10. *ἐμὲ γὰρ ἐκείνη ἡ ἀρχή*, *κ.τ.λ.*, *for me* (emphatic both in form and position) *that government* (of the thirty), *strong as it then was*, *did not so terrify*. 13. *ἤγαγον Λέοντα*. He was put to death. Xen. Hel. II, 3, 39. *ᾠχόμην ἀπιὼν οἴκαδε*, *went immediately home*. 15. *διὰ ταχέων* = *ταχέως*. The government of the Thirty Tyrants lasted only about eight months before Thrasybulus advanced against them. It was then some months later before peace was established.

E. 17. *τοσάδε ἔτη*, *so many years* as I *have* lived. 18. *ἔπραττον*. The imperf. denotes *continued* action. 19. *τοῖς δικαίοις*, the things that are just = justice. *ὥσπερ χρή*, *as one ought* always to do—this is implied in the present. 21. *οὐδὲ γὰρ ἂν ἄλλος ἀνθρώπων οὐδείς*, sc. *διεγένετο*, would have lived so many years.

A. 23. *τοιοῦτος φανοῦμαι*, *shall be found* (on examination) 33 *such a man*, sc. one who has never fallen in with any one in anything contrary to justice, as explained by the following clause. 26. *ἐμοὺς μαθητὰς εἶναι*. Socrates was charged by his enemies with the crimes of Critias and Alcibiades, the one the prince of demagogues and the other the leader of the Thirty Tyrants. They had indeed listened to his conversations; but neither they nor indeed any other man (he proceeds to say) were his *disciples*, for he had no disciples, and never professed to be a teacher. Hence he never called his hearers *μαθηταί*, but *οἱ συνόντες*. See this whole topic discussed at length, Xen. Mem. I, 2. 27. *τὰ ἐμαυτοῦ*, my proper

Page 67 business, my appointed mission, already described as assigned him by Apollo.

Page 68 B. 1. οὐδέ gives emphatic denial to both clauses as unified by μέν and δέ. 2. μὴ λαμβάνων δὲ οὔ, sc. διαλέγομαι, *but in case I do not receive pay, not converse.* 3. παρέχω . . . ἐρωτᾶν, *I give liberty to question me to rich and poor alike, and if any one choose to answer* my question, *and hear what I may say,* I give him liberty to do that. παρέχω ἐμαυτόν is to be supplied from the previous clause. For the voice of ἐρωτᾶν, cf. G. 261, 2, R; H. A. 952, a. Compare Gorgias, 480, D, ἐὰν μέν γε πληγῶν ἄξια ἠδικηκὼς ᾖ τύπτειν παρέχοντα. 5. τούτων . . . ὧν . . . μηδενί. *Of* (in respect to) *these* (alleged disciples) *I should not justly bear the responsibility, to no one of whom I ever promised,* etc.

C. 13. ὅτι ἀκούοντες χαίρουσιν, κ.τ.λ. The same *words* are used above, 23, C. There, however, the participle ἀκούοντες stands last, and is followed by its proper case, the genitive, ἐξεταζομένων, κ.τ.λ., while here the verb χαίρουσιν follows the participle and is followed by its appropriate case, the dative, viz., ἐξεταζομένοις, κ.τ.λ., *I told you the whole truth,* viz., *that they enjoy hearing examined those who think they are wise but are not.* 16. τοῦτο, sc. to examine those who suppose that they are wise but are not. ὡς ἐγώ φημι, resumptive of the claim as made before. 17. παντὶ τρόπῳ. Among these ways, Xenophon (Mem. I, 1, 3) specifies οἰωνοῖς, θυσίαις, φήμαις, συμβόλοις. 20. εὐέλεγκτα, strictly, *easy to be confuted;* but here, *easy to be tested and proved.* εἰ γὰρ δή, *for if really.*

D. 21. χρῆν δήπου, *they ought surely.* The imperf. implies that they were not doing it. G. 222, N. 2; H. A. 897. εἴτε τινὲς αὐτῶν πρεσβύτεροι γενόμενοι . . . νέοις οὖσιν αὐτοῖς, κ.τ.λ., *both if any of them, after having become older, became conscious that when they were young,* etc. Instead of εἴτε the correlative member of the sentence begins with the more emphatic εἰ δέ. So below, 40, D, E, εἴτε δὴ μηδεμία αἴσθησις . . . εἰ δ' αὖ οἷον ἀποδημῆσαι. So δέ is sometimes antithetic to τέ, and οὐδέ to οὔτε. 25. αὐτοί, *themselves,* in contradistinction from their relatives. So αὐτούς in the previous clause. 28. μεμνῆσθαι depends on χρῆν in the antithetic member of

the sentence, the force of which still continues. 1. ἐνταυθοῖ. Page 33
H. A. 788, b. 2. Κρίτων οὑτοσί, *this Crito here.* His name has become identified with that of Socrates, as his friend and patron, and is perpetuated in the Platonic dialogue, or rather monologue, called Crito. He was a wealthy Athenian, of the same *deme* (δημότης) or ward as Socrates, viz., Alopece, and now, it seems, like him, far advanced in life. The son Critobulus seems to have evoked great admiration for his beauty, but as an example of enlarged manhood to have done little credit either to his father or his teacher. Cf. Xen. Mem. I, 3, 8 seqq.; Athen. 220, A; Xen. Symp. IV, 10.

E. 3. Λυσανίας. Cf. Diog. Laert. 2, 60. ὁ Σφήττιος, of the deme Sphettus. It was customary at Athens to add by way of distinction to the name of the individual the ward to which he belonged, and often also the name of his father. The same object was accomplished at Rome, as it also is in modern times, by several names. 4. Αἰσχίνου, usually called the Socratic, to distinguish him from the orator of the same name. He established no school of philosophy, but taught the doctrines of his master for money, and wrote Socratic dialogues. The extant dialogues, however, which bear his name are not genuine. ὁ Κηφισιεύς, *of the deme Cephisia.* This Antiphon is to be distinguished from the orator and from several others of the same name. The son, Epigenes, is mentioned by Xenophon (Mem. III, 12), as well as by Plato in his Phædo, 59. 5. τοίνυν, *moreover*, is not inferential but transitional, as it often is in the orators as well as the philosophers. Cf. Stallb. ad loc., also Schaefer ad Demosth. Several of the names which follow are found only here, e. g., Nicostratus, Theodotus, Paralus, and Æantodorus. Touching Demodocus, see Theag. 127, E; Adeimantus, brother of Plato, de Repub. 357–368, 548; Apollodorus, Phæd. 59, A, 117, D; Xen. Mem. III, 11, 17. Apollodorus was a most ardent and devoted follower of Socrates. Theages and Plato also were favorite disciples. 8. καταδεηθείη = Latin, deprecari, sensus est: non potest Theodotus Nicostratum fratrem rogare, ne me accuset et contra me testetur. Stallb.

A. 13. μάλιστα μέν is correlative to εἰ δὲ τότε. The *best* 34

Page 69 time for Meletus to call some of these witnesses—the time when he *ought especially* to have called them—was in the course of his *argument* before the court; *but if he forgot it then*, etc. 15. παραχωρῶ, *give way*, *yield him the floor*, as we say, or in the technical language of the Greek bar, let him speak or testify during my water (the measure of *time* by the clepsydra). Cf. Mahaffy, Primer of Old Greek Life, sect. 98.

B. 20. ἂν λόγον ἔχοιεν βοηθοῦντες, *might have a reason for helping me*, i. e., for defending me, right or wrong. 22. ἀλλ' ἤ. Cf. note, 20, D. 23. ξυνίσασι Μελήτῳ, κ.τ.λ. *They know as Meletus knows*, etc. Comp. note, 21, B. 25. Εἶεν. Cf. note, 19, A. Socrates here concludes his direct defense, ἃ μὲν . . . ἀπολογεῖσθαι . . . τοιαῦτα, and proceeds to justify himself in not resorting to the ordinary means of moving the compassion of his judges and so saving his life. Cf. Mahaffy, Primer of Greek Life, sect. 96. 27. Τάχα δ' ἄν, κ.τ.λ. Such means of acquittal were expressly prohibited by law. Cf. Demos. adv. Timocr.; Xen. Mem. IV, 4, 4. But the law was disregarded, and it was the prevailing practice to bring in the wives and children of the accused, and to resort to all possible ways of exciting the compassion of the judges, as is manifest from many passages of the orators and of Aristophanes, e. g., Vesp. 568 sqq.; Demost. in Mid. 99; Isoc. de Perm. 31. Ast thinks the Apology here a manifest imitation of Isocrates in the passage last cited, and therefore not genuine; but with how little reason, see Schleiermacher ad loc.

Page 70 C. 4. ἐγὼ δὲ οὐδὲν ἄρα, κ.τ.λ., *while I*, as ought to have been expected (ἄρα), *will do none of these things*. 5. καὶ ταῦτα, *and that, too, when incurring*, etc.

D. 9. οὐκ ἀξιῶ μὲν γὰρ ἔγωγε, εἰ δ' οὖν, *for I for my part do not expect it, but if, I say, any one of you is in such a state of mind*. For ἀξιῶ, cf. 19, D; for οὖν, 21, A. 11. καὶ γὰρ τοῦτο αὐτὸ τὸ τοῦ Ὁμήρου, *and* well I may have, *for in the very language of Homer*. Acc. in apposition with a sentence, G. 137, N. 3; H. A. 626, b. So quotations, especially proverbs, are often introduced. The quotation is from Od. 19, 163, where Odysseus, in the guise of a beggar, is thus addressed by Penelope. The expression is proverbial, and denotes that the person to whom it is applied is a man among men, sprung from men and related to them. 14. υἱεῖς . . . τρεῖς, *and sons even, men of Athens, three* of them, cf. Crit. 47, B, note. μειράκιον, *a young man*, sc. Lamprocles, who is called μέγας in Phæd. 65, and is introduced in Xen. Mem. II, 2, holding a conversation with his father touching his filial duty to his termagant mother. 15. παιδία, *small children*, sc. Sophroniscus and Menexenus, cf. Phæd. 3, where they are called σμικροί. Seneca (Epis. 104) says that the sons of Socrates resembled their mother rather than their father. Page 70

E. 18. ἀλλ' εἰ μέν, κ.τ.λ., *but whether I can meet death with confidence or not is another question.* He barely *hints* at this as one reason for his course, but modestly dismisses it as not exactly pertinent on the present occasion. 20. πρὸς δ' οὖν δόξαν, *however that may be, for reputation both mine and yours*, etc. Cf. note, 17, A. So just below, ἀλλ' οὖν δεδογμένον, *but whatever may be the fact, it is at least supposed.* 22. τηλικόνδε, sc. seventy, cf. 17, D. τοῦτο τοὔνομα, sc. σοφός, cf. 23, A. 23. ψεῦδος, the subs. is often associated with the adj. ἀληθές, as shown by Heindorf, Ast, and Stallbaum. Page 71

A. 28. τι εἶναι. H. A. 703, a. 2. ὥσπερ . . . ἐσομένων. 35
G. 277, N. 3; 278, 1, N.; H. A. 978, a; 972, a. 9. καὶ ὁτιοῦν εἶναι, *to be even anything whatever*, i. e., to have any weight of character, however inconsiderable. 14. χωρὶς δὲ τῆς δόξης, but irrespective of *the* reputation, sc. which attaches to me and of which we have been speaking. Observe the force of the article. The emphatic negative οὐδέ should also be noticed; it appears to me that it is *not even* right. The second οὐδέ is not merely correlative to the first, but emphatic = *no nor*, or *nor even.*

C. 17. καταχαρίζεσθαι τὰ δίκαια is *to pervert justice for the sake of pleasing.* So κατα-χρᾶσθαι = mis-use or abuse. 18. ταῦτα, sc. τὰ δίκαια = *justice.* ὀμώμοκεν. The oath of office taken by the δικασταί, and the security it afforded, are very often adverted to, particularly by the Attic orators, e. g., Demos. de Cor. 2 and 6. The substance of the oath was that they would administer justice according to the laws so far as

Page 71 there were laws, and where no laws existed, according to their own best judgment of what was right. Cf. Poll. Onom. 8, 122; Demos. adv. Lept. 118. 21. ἐθίζεσθαι. The passive has permissive meaning, ***nor should*** you permit yourselves to be accustomed. Cf. Crito, 48, D: ἀγόμενοι, permitting ourselves to be taken away.

D. 24. ἄλλως τε μέντοι . . . πάντως καί, ***both every other way, to be sure, but especially when accused of impiety***, etc., cf. note on ἄλλως τε καί, 26, E. The expected order is broken suddenly to emphasize the utter inconsistency of such a proposition. 25. σαφῶς γὰρ ἄν, cf. note, ὥσπερ οὖν ἄν, 17, D. 27. θεοὺς . . . εἶναι. Observe the emphatic position of these words, the one at the beginning, the other at the end of the clause: ***I should teach you not to believe in the existence of***
Page 72 ***the gods.*** 2. νομίζω τε γάρ, sc. θεούς, ***for I both believe in them.*** ὡς οὐδείς = ***more than any.*** 3. καὶ ὑμῖν ἐπιτρέπω καὶ τῷ θεῷ κρῖναι, ***and I commit it to you and the god to decide.*** This clause is to be closely connected with its correlative clause (νομίζω τε . . . καὶ . . . ἐπιτρέπω), and in that connection it implies, that he ***shows*** his belief in the gods practically by his calm reliance on the providence of God in this trial for his life. It will be observed that Socrates here uses the singular τῷ θεῷ, though he has been using the plural just before. He may refer to the god at Delphi, of whom he has often before spoken particularly, and in the singular number (cf. τὸν θεὸν τὸν ἐν Δελφοῖς, 20, E, sqq.), and who, having indirectly, by means of the oracle, involved him in difficulty, would now provide for the best result; or he may refer to the supreme God, whom he often, as represented in the writings both of Plato and Xenophon, singles out and distinguishes from the inferior deities (cf. Xen. Mem. IV, 3, 13).

With the above words of pious resignation and confidence, Socrates concludes the first and principal part of his defense, and submits the question of guilty or not guilty to his judges. They pronounce him guilty by a small majority of votes. The question still remained, what punishment should be inflicted. In all those cases, where the laws do not prescribe the penalty (ἀγῶνες ἀτίμητοι)—and charges of impiety were of this sort, cf. Dem. in Timoc. 702, 5—it was customary for the accuser to propose what he deemed a suitable penalty (τιμᾶσθαι), and the accused, if he chose, to propose some other punishment (ἀντιτιμᾶσθαι or ὑποτιμᾶσθαι), and then the judges decided between these two, no third proposition being admissible. Cf. Grote, vol. viii, chap. 68; also Boeckh, Meier and Schömann, and Smith's Dic. Antiqq.: Ἀγῶνες ἀτίμητοι καὶ τιμητοί. The accusers of Socrates pronounced him worthy of death. Had Socrates chosen to propose banishment, for instance, instead of death, he might doubtless have escaped the extreme penalty, cf. 37, C; Crit. 52, C. But when he disdained to acknowledge guilt by any counter-proposal, and even claimed reward instead of punishment as his due, the judges took offense and sentenced him to death. His remarks on what he thought the proper sentence constitute the second part of the Apology, capp. 25–29. Page 73

A. 6. τὸ μὲν μὴ ἀγανακτεῖν depends on ξυμβάλλεται. The infinitive is emphatic in its position, and suggests a word of prevention, as in the mind. ξυμβάλλεται would regularly take a preposition—εἰς or possibly πρός, cf. Rep. 1, 331, B, where the inf. is repeated in εἰς τοῦτο. The article simply marks the infinitive a little more distinctly as the object of the main action; otherwise we should expect the infinitive alone. The μέν is correlative to δέ at the commencement of the next chapter: Τιμᾶται δ' οὖν. 7. μου. G. 173, 2, N.; H. A. 752. ἄλλα τε . . . καί, *both many other things conspire to cause, and* especially the fact that *it has happened to me not unexpectedly*, cf. note on ἄλλοι τε καί, 28, C. The full and regular construction would have been καὶ δὴ καὶ τοῦτο ὅτι οὐκ ἀνέλπιστον, κ.τ.λ. ἐλπίς and its derivatives are used with reference to objects of fear as well as hope. So spes and sperare in Latin, cf. Verg. At *sperate* Deos memores fandi atque nefandi. 11. παρ' ὀλίγον . . . παρὰ πολύ. παρά implies *comparison*, *for I, for my part, did not suppose it would be thus by little*, but *by much*, sc. that the votes against me would exceed those in my favor. Cf. H. A. 802, near the end. οὕτω belongs to ὀλίγον, cf. 40, A: πάνυ ἐπὶ σμικροῖς, where πάνυ goes with σμικροῖς. 12. εἰ τριάκοντα μόναι, κ.τ.λ. We have accepted here the reading of 36

Page 72 Stallbaum, Cron, and the best MSS., instead of the common reading τρεῖς. If a *change* of thirty votes would have turned the scale, the *majority* against Socrates must have been sixty. Diogenes Laertius, II, 41, as usually interpreted, says that the number of votes against him was 281. Deducting 60 from this number, we have 221 for the number of votes in his favor, and 502 for the whole number of votes cast. But the sections of the Heliastic courts usually consisted of 500 each, or a multiple of 500, with one additional dicast to avoid a tie vote. And if 281 of the 501 dicasts voted against Socrates, only 220 could have voted for him, and then a transfer of 30 votes would not have secured his acquittal. We may suppose, however, that he was content with an approximate statement in round numbers. 12. *μετέπεσον*, fallen over, sc. into the other urn, which received the votes for acquittal. 13. *ἀποπεφεύγῃ*. For this form of the plup. see note, 31, E. 15. *ἀνέβη*, etc. Upon the *βῆμα* to aid Meletus in the advocacy of his cause, cf. note, 18, B. 17. *χιλίας δραχμάς*. The prosecutor, unless he received a fifth part of the votes, was liable to a fine of a thousand drachmas and also a forfeiture (*ἀτιμία*) of the right to appear as prosecutor in future—a very useful and very necessary check on the virulence of public prosecutions in the Athenian courts. Cf. Dem. de Cor. 103; in Mid. 23; Boeckh, Pub. Econ. Ath., chap. ix, 11. Socrates argues that Meletus (not being the most popular or influential of the three accusers), if he had been the sole prosecutor, would not have carried more than a third as many votes as were actually gained by the joint influence of the three, and consequently would not have received a fifth part of all the votes. Cf. Schleier. ad loc. *τὸ πέμπτον μέρος*. Observe the force of the article, *the* required fifth according to the well-known law. Demosthenes (de Cor. 103) uses simply *τὸ μέρος* in the same way, *the* required *portion*.

B. 19. *ὁ ἀνήρ*, sc. the accuser, of whom he had just been speaking in the foregoing chapter. *τιμᾶται* is middle voice. The usage in regard to the penalty and counter-penalty (*τιμᾶσθαι* and *ἀντιτιμᾶσθαι*) has been explained above. 20. *ὑμῖν* can be taken as ethical dative. *τῆς ἀξίας* is gen. of price after ἀντιτιμήσομαι, to be supplied from the question. 21. ἢ δῆλον, *or* is it needless to ask—*is it evident*, etc. 22. παθεῖν refers to corporal punishment, ἀποτῖσαι to a pecuniary penalty. The question is asked in the words of a judicial formula, cf. Dem. in Timoc. 105. ὅ τι μαθὼν differs from τί μαθὼν only in being relative and indirect. It may be rendered *because*, but further indicates surprise or censure. This implication can be expressed in English only by a parenthesis: *because I did not keep quiet* (*and what had I taken into my head*, literally, learned, *that I did not*). Cf. M. and T. 109, N. 7, b, near the end; H. A. 968, c. 23. ὧνπερ οἱ πολλοί, sc. ἐπιμελοῦνται, supplied from ἀμελήσας, as often a positive from a corresponding negative word, *not caring for those things which the mass* care for. 25. τῶν ἄλλων ἀρχῶν, not the *other* magistracies, for the specifications which precede are not all magistracies, but *the rest*, sc. *the magistracies*, or the magistracies besides. So Gorg. 473, C: πολιτῶν καὶ τῶν ἄλλων ξένων=the citizens and the rest, viz., the strangers. So οἱ ἄλλοι is often used. See Lex. ἄλλος II, 8. ξυνωμοσιῶν καὶ στάσεων. Conspiracies and factions abounded at Athens in the age of Socrates. 27. ἐπιεικέστερον . . . σῴζεσθαι, *too upright a man to be safe if I went into these things*. ὄντα is better established than ἰόντα. Its pregnant meaning with εἰς has a parallel in πάρεισιν ἐνταυθοῖ, 33, D. Notice also ἐνταῦθα with ᾖα in the next line. For both, cf. H. A. 788. Page 72

C. 1. ἐνταῦθα here is equivalent to ἐπὶ τοῦτο, answering to ἐπὶ τὸ εὐεργετεῖν, and ἰὼν is redundant: *but to go and confer on each individually the greatest benefit*, to this (literally, *there*) *I went*. 8. τῶν τε ἄλλων . . . ἐπιμελεῖσθαι, that is, on the principle that the man is more than his property, the state more than its possessions, and in general persons or things more than their appurtenances. The same great principle is often inculcated by our Lord in the gospels, cf. Mat. VI, 25, 33. Page 73

D. 11. τιμᾶσθαι here also is mid. = *to amerce myself*. Compare E, below: εἰ οὖν δεῖ με κατὰ τὸ δίκαιον τῆς ἀξίας τιμᾶσθαι. 12. τοιοῦτον ὅ τι, instead of τοιοῦτον οἷον, to make it more indefinite; *such a good of whatever kind it may be, as*, etc. Below we have a still more singular mixing of correlatives: μᾶλλον πρέπει οὕτως, ὡς, where we should expect

Page 36 μᾶλλον . . . ἤ or οὕτως ὡς, but find both forms brought together. A similar construction occurs at 30, A: πρότερον μηδὲ οὕτω σφόδρα ὡς, except that there μηδέ is interposed between πρότερον and οὕτω, and makes the construction somewhat less concise and abrupt. 13. πένητι. Cf. note, 23, B. εὐεργέτῃ, *a public benefactor*, a term of honor, which the Athenians conferred by formal vote on those who had deserved well of the state, and which foreigners, and even foreign kings and princes, were ambitious to receive. So in Egypt, Ptolemy Euergetes. ἐπὶ τῇ ὑμετέρᾳ παρακελεύσει, *for your admonition*, i. e., to instruct you, the adj. taking the place of the *objective* gen. 14. μᾶλλον πρέπει, see above. 15. ἐν πρυτανείῳ σιτεῖσθαι. The Prytaneum was a sort of city hall or state house, where the laws and public archives were kept, where some of the magistrates had their meals, and entertained, at the public expense, not only ambassadors from foreign states, but citizens who had deserved well of the state. Cron says, "as table companion of certain officials. Not of the archons who ate in the θεσμοθέσιον, nor of the prytanes who ate in the θόλος, but apparently of certain priests." To be thus entertained was the highest honor. Socrates claims it as a εὐεργέτης who has rendered the most useful services to the state, and also as affording him the requisite leisure, that he might devote himself wholly to the instruction of the citizens. 16. πολύ γε μᾶλλον. Victors in the public games were honored with entertainment at the Prytaneum. Socrates claims the honor as due to himself *much more at least* than to such. ἵππῳ, a *race-horse* under a rider; ξυνωρίδι, *a two-horse chariot;* ζεύγει, a general term for carriage, here denotes especially a chariot drawn by more than two horses, and may be rendered *four-horse chariot.* 17. Ὀλυμπιάσιν, *at the Olympic games.* The acc. (Ὀλυμπιάδα or Ὀλύμπια) more frequently follows νικᾶν. See Lex. under νικάω. 18. δοκεῖν εἶναι . . . εἶναι. Socrates was an uncompromising enemy of all *seeming*, and often exposes the *folly*, as well as the baseness of it, since the best way to *seem* to be good (in whatever excellence), is to *be* good. Cf. Xen. Mem. I, 7, 1. Compare the immortal verse of Æschylus, 592, Ἕπτα Ἐπὶ Θήβας: Οὐ γὰρ δοκεῖν ἄριστος

ἀλλ' εἶναι θέλει. 19. ὁ μὲν τροφῆς οὐδὲν δεῖται, ἐγὼ δὲ δέομαι, Page 73
sc. because he is rich, as the victor in a chariot must be, while I am poor. He here has respect to the πένητι above, as in the preceding clause he refers to the εὐεργέτῃ. He is a *real benefactor*, and he is *really poor*. He both deserves and needs to be provided for in the Prytaneum.

A. 22. παραπλησίως . . . ὥσπερ περὶ τοῦ οἴκτου καὶ τῆς 37
ἀντιβολήσεως. The reference is to chap. xxiii, where he scorns to resort to supplications or appeals to compassion, and yet denies that he does this αὐθαδιζόμενος, *from arrogance.* Here he employs the rare word ἀντιβόλησις instead of the usual ἱκετεία. 25. τοιοῦτον ἀλλὰ τοιόνδε, not *such as that*, but *such as this;* not *such as you suppose*, but *such as I proceed to explain* (cf. note, 21, B), i. e., it is not arrogance but truth and duty that impels me. 26. ἑκὼν εἶναι is stronger than ἑκών alone. It means, *so far as depends on my will.* Cf. G. 268, N.; H. A. 956, a. 27. πείθω sometimes takes two acc. διειλέγμεθα. The perf. has respect to this apology, which he regards as virtually finished—it was finished so far as the question of guilt or innocence was concerned. 28. ὥσπερ καὶ ἄλλοις ἀνθρώποις. He probably has particular reference to the Lacedemonians, whose laws Socrates, in common with most of the philosophers, highly reverenced, and who, as Thucydides and Plutarch inform us, never decided *capital* trials hastily, but extended them over several days.

B. 5. ἀδικήσειν. G. 202, 3, b. 6. του κακοῦ, *some evil*, Page 74
i. e., *any punishment.* So τοιούτου τινός, *anything of this sort.* It is gen. of *price* or *penalty*, and is accompanied with the dat. of the *person* (ἐμαυτῷ) on whom the penalty is assessed. The same construction is seen in οὗ Μέλητός μοι τιμᾶται, et passim. Ad rem, cf. note, 38, B. 7. ἢ μὴ πάθω. ἢ is interrogative: shall I do it through fear that I may suffer death, when I am so ignorant of death that I do not know whether it is a good or an evil? 9. ἕλωμαι, subj. aor. in a deliberative question. It is to be rendered by the future. It is followed by a partitive genitive: *shall I choose* OF *those things which I know to be evil*, sc. imprisonment, banishment, etc. We have in this sentence another example of that usage

Page 74 which occurs so often in Plato—two constructions condensed into one. The author might have said: ἕλωμαί τι τούτων ἃ εὖ οἶδα ὅτι κακά ἐστιν, or ἕλωμαί τι τούτων ἃ εὖ οἶδα κακὰ ὄντα, or with attraction of the rel., ὧν εὖ οἶδα κακῶν ὄντων. But instead of either we have parts of both.

C. 11. τῇ ἀεὶ καθισταμένῃ ἀρχῇ, *the ever-shifting government.* The Eleven who had charge of the prisons, executions, etc., were chosen *annually* (one from each of the ten tribes, with a secretary). Socrates implies that it were hardly worth while to live subject to the caprice of such a succession of petty tyrants as might chance to be *established from time to time* (such is the exact force of ἀεὶ καθισταμένῃ) over the public prisons. Cf. note on ἀεί, 25, C. 12. δεδέσθαι. M. and T., 18, 3, N. 13. ἀλλὰ ταὐτόν . . . ἔλεγον, sc. perpetual imprisonment, because he had no money and therefore would never be released. 15. τιμήσωμαι . . . τιμήσαιτε. Observe the change of voice. The middle voice is used of the *accuser* and *the accused*, and the active of the *judges*.

D. 20. βαρύτεραι, *too burdensome.* It is fem. as referring to διατριβάς. 21. ἄλλοι δὲ ἄρα, κ.τ.λ., *will others, then* (or *forsooth*), bear them easily? The clause is an irregular apodosis to ὑμεῖς μὲν ὄντες, κ.τ.λ. 27. κἂν μὲν τούτους ἀπελαύνω, κ.τ.λ., *and if on the one hand I do repulse them, they will themselves drive me out of the city.* ἐξελῶσι is Attic fut. G. 110, II, 2, N. 1 (b); H. A. 424.

Page 75 E. 4. ἡμῖν, Eth. Dat., *please tell us*, is inserted simply to make the discourse more emphatic and subjective. G. 184, 3, N. 6; H. A. 770. 5. ἐξελθών, sc. into exile. 8. ὡς εἰρωνευομένῳ, *supposing that I spoke ironically.*

38 A. 12. ὁ δὲ ἀνεξέταστος, κ.τ.λ., *and that a life without investigation is not worth living*, literally, not to be lived. This clause depends on λέγω ὅτι, and ἀνεξέταστος, contrary to the prevailing usage, is to be taken in an active sense. The active meaning, however, carries with it the passive. 13. ταῦτα δ', *this on the other hand.* δέ emphasizes the apodosis in the latter of the two supposed cases. M. and T. 57.

B. 18. ὅσα ἔμελλον ἐκτίσειν, as much as I was about to pay, i. e., as much as I should be likely to be able to pay.

οὐδὲν γὰρ ἂν ἐβλάβην implies that he would have considered the loss of property, if he had it, no real loss. This accords with what he had said above (37, B), that he would not amerce himself to the amount of *any evil*, for he did not deserve it. 19. *νῦν δὲ οὐ γάρ*, *but now* I can not amerce myself in a sum of money, *for I have not got it.* It is usually printed thus: *νῦν δέ—οὐ γάρ*, and treated as a case of aposiopesis. But this reading of Cron comes to the same thing. 25. *αὐτοὶ δ' ἐγγυᾶσθαι.* Intell. *φασί*, quod continetur præcedenti verbo *κελεύουσι.* Stallb. 26. *ἀξιόχρεῳ.* Cf. note, 20, E. The comparatively small fine in which Socrates here proposes to amerce himself (only half a talent, or about $500), and the whole strain of his remarks on the subject, prove that he was not in earnest. Accordingly the Apology ascribed to Xenophon denies that he proposed a counter and lower assessment. He was not really desirous to preserve his life. He must have foreseen that his judges would not accept such a substitute for the death penalty, which the accusers had named in their indictment. He must also have known that his freedom of speech, his playful irony, and especially his assumption of entire innocence which merited reward instead of punishment, would provoke the hostility of those judges at least who had already pronounced him guilty, and, as they had to choose between the penalties proposed by the parties, they would certainly choose that of the accusers and put him to death. According to Diogenes Laertius, eighty who had voted for his acquittal now passed over to the majority and voted for his death. Cf. Cic. Orat. 1, 54: Socratis responso sic judices exarserunt, ut capitis hominem innocentissimum condemnarent. Page 75

Here ends the second part of the Defense. The vote is now taken touching the penalty, and Socrates is condemned to death by an increased majority. He then concludes his speech in a tone of conscious innocence and moral heroism, in which, as Cicero says, he appears, not so much in the attitude of a culprit or a suppliant before his judges, as of their master and lord.

C. 1. *Οὐ πολλοῦ . . . χρόνου.* The remainder of the life of Socrates (now 70 years of age) was so short, that it was Page 76

Page 76 hardly worth their while to incur so much dishonor for the sake of extinguishing what would soon have terminated in the course of nature. 2. ὄνομα ἕξετε καὶ αἰτίαν, *you will have the name and blame*, both here in a bad sense, though often in a good one. For ὑπό, cf. note, 17, A.

D. 15. τόλμης καὶ ἀναισχυντίας, i. e., what Socrates would consider audacity and shamelessness, viz., daring to say and do such things, whether true or false, noble or ignoble, as would disgrace him, while persuading them. Cf. ἐάν τις τολμᾷ πᾶν ποιεῖν, below, 39, A.

E. 20. τότε, sc. while making my defense, before sentence was pronounced. 23. ἐκείνως, sc. ἀπολογησάμενος, *having de-*
Page 77 *fended myself in that way.*

39 A. 3. μή οὐ . . . ᾖ. G. 218, N. 2; H. A. 867. 5. θᾶττον γάρ, κ.τ.λ. Cf. Homer's Ἄτη, Il. ix, 505.

B. 6. ἅτε . . . ὤν, *as . . . being* = inasmuch as I am. ὑπό τοῦ βραδυτέρου. Cf. Od. viii, 329: οὐκ ἀρετᾷ κακὰ ἔργα· κιχάνει τοι βραδὺς ὠκύν. 7. δεινοί is the opposite of πρεσβύτης, and ὀξεῖς of βραδύς. The swifter pursuer, viz., vice, is represented as overtaking the swifter party, viz., the judges who condemned Socrates; while Socrates himself, tardy with years, is seized upon by the more tardy pursuer, viz., death. 9. θανάτου δίκην ὀφλών, *having incurred sentence of death.* ὑπὸ τῆς ἀληθείας, sc. as judge. Compare Maximus Tyrius (Diss. 9), where he says: Socrates was, indeed, put to death, but the Athenians were condemned, and God and truth was their judge. 10. ὠφληκότες μοχθηρίαν καὶ ἀδικίαν = *having been convicted of wickedness and injustice.* 12. μετρίως ἔχειν, *to be suitable*, i. e., well.

C. 14. τὸ μετὰ τοῦτο, the after this, i. e., the sequel, or consequence. 16. χρησμῳδοῦσιν, ὅταν μέλλωσιν ἀποθανεῖσθαι. This idea, that the soul, when about to leave the body, shows its divine nature and prophetic power, was widely prevalent among the ancients. Thus Patroclus predicts the death of Hector (Il. xvi, 851 sqq.), and Hector prophesies the death of Achilles (Il. xxii, 358 sqq.); cf. also Phæd. 84, E; Xen. Apol. 30; Cic. de Div. I, 30; Sex. Empir. Math. ix, 20. 19. οἵαν ἐμὲ ἀπεκτόνατε. For the double acc., cf. G. 159, N. 4; H. A.

725. 21. *τοῦ διδόναι ἔλεγχον τοῦ βίου*, from giving proof of your life, i. e., *from the necessity of letting your manner of life be put to the proof.* Page 77

D. 26. *ἀποκτείνοντες ἀνθρώπους*, *by putting men to death.* 28. *οὐ γὰρ ἔσθ' αὕτη.* G. 28, 3, N. 1; H. A. 480, 3.

E. 6. *ὑπέρ*, notice the preposition *ὑπέρ* rather than *περί*, Page 78
as if he would defend the conclusion. 6. *ἐν ᾧ οἱ ἄρχοντες ἀσχολίαν ἄγουσι*, *while the magistrates are busy, and I do not yet come, whither when I have come, I must be put to death*, i. e., before the Eleven (cf. note, 37, C) are ready to lead me away to prison.

A. 12. *τί ποτε νοεῖ*, what in the world it means, or what 40
can be its meaning. Cf. note, 20, D. *ὦ ἄνδρες δικασταί.* He has habitually addressed the court hitherto as *ἄνδρες Ἀθηναῖοι.* The change here is intentional, since that portion of the court whom he now addresses were *judges* indeed, that is, administrators of *justice.* 14. *ἡ γὰρ εἰωθυῖά μοι μαντικὴ ἡ τοῦ δαιμονίου*, *for the customary prophetic voice of the divinity.* Cf. 31, D, note ibid. Schleiermacher considers *ἡ τοῦ δαιμονίου* as a gloss, because Plato elsewhere calls the voice itself *τὸ δαιμόνιον*, and where a genitive of source is added to *μαντικῇ*, *φωνῇ*, etc., it is not *τοῦ δαιμονίου*, but *τοῦ θεοῦ.* Stallbaum admits that the combination here is unusual, but does not, for that reason, feel at liberty to depart from the established reading. 16. *καὶ πάνυ ἐπὶ σμικροῖς*, *even on very trifling occasions.* *πάνυ* is often placed thus before the preposition for the sake of emphasis. 18. *ἅ γε δὴ οἰηθείη ἄν τις καὶ νομίζεται*, *which one might certainly suppose to be, and are in fact usually considered.* The relative is the object of the first verb and the subject of the second. The former verb is optative, to denote what any one might naturally suppose; the other is indicative, to denote what is in fact the prevailing sentiment. The reader will observe the difference between *οἴομαι* and *νομίζω* here implied and habitually observed.

B. 27. *τοῦτο ἀγαθὸν γεγονέναι.* In a conversation with Hermogenes, recorded by Xenophon (Mem. IV, 8), Socrates assigns several reasons why, aside from his hopes for another world, he deemed it better for his happiness in this life, and

Page 78 better for his reputation, that he should die then rather than live to a more advanced age. Add to these the considerations touching a future life, which follow in the next chapter of the Apology, and we have the most complete demonstration of his deliberate preference to be condemned rather than to be acquitted, and thus a justification of the otherwise inexplicable manner and spirit of his defense.

Page 79 C. 4. Few passages in the Greek classics have been oftener cited, translated, and commented upon in ancient or modern times, than the chapter on which we now enter. Cf. Plut. Cons. ad Apol.; Xen. Cyrop. viii, 7, 18 sqq.; Cic. Tusc. Quæst. i, 41, where it is translated; also the Christian Fathers, Eusebius, Theodoret, etc., etc. 5. **δυοῖν γὰρ θάτερον.** Stallbaum remarks, that here we doubtless have the true Socratic doctrine of a future state, whereas the Phædo and other Dialogues exhibit Plato's views on the subject. Accordingly Xenophon in his Cyropædia, as above cited, makes Cyrus on his death-bed discourse in exact accordance with the passage before us. 6. **οἷον μηδὲν εἶναι**, *of such a nature as to be nothing*, i. e., to be annihilated. So below, D: **οἷον ὕπνος**, and E: **οἷον ἀποδημῆσαι.** 7. **κατὰ τὰ λεγόμενα**, according to what is said, i. e., the common opinion. 8. **τῇ ψυχῇ**, dat. for the gen. G. 184, 3; H. A. 767. The gen. would represent the subject of the action. 9. **τοῦ τόπου.** The gen. of the *place from which*, without a preposition, may follow a verbal noun as well as a verb. **τοῦ ἐνθένδε**, for **τοῦ ἐνταῦθα**, because of the motion expressed by **μετοίκησις.**

D. 9. **εἴτε μηδεμία.** This **εἴτε** has its correlative in **εἰ δ' αὖ** below, E, which is only more emphatic than another **εἴτε.** Compare **οὔτε . . . οὐδέ γε**, 19, E, and note ibid. 10. **οἷον ὕπνος.** Cf. Od. xiii, 79, 80: **νήδυμος ὕπνος . . . θανάτῳ ἄγχιστα ἐοικώς.** 12. **ἐγὼ γὰρ ἂν οἶμαι** introduces a long and involved sentence. The force of the **ἂν** falls on **εὑρεῖν** several lines below, where it is repeated (cf. notes, 17, D, and 23, B). **οἶμαι** itself and **δέοι** are also repeated. 13. **μὴ ὅτι ἰδιώτην**, *not only a private individual.* H. A. 1035, a. The reader need not be informed that by the great king the Greeks mean the king of Persia, the richest and most powerful sovereign with whom they had to do in all their early history. The comparison of death to night and sleep has always been, as it is now, common especially with the poets. Cf. Hom. Il. xiv, 231; xvi, 672; Od. xiii, 80; Catul. v, 5; Hor. Od. i, 28, 15. Page 79

A. 26. εἰς Ἅιδου, to Pluto's, sc. house or realm. So we 41
omit the word house after the owner's name, and the word church after the name it bears. 1. Μίνως τε καὶ Ῥαδάμανθυς, Page 80
nom. by attraction to the relative οἵπερ. Minos and Rhadamanthus were brothers (hence closely connected by τε καί), both sons of Jove, and celebrated kings, judges, and lawgivers, the former in Crete and the latter in the islands of the Ægean. Æacus, who reigned in Ægina, was also a son of Jupiter, and the father of Peleus and Telamon. Triptolemus was the favorite of Demeter, the inventor of the plow and agriculture, and the great hero in the Eleusinian Mysteries. We find Minos represented as performing the office of judge in the lower regions in the Homeric poems (Od. xi, 568 sqq.); Rhadamanthus in Pindar (Olymp. ii, 137 sqq.); when Æacus was first added to the number, we do not know. In the Gorgias (523, E) these three are represented as administering justice at the entrances to Tartarus and to the Isles of the Blessed: Rhadamanthus to souls from Asia, Æacus to those from Europe, and Minos, as president judge, to decide in doubtful cases. Triptolemus is assigned that office only in this passage, though in the Homeric Hymn to Demeter (153) he sits in judgment on earth. Perhaps he is introduced here to give prominence to the Eleusinian hero, or since *others*, whose names are not mentioned, are here said to be judges in the lower world, we may perhaps suppose that the common opinion ascribed to Triptolemus and others the same office and occupation there which they held on earth. The conception is, however, limited here to those early and just judges and lawgivers whom the imagination of the Greeks had invested with the dignity of demigods (ὅσοι τῶν ἡμιθέων δίκαιοι ἐγένοντο ἐν τῷ ἑαυτῶν βίῳ). 5. ἐπὶ πόσῳ ἄν τις δέξαιτ' ἂν ὑμῶν; Quanti tandem æstimatis. So Cicero renders it. Tusc. Quæst. i, 41, 98. 7. ἐπεὶ ἔμοιγε, κ.τ.λ., *for to myself also the converse there would be delightful, where I might converse with Pala-*

Page 80 *medes and Ajax the son of Telamon.* Both these Grecian heroes had come to a tragical end, the former at the hands of the army, the other by his own hands, in consequence of unjust decisions brought about by the wiles of Odysseus. The story of Ajax is found in Homer (Od. xi, 541 sqq.); that of Palamedes in the Tragic Poets, especially Euripides.

B. 10. **ἀντιπαραβάλλοντι . . . οὐκ ἂν ἀηδὲς εἴη.** This clause is explanatory of the foregoing, hence it is without a connective, and hence also the participle in the dative answering to **ἔμοιγε.** 11. **τὸ μέγιστον** is in apposition with the following proposition. G. 137, N. 3; H. A. 626, b. In this proposition the participle **ἐξετάζοντα** is in the accusative, agreeing with the subject of **διάγειν,** with which **οὐκ ἂν ἀηδὲς εἴη** is again understood. 15. **τὸν ἐπὶ Τροίαν ἄγοντα,** sc. Agamemnon, to see whether he was really as great, and Odysseus as wise, and Sisyphus as crafty, as the Poet represents them to have been. Hom. Il. iii, 178; Od. ix, 19; Il. vi, 153.

C. 18. **ἀμήχανον ἂν εἴη εὐδαιμονίας,** *would be an immense* sum *of happiness.* The genitive is partitive. Or it can be, as Ast supposes, a genitive of specification = in respect of happiness. 19. **τούτου γε ἕνεκα,** sc. for conversing with men and examining them—*they do not, methinks, for this put men to death there,* as they do here. 25. **ἕν τι τοῦτο** = *one thing,* viz., *this.* The **τι** first states it indefinitely; then **τοῦτο** is added to define it.

Page 81 D. 2. **ἀπηλλάχθαι πραγμάτων,** *to be set free from the business and troubles of life.* The perfect is used as referring to a completed condition or state, and that conceived, not actual. 4. **βέλτιον ἦν.** The tense in anticipation looks at the result as already reached; *it was better* as conceived, in anticipation by an overruling Providence.

E. 9. **ταὐτὰ ταῦτα λυποῦντες ἅπερ ἐγὼ ὑμᾶς ἐλύπουν,** i. e., besiege them with warnings and expostulations. **λυπεῖν** here takes a double accusative, as a verb of *doing ill.* G. 165; H. A. 725, a. 12. **ἐὰν δοκῶσί τι εἶναι μηδὲν ὄντες,** *if they think they are something when they are nothing.* The same idea is expressed in the same words by Paul, Gal. vi, 3.

CRITO.

Page 62

A. 1. τηνικάδε, *at this time of day*, that is, at so early an 43
hour. τηνίκα and its corresponding relative and demonstrative words, together with their derivatives, have respect, in Attic usage, not to time in general, but to the *hour of the day*, or, figuratively, to the precise day or hour of some event. ἢ οὐ πρῴ ἔτι ἐστίν, *or is it not still early in the morning?* Buttman writes πρώ (without the iota subscript); Fischer πρῷ; the earlier editions πρωΐ, which Bekker, Ast and Stallbaum shorten into πρῴ after the authority of the poets and the old grammarians. 2. πάνυ μὲν οὖν, *certainly it is*, is the most common expression of full assent in Plato's Dialogues. Sometimes it stands in construction with a verb, as in Apol. 26, B, but more frequently by itself, as here. πάνυ γε is also frequent in affirmative answers, cf. Apol. 25, C. The πάνυ expresses assent, the μέν and γε restriction, and οὖν accordance = certainly so far (it is) as you say. 4. πηνίκα μάλιστα, *what time of day about*. μάλιστα, with words of number, denotes uncertainty, or indefiniteness. 5. Ὄρθρος βαθύς, *very early dawn*. πρῴ is simply morning; ὄρθρος is the dawn or *rising* of the day. βαθύς adds emphasis, *very early*. We speak of midnight deep, deep night, etc. The Greeks extend the same figure to morning and evening—the former in its earliest, and the latter in its latest stages. 6. τοῦ δεσμωτηρίου. I have said in the Preface, *perhaps* the same cell, hewn out of the solid rock, near the old Agora, which now bears the name of "the Prison of Socrates." Professor Felton says: "*undoubtedly;* I read the Phædo there, and when I came to the passage where Crito says, *the sun is yet upon the mountains*, I stepped to the entrance of the cell, and lo! the shadows

Page 82 covered the valleys, but the sun still lingered on Mars' Hill, the Acropolis, and Lycabettus." 7. ὑπακοῦσαι, *to hearken* and hence *open* the door for admittance. ὅπως gives emphasis to the expression of surprise: I wonder *how it happened that* he was willing to admit you, sc. at so very early an hour, as he was not accustomed to open the prison gate very early, cf. Phædo, 59, D. 9. καί τι καὶ εὐεργέτηται, *and he has also been somewhat obliged by me.* The augment in this verb is commonly omitted, but no rule can be recognized. 12. Ἐπιεικῶς πάλαι, *a considerable time since.*

B. 13. εἶτα πῶς, *then how did it happen, that*, etc., expressive of surprise. 15. οὐδ' ἂν αὐτὸς ἤθελον, *I should not myself prefer to be in so much sleeplessness and sorrow*, sc. if I had been at liberty to choose simply for *myself;* but for *your sake* I felt constrained not to disturb your quiet slumbers. This reason is implied here and more fully expressed below: ἐπίτηδές σε οὐκ ἤγειρον, ἵνα ὡς ἥδιστα διάγῃς. 16. ἐν τοσαύτῃ, sc. so much as I have suffered, while I have been watching your peaceful slumbers. τε *preceding* ἀγρυπνίᾳ shows that τοσαύτῃ belongs not only to ἀγρυπνίᾳ, but also to λύπῃ = so much both sleeplessness and sorrow. 17. ὡς ἡδέως = ὅτι οὕτως ἡδέως. So below, ὡς ῥᾳδίως = ὅτι οὕτω ῥᾳδίως.
Page 83 Stallb. 1. διάγῃς. G. 218; H. A. 881, a. 2. τρόπου, turn of mind, or manner of life, hence = *character*, Lat. mores. For the gen., see G. 173, 1; H. A. 744. As to the sentiment, compare Xen. Mem. IV, 8, 2. 6. τηλικοῦτον ὄντα, *a man of my age*, sc. 70, Apol. 17, D.

C. 8. ἀλλ' οὐδὲν αὐτοὺς ἐπιλύεται, κ.τ.λ., *but not at all does their age set them free from grieving at their present fortune*, literally, as to not grieving, or so as not to grieve. τὸ ἀγανακτεῖν is acc. of specification, and does not differ essentially from ὥστε ἀγανακτεῖν. μὴ οὐχί = ne non, or quo minus. G. 283, 6 and 7; H. A. 1034, a. Instead of αὐτούς, αὐτοῖς was the reading previous to Bekker. 14. ὡς ἐμοὶ δοκῶ. Cf. note, 18, A. 15. ἐν τοῖς βαρύτατ'. This is one of several ways in which the superlative is strengthened by the Greeks. The origin of the formula is variously explained. In such passages as this, it may be analyzed as Stallbaum does, viz., = ἐν τοῖς βαρέως φέρουσιν ἐγὼ βαρύτατ' ἂν ἐνέγκαιμι. In other passages, τοῖς seems to be neuter, and to be used like a pronoun, i. e., ἐν τοῖς = ἐν τούτοις. H. A. 652, a. 16. τίνα ταύτην, sc. φέρεις = τίς ἐστιν αὕτη ἡ ἀγγελία, ἣν φέρεις. ἢ τὸ πλοῖον, κ.τ.λ., *or has the vessel arrived*, etc. The ἤ in such interrogative sentences is restrictive of a more general question, or corrective of the foregoing context = but why do I ask? The vessel here mentioned is that in which Theseus returned from Crete, bringing back in safety the seven young men and seven maidens whom the Athenians were obliged to send every year as a tribute to Minos, the Cretan king. Ever after this unexpected deliverance, the same vessel (patched and repaired till its identity became a vexed question for the speculative philosophers) was sent every year in sacred procession to the island of Delos, as a thank-offering to Apollo. And from the moment when the sacred stern was crowned with garlands till its return, it was unlawful to defile the purified city with any public execution. It so happened that the vessel set sail for Delos the very day before the condemnation of Socrates. He thus gained a respite of some thirty days, which he spent in prison, but in free conversation with his friends. See the whole thing explained in full, Phædo, 58. Cf. also Xen. Mem. IV, 8, 2; Plut. Vit. Thes., etc. Page 83

D. 18. δοκεῖ μέν. μέν is not unfrequently used, especially after δόκει, οἶμαι, and the like verbs, without the corresponding δέ expressed, but implying some such clause as σαφῶς δ' οὐκ οἶδα. It may indeed be taken as simply the same with the longer form μήν. Here δοκεῖ μέν is employed with that Attic urbanity which avoids positive assertions, even when no doubt is intended, for just below he says: δῆλον οὖν, ὅτι ἥξει τήμερον. Sunium was the southeastern promontory of Attica. 23. τύχῃ ἀγαθῇ. G. 188, 1; H. A. 776. A formula of prayer or well-wishing, often used by the Greeks in entering upon any enterprise or at the mention of any anticipated event, equivalent to the Latin, quod bene vertat. The use of it by Socrates in this connection is a striking illustration of his cheerfulness and hopefulness in view of death.

A. 27. που, *I suppose*, ni fallor. τῇ ὑστεραίᾳ ἢ ᾗ ἂν ἔλθῃ = 44

Page 83 *the next day after the ship may arrive.* ὑστεραίᾳ is followed Page 84 by ἢ because it involves a comparative. 1. Φασί γέ τοι δή, *so say, at least, to be sure, those who have the disposal of these things*, sc. the Eleven. φασί is emphatic, they *say so, to be sure*, though Crito would fain doubt it and show them to be mistaken, if he can but persuade Socrates. 2. τῆς ἐπιούσης ἡμέρας, the coming day, i. e., the day about to dawn = *to-day*. G. 179, 1; H. A. 759. 3. τῆς ἑτέρας, the second day = *to-morrow*. Socrates means, of course, the same days which Crito above calls τήμερον and αὔριον. 4. ὀλίγον πρότερον, a little while ago, of course after midnight; dreams before midnight the ancients deemed false. 5. κινδυνεύεις = δοκεῖς in Attic writers. How it came to have that meaning, see explained in Stallb. ad loc., and in the Lexicons. ἐν καιρῷ τινι, *quite opportunely*.

B. 9. ἤματί κεν τριτάτῳ, κ.τ.λ. These are the words of Achilles declaring to Agamemnon his intention to return home to Phthia, and his expectation to arrive there on the third day. Hom. Il. ix, 363. Socrates finds in them a beautiful accommodation to his own departure to his heavenly home. This dream is not to be set down as a mere fiction of Plato. Besides the general truthfulness and trustworthiness of this dialogue, Socrates was a notorious dreamer of dreams or seer of visions, and a full believer in their divine significance. Moreover, he was a great reader and admirer of Homer. What, then, could be more natural or probable than that his approaching departure to another world, which he talked of by day and meditated on by night, should present itself before him in his dreams and clothe itself in the familiar language of the Homeric Poems? 11. ἐναργές, clear, i. e., easy to be understood. μὲν οὖν = imo vero, *nay but.* 12. δαιμόνιε is used as a form of address, in itself respectful, and in its own proper signification *only* respectful, yet sometimes applied in such a connection, and spoken in such a tone of irony or severity, that some lexicographers have erroneously concluded that it was in its nature a term of reproach as well as of honor. Compare ὦ μακάριε Κρίτων below, and our *My dear sir, My excellent fellow.* 13. ἔτι καὶ νῦν, *yet even now*, implies that Crito had

previously plied Socrates with unavailing arguments of the Page 84
same kind. 14. οὐ μία, *not one merely*. Al. οὐδεμία. 15. χωρὶς μὲν . . . ἔτι δέ, *besides in the first place* sustaining the loss of an invaluable friend, I shall *in the second place* incur the reproach of many. The unusual concurrence of μέν and δέ in the same proposition, sets forth strongly the *twofold* evil. The correction of Wolf, τοῦ ἐστερῆσθαι for σοῦ ἐστερῆσθαι of the MSS. is with good reason adopted in all the recent editions. 16. οὐδένα μή ποτε. This combination has the same emphasis of negation as οὐ μή = *such as there is no reason to expect that I shall ever find*. G. 257; H. A. 1032. 17. ὡς οἷός τε ὢν σε σῴζειν. The ὡς belongs with the participle ὤν, not, as Buttmann and some others have taken it, with the infinitive ἀμελῆσαι, and performs here the office which it usually performs with a participle, viz., of denoting the *ground or supposition* on which Crito would appear to many to have neglected the preservation of the life of Socrates: *as if I was able*, i. e., *supposing that I was able to save you*—a supposition which, in this case, was contrary to the fact, since the inflexible will of Socrates rendered it impossible for Crito to save him. Cf. G. 277, N. 2, a; H. A. 978.

C. 19. τίς ἂν αἰσχίων εἴη ταύτης δόξα, ἢ δοκεῖν, *what reputation could be more dishonorable than this—than to be reputed*. Here the comparative is first followed by a genitive, and then by an explanatory clause with ἤ. It will be observed that δόξα and δοκεῖν have the same root. 26. ὥσπερ ἂν πραχθῇ, *just as they may chance to be done*, however that may be. H. A. 914, B.

D. 28. αὐτὰ δὲ δῆλα τὰ παρόντα. Al. δηλοῖ by conjecture. But the emendation is not necessary. The passage is explained by Stallbaum, Jacobs, and others, as an example of anacoluthon: Nam Crito quum additurus esset haec: ὅτι ὑπὸ τῶν πολλῶν ἐξειργασμένα ἐστίν, constructione repente mutata, rem multo gravius eloquitur, dicens: ὅτι οἷοί τέ εἰσιν οἱ πολλοί.
Stallb. 4. εἰ γὰρ ὤφελον. G. 251, 2, N. 1; H. A. 871, a. 5. Page 85
ἵνα . . . ἦσαν. The past tense of the indicative here implies that they are *not* able. G. 216, 3; H. A. 884. 7. οὔτε γὰρ φρόνιμον, κ.τ.λ. The noble sentiment is here implied, that so

Page 85 long as the multitude can not alter a man's *character* for better or worse, all else is of no account. The concluding clause in this chapter, ποίουσι . . . τύχωσιν, means, that the multitude are governed by mere chance and caprice instead of fixed principle.

E. 10. ἆρά γε μὴ ἐμοῦ προμηθεῖ, *you do not, do you, feel anxious for me*, etc., in form expecting a negative answer, yet implying a suspicion or a fear that he does. G. 282, 2; H. A. 1015; cf. also 25, A. 11. οἱ συκοφάνται. The word is well explained in the Lexicon of Liddell and Scott, and the class of men in Smith's Dictionary of Antiquities. 12. πράγματα παρέχωσιν, *make trouble*. Notice here present of continued action; with ἀναγκασθῶμεν, aorists of single act. 13. ἢ καὶ πᾶσαν, κ.τ.λ., *either to lose even all our property, or at least large sums of money, or even to suffer some additional* heavier penalty, such as imprisonment, exile, or death, cf. below, 53, B. 15. ἔασον αὐτὸ χαίρειν, *bid it farewell*, that is, dismiss the fear.

45 A. 16. ἡμεῖς γάρ που δίκαιοί ἐσμεν, cf. H. A. 944, a. For που, cf. note, 44, A. 18. ἀλλὰ ἐμοὶ πείθου. ἀλλά with the imp. suggests an anticipated unwillingness or objection. 21. μήτε τοίνυν φοβοῦ. The sentence, interrupted by a long explanation, is resumed in μήτε ταῦτα φοβούμενος, below, B, and is there followed by the correlative clause, μήτε ὃ ἔλεγες. 23. τούτους is contemptuous, like the Latin iste, cf. below, 48, C: τούτων τῶν πολλῶν, and Demosthenes, passim. 24. ὡς εὐτελεῖς, sc. εἰσιν, *how easily they can be bought*. Crito knew this from his own experience, cf. Xen. Mem. II, 9, 1. ἐπ' αὐτούς, *for them*, sc. to bribe them.

B. 25. σοί is made emphatic by its position. ὑπάρχει, *is ready for your use*. ἱκανά is added to express the idea that his property alone is, in his opinion (ὡς ἐγῷμαι), *sufficient*. Crito was wealthy, cf. note, 33, D. 27. ξένοι. Simmias and Cebes were Thebans, cf. Phæd. 59, C. Notice the omission of the article; ξένοι are mentioned only as a class, and are then particularized by οὗτοι. *If you do not think proper to* Page 86 *spend my money, there are strangers, these*. 3. ἀποκάμῃς, *fail*, or *hesitate*. ἀποκάμνω is more frequently followed by a participle, though sometimes, as here, by an infinitive. H. A. 983 Page 86 and 986. 4. ὃ ἔλεγες ἐν τῷ δικαστηρίῳ, cf. Apol. 37, C, D. 5. ὅ τι χρῷο σαυτῷ, *what to do with yourself.* G. 188, N. 2; H. A. 777, a. 6. ἄλλοσε, by attraction for ἀλλαχοῦ. G. 153, N. 4 and 3; H. A. 1003.

C. 10. οὐδὲ δίκαιον. οὐδέ is emphatic, *not even right.* 13. σπεύσαιέν τε καὶ ἔσπευσαν. See the same combination of the opt. with the ind.—of the probable with the actual—Apol. 40, A: οἰηθείη ἄν τις καὶ νομίζεται.

D. 16. οἰχήσει καταλιπών. G. 279, 4, N. It is an emphatic form, as if Socrates were in *haste* to leave his children orphans. Observe the force of the ἐκ in ἐκθρέψαι and ἐκπαιδεῦσαι, to bring up and educate *completely.* 16. τὸ σὸν μέρος, *so far as you are concerned.* Orphans at Athens were provided for by the state, and intrusted to the care of the Archon Eponymus. Still they must, of course, be subjected to many inconveniences (cf. Hom. Il. xxii, 490); and *so far as Socrates was concerned,* his children would be left *to do well or ill, just as they might chance to do.* 19. χρή. Al. χρῆν. 21. ῥᾳθυμότατα is the opposite of ἀγαθὸς καὶ ἀνδρεῖος. 23. φάσκοντά γε δή, *especially if one claims.*

E. 27. Καὶ ἡ εἴσοδος τῆς δίκης, κ.τ.λ., *both the coming in of the case into court,* cf. Demos. adv. Phorm.: μελλούσης τῆς δίκης εἰσιέναι εἰς τὸ δικαστήριον. 28. ὡς εἰσῆλθεν. Later editors and the best MSS. read thus instead of εἰσῆλθες, the reading of Stallbaum. ἐξὸν μὴ εἰσελθεῖν. G. 278, 2; H. A. 973. He could have avoided the trial, either by flight and voluntary exile, or by inducing, as he might easily have done, the accusers to withdraw the charges before the trial had commenced. αὐτὸς ὁ ἀγών, κ.τ.λ., *the entire management of the case.* Socrates did not employ advocates, or resort to any of the ordinary means of influencing the judges. 2. καταγέλως. Page 87 Cornar, with the approval of Schleiermacher, Stallbaum, and others, suggests that there is an allusion in this word to the absurd and ridiculous conclusion of a comedy, which has its three parts, the πρότασις, ἐπίτασις, and καταστροφή, corresponding with the εἴσοδος, ἀγών, and καταγέλως of the Socratic drama, as it is here represented. 3. διαπεφευγέναι ἡμᾶς δοκεῖν

Page 87 is epexegetical of τὸ τελευταῖον τουτί: *and finally this almost farcical conclusion of the matter, that it should seem to have slipped out of our hands, through some sloth and unmanliness of ours.*

46 A. 4. εἴ τι . . . ὄφελος ἦν. Cf. note, Apol. 28, B. The force of the perfect is seen not only in βεβουλεῦσθαι, but also in πεπρᾶχθαι = *to have consulted, to have been done.* 10. ἀδύνατον, κ.τ.λ., *impossible* (for us) *and no longer practicable.*

B. 13. ἡ προθυμία, κ.τ.λ. For the omission of the copula (ἐστίν), cf. H. A. 611. For the sentiment compare the words of Paul to the Galatians, iv, 17: καλὸν δὲ ζηλοῦσθαι ἐν καλῷ. 17. τῶν ἐμῶν μηδενὶ ἄλλῳ πείθεσθαι ἢ τῷ λόγῳ. The strongest argument, in other words, the truth as it appears to his mind after careful consideration, is here beautifully represented by Socrates as his best *friend*, and the only one to whom he yields a controlling influence. See Lex., ἐμός, II, 2.

C. 24. πλείω limits μορμολύττηται, as it is construed by Stallbaum; not ἐπιπέμπουσα, as it is construed by Buttmann. 26. δεσμοὺς καὶ θανάτους. Observe the force of the plural. All these in their worst forms and degrees are mere bugbears to frighten children—such is the spirit of the passage. See Gorgias, 473, D, where to Polus' fearful array of punishments, the rack, castration, crucifixion, covering with pitch and burning alive, Socrates replies: Μορμολύττει, You are bringing up bugbears, not proofs. Compare Paul's emphatic enumeration of his sufferings, 2 Cor. xi, 23: ἐν κόποις, ἐν πληγαῖς, ἐν φυλακαῖς, ἐν θανάτοις. 27. μετριώτατα σκοποίμεθα. Cf. note, Apol. 39, B. This question, in many editions, is put into the mouth of Crito. But it seems more appropriate to Socrates, who, in the next sentence, answers himself, as he often does.

Page 88 1. ἀναλάβοιμεν, *resume* for further consideration. 2. ἑκάστοτε, *in every instance*, sc. when we were discussing the subject in our frequent former conversations. Hence the imp. ἐλέγετο here and below repeatedly.

D. 3. πρίν governs δεῖν. 4. Κατάδηλος is for κατάδηλον, being attracted by λόγος. ἄρα = *forsooth, as it seems.* H. A. 1048, 1, and note, Apol. 34, B. ἄλλως = temere, *without reason.* 8. ᾧδε ἔχω, sc. in danger of losing my life. 10. τι λέγειν, *to say something*, sc. to some purpose, of some importance, cf. Xen. Mem. II, 1, 12. Page 88

E. 14. ὅσα γε τἀνθρώπεια, *in all human probability*. 27. ἱκανῶς is explained below by καλῶς.

B. 27. τὰ τοιαῦτα, *such things as these*. 28. τοῦτο πράττων, *practicing this, making a business of it*. Cf. Herod. VI, 125: ἡμεροδρόμον τε καὶ τοῦτο μελετῶντα. So πρακτέον, below. We see here Socrates' fondness for illustrations drawn from the common pursuits of life. 10. καὶ ἐδεστέον γε, *yes, and eat* and drink. γε = *yes*. So καὶ υἱεῖς γε, Apol. 34, D, might be rendered, *yes, and sons*. The eating and drinking here come within the province of the ἰατρός, as the gymnastic exercises come under the direction of the παιδοτρίβης. 47 Page 89

D. 1. αἰσχύνεσθαι καὶ φοβεῖσθαι. These verbs are often followed, as they are here, by an accusative of the person *before whom* one *must be ashamed and afraid*, especially to do anything dishonorable or wrong. 3. ἐγίγνετο . . . ἀπώλλυτο. The imperfect has reference to what *was said* in former discussions, cf. ἐλέγετο ἑκάστοτε above, and below: πῶς αὖ τὰ τοιαῦτα ἐλέγετο. H. A. 833; M. and T. 11, N. 6. Page 90

E. 8. πειθόμενοι μὴ τῇ τῶν ἐπαϊόντων δόξῃ, *by obeying not the opinion of the wise*; but of the unwise, is implied in the antithesis by the position of μή. Cf. Xen. Mem. III, 9, 6: καὶ μὴ ἃ οἶδε δοξάζειν = *not what he knows*, but what he does not know. 16. ᾧ . . . λωβᾶται, *which the unjust injures*. The editions before Bekker changed ᾧ to ὅ. But the MSS. have ᾧ, and λωβᾶσθαι may be followed either by the accusative or the dative. 17. φαυλότερον = cheaper, *less valuable*, the opposite of τιμιώτερον, below.

A. 24. τί . . . ἡμᾶς. τί for ὅ τι, cf. G. 282, 1; H. A. 1011; For the two acc. cf. G. 165; H. A. 725, a. 1. μέν = μήν. 48 Page 91

B. 5. οὗτός τε ὁ λόγος, κ.τ.λ., is correlative to καὶ τόνδε αὖ σκόπει. To the suggestion, that the multitude have power to put him to death, Socrates has a twofold answer: in the first place, that does not invalidate the argument which we have gone through with, nor make it any less conclusive, or in any way different from what it was, before his life was endangered; and in the second place, he says, *consider also*,

Page 91 *whether this doctrine*, once admitted by us, *abides or not, that we must not set the highest value on mere living, but on living well.* 11. Τὸ δὲ εὖ, κ.τ.λ. *And does it still remain true that to live well is the same thing as to live honorably and justly, or does it not remain true?* πρότερον, *aforetime*, i. e., in former discussions.

C. 18. σκέψεις. G. 154; H. A. 995. ἀναλώσεως χρημάτων, 44, E, seqq.; δόξης, 45, B, seqq.; παίδων τροφῆς, 45, C, D. 19. μή, sc. ὅρα. G. 218, N. 2; H. A. 867. ὅρα is expressed below, 49, D. 20. ῥᾳδίως, lightly, *rashly*. 21. καὶ ἀναβιωσκομένων γ' ἄν, *yes, and would restore them to life again.* For the force of ἄν with the participle, cf. G. 211; H. A. 987, b. 22. τούτων τῶν πολλῶν is added to express contempt, and, in connection with οὐδενὶ ξὺν νῷ, it implies, that it is characteristic of the multitude to act thus without reason. ὁ λόγος αἱρεῖ, *the argument so establishes the point.* This use of αἱρεῖ arises from its use to express a victory at the games, or a conviction in a court of justice. Cf. *ratio vincit*, Hor. Sat. i, 3, 115, et al. αἱρεῖ, see Lex. A, 5. 24. καὶ χρήματα τελοῦντες . . . καὶ χάριτας. Zeugma, τελοῦντες being strictly applicable only to χρήματα, and ἄγοντες being required with χάριτας. 25. καὶ αὐτοί, κ.τ.λ., *and* whether we shall do right *ourselves both in leading out* of prison, *and in being led out.*

D. 28. μὴ οὐ δέῃ, κ.τ.λ., *we must not consider the question, whether we must die, if we remain in* prison *and keep quiet, nor* whether we must *suffer anything else, however dreadful, rather than do wrong*, i. e., we must not take the *consequences* into the account at all, but only the question of right and wrong. Before μὴ οὐ, there is an ellipsis of a verb of seeing, or fearing, and the meaning is, I fear, that we must *not* take into account, etc. G. 218, N. 2; H. A. 867.

Page 92 E. 9. ὡς ἐγὼ περὶ πολλοῦ, κ.τ.λ., *as I esteem it of great importance to do this with your consent.* 11. ἐάν. H. A. 1016, c; M. and T. 71, N. 1. σοι ἱκανῶς, *to your satisfaction.*

49 A. 14. ἑκόντας ἀδικητέον εἶναι = ἑκόντας ἀδικεῖν δεῖν ἡμᾶς. G. 281, 2; H. A. 991, a. 20. καὶ πάλαι . . . ἄρα, *and so for a long time we, men of such advanced years.*

B. 22. *ἢ παντὸς μᾶλλον, or rather.* The repeated and Page 92
pressing questions mark the reluctance of Crito to accept the conclusion. 25. *ὅμως, yet,* i. e., whatever may be the consequences. 26. *τυγχάνει ὄν, turns out to be.* 3. *ὡς οἱ πολλοὶ* Page 93
οἴονται. The general sentiment of antiquity not only justified but required retaliation, as just and manly, cf. Meno. cap. iii: *αὕτη ἐστὶν ἀνδρὸς ἀρετή, ἱκανὸν εἶναι τὰ τῆς πόλεως πράττειν, καὶ πράττοντα τοὺς μὲν φίλους εὖ ποιεῖν, τοὺς δ' ἐχθροὺς κακῶς.* Eurip. Fragm.: *ἐχθρὸν κακῶς δρᾶν ἀνδρὸς ἡγοῦμαι μέρος.* Xen. Mem. II, 6, 35. A similar view is also taken in Plato's Republic, B. I. But Socrates in the Gorgias, 469, A, insists that it is far better to suffer wrong than to do wrong.

C. 5. *οὐ φαίνεται, it appears not,* that is, it is clear from the argument that we must in no case do an injury. 15. *οὐδ' ἂν ὁτιοῦν, κ.τ.λ., not even if he suffer anything however severe by them.* 21. *κοινωνεῖς, whether you hold* these opinions *in common with me, and think as I do.*

D. 16. *καθομολογῶν, admitting* to your detriment. So L. and S. But perhaps *καθομολογῶν* differs from *ὁμολογῶν* only in emphasis or extent = *in admitting all this.* 25. *τῆς ἀρχῆς,* the *premise* or *first principle* of the argument, sc. that it is never right to do an injury, etc. To *τῆς ἀρχῆς*, as the *premise, τὸ μετὰ τοῦτο* stands opposed as the *conclusion.* Page 94

A. 7. *ἀπιόντες ἐνθένδε, in going out hence,* sc. from prison, 50
This clause is to be connected, not only with *ποιοῦμεν,* but also with *ἐμμένομεν, whether in going out hence . . . we abide by what we have admitted to be right.* 12. *Οὐ γὰρ ἐννοῶ.* "One might almost think that Crito will not understand because he dreads the repugnant conclusion." Cron. 14. *ἀποδιδράσκειν*; used of stealthy flight, and so especially of slaves. 15. *τὸ κοινὸν τῆς πόλεως, the commonwealth.* So Cic. in Verr. ii, 46, 114; a communi Siciliæ. For an imitation of this personifying of the state, see also Cic. in Cat. i, 7, 18. 17. *ἄλλο τι ἤ = nonne, do you not.* G. 282, 3; H. A. 1015, b.

B. 20. *ἀνατετράφθαι, be immediately and utterly subverted.* For this force of the *perfect,* cf. H. A. 849, a. *αἱ γενόμεναι δίκαι, the judgments that have been rendered.* 24. *ὑπὲρ . . . ἀπολλυμένου*; *in behalf of this law which is threat-*

Page 94 *ened with destruction.* The present participle, as often, denotes expectation or apprehension. Cf. M. and T. 10, 1, N. 7.

C. 26. ὅτι ἠδίκει γὰρ ἡμᾶς. The ὅτι in direct quotations is pleonastic. The γάρ refers to an implied clause: we do right to escape, *for the state did us an injustice*, sc. when it
Page 95 pronounced sentence against us. 6. τῷ ἐρωτᾶν τε καὶ ἀποκρίνεσθαι. The reader will recognize here an allusion to the well-known method of discussion, which was so characteristic of Socrates as to be called "the Socratic method."

D. 8. πρῶτον μέν. The *second* question, which answers to this as the first, is found in ἀλλὰ τοῖς περὶ τὴν τοῦ γενομένου τροφήν, κ.τ.λ., and is introduced with ἀλλά instead of ἔπειτα, in consequence of the intervening question, μέμφει τι, κ.τ.λ. 9. ἐλάμβανεν, *imperfect* to denote the *process* through which the wife was obtained. The editions previous to Buttmann had ἔλαβε. 12. ἔχουσιν, participle. 16. ἐν μουσικῇ καὶ γυμναστικῇ, i. e., in physical and mental education, cf. Repub. 376, E: ἡ μὲν [παιδεία] ἐπὶ σώμασι γυμναστική, ἡ δ' ἐπὶ ψυχῇ μουσική. The former comprehended the whole *exercise* and *training* of the body, in which the Greeks so excelled; the latter the entire *discipline* and *culture* of the mind, or, as the word denotes, the department of the *muses.* The prominence which the Greeks gave to the cultivation of the *taste* and the *emotions*, helps to explain the name by which they called this department of education. Some writers add a third department, viz., γράμματα, letters, or primary education. Cf. Smith's Dic. of Antiqq., *Gymnasium.* Aristotle, in his Politics, viii, 2, makes four departments, adding to letters, gymnastics, and music, the department of drawing and painting, γραφική.

E. 19. δοῦλος. Cf. Cic. pro Cluentio, 53: Legum omnes *servi* sumus, ut liberi esse possimus. 23. ἦ πρὸς μὲν ἄρα σοι τὸν πατέρα. The unusual position of σοι (hyperbaton) is explained by the fondness of the Greeks for bringing contrasted
Page 96 words into juxtaposition. σοι is dat. after ἐξ ἴσου.
51 A. 28. ἄρα. Cf. note, 46, D. 2. καὶ σὺ δὲ ἡμᾶς, κ.τ.λ., is an emphatic repetition of πρὸς δὲ τὴν πατρίδα, etc., above.

4. ὁ τῇ ἀληθείᾳ τῆς ἀρετῆς ἐπιμελόμενος is ironical. 7. ἡ πατρίς. Page 96
We insert the article, contrary to our former reading. It seems necessary to mark the particular fatherland of any individual.

C. 18. πείθειν depends on δεῖ, implied in ποιητέον.

D. 1. τῷ ἐξουσίαν πεποιηκέναι, *by having given liberty.* Page 97
2. δοκιμασθῇ, when he has been examined and approved, i. e., admitted to the rank of a citizen, al. δοκιμάσῃ. 4. ἐξεῖναι depends on προαγορεύομεν.

E. 12. ὡμολογηκέναι ἔργῳ denotes a "*tacit compact,*" but one of a very different kind from that fiction, in which some political philosophers of modern times find the *origin* of society and government.

A. 17. προτιθέντων ἡμῶν, sc. ἢ πείθεσθαι ἢ πείθειν, *al-* 52
though we refer it to your choice, i. e., lay it before you for consideration, the allusion being to the peculiar rights and privileges of an Athenian citizen in canvassing laws when they are proposed, and moving for their repeal afterward, if they are found to be oppressive. The style is intentionally repetitious in imitation of the style of conversation. 21. ἐνέξεσθαι = *will be implicated in*, or *obnoxious to.* So ἔνοχος = obnoxious, cf. Xen. Mem. I, 1, 64: πῶς οὖν ἔνοχος ἂν εἴη τῇ γραφῇ. 22. ἐν τοῖς μάλιστα. Cf. note, 48, C: ἐν τοῖς βαρύτατ'.

B. 1. διαφερόντως, *pre-eminently above.* 2. θεωρίαν, a Page 98
spectacle, such as the games and religious festivals. As these were attended by the leading men from all Greece, the non-attendance of Socrates, with the single exception of going once to the Isthmian games, might well be remarked as an indication of singular satisfaction with Athens. 4. στρατευσόμενος. Cf. ἐν Ποτιδαίᾳ καὶ ἐν Ἀμφιπόλει καὶ ἐπὶ Δηλίῳ, Apol. 28, E, and note, ibid. 6. ἐπιθυμία first governs πόλεως and νόμων in the gen., and then is followed by the infin. εἰδέναι, with which is to be understood a pronoun in the acc., referring to those genitives, *a desire of another city or other laws—to know them;* classed by Cron as a case of prolepsis. H. A. 878.

C. 9. τά τε ἄλλα καί, *besides all the rest,* sc. of your

Page 98 acts, which prove your preference for Athens. Cf. note on ἀλλά τε . . . καί, Apol. 36, A. 11. φυγῆς τιμήσασθαι. Cf. note, Apol. 37, C. 16. αἰσχύνει, *respect*, lit., feel ashamed before. ἐντρέπει, *regard*, lit., turn yourself toward.

E. 26. Ἄλλο τι οὖν ἂν φαῖεν ἤ, *do you not then, they would say, violate*, etc., lit., do you do anything else than violate. The ἂν would regularly follow φαῖεν; but when two clauses are incorporated in one (especially with φαίη or φαῖεν), the particle is often attracted out of its place, cf.
Page 99 Hermann on the particle ἄν. 1. ἐν ἔτεσιν ἑβδομήκοντα. Cf. Apol. 17, D. 4. οὔτε Λακεδαίμονα . . . οὔτε Κρήτην. These states were often cited as models of law and order by Plato and other political philosophers of the day, cf. Repub. 544, C; Legg. 634. δή = scilicet. ἑκάστοτε = quotiescunque de iis loqueris. Stallb.

53 A. 11. ἐάν ἡμῖν γε πείθῃ. Sub. ἀλλ' ἐμμενεῖς.

B. 21. τῇ τούτων πολιτείᾳ, *to the polity of these men*, instead of these states, as if πολιτῶν, instead of πόλεων, had preceded. Examples of this figure (*synesis*) are frequent in Plato. 24. βεβαιώσεις τοῖς δικασταῖς, κ.τ.λ., that is, will confirm others in an opinion favorable to the judges, so that they will be regarded as having decided the case right. 28. τάς τε εὐνομουμένας . . . τοὺς κοσμιωτάτους, *the cities that have good laws, and the men who have the most regard for law*
Page 100 *and order*. 3. τίνας λόγους, *what discourses, Socrates? such forsooth as you utter here, that*, etc. ἤ is strictly *or*, and ἀναισχυντήσεις διαλεγόμενος is understood after it. 5. ἂν φανεῖσθαι. Cf. note on ἂν . . . διαφθαρήσονται, Apol. 29, C.

D. 7. ἀπαρεῖς, *you will depart*, lit., carry away, remove. 9. ἐκεῖ γὰρ . . . ἀκολασία. The Thessalians were infamous for their social and political vices. Cf. Demos. Ol. i, 22: ταῦτα γὰρ (τὰ τῶν Θετταλῶν) ἄπιστα μὲν ἦν δήπου φύσει καὶ ἀεὶ πᾶσιν ἀνθρώποις; and Athenæus, vi, 260, B: ἀκόλαστοι καὶ περὶ τὸν βίον ἀσελγεῖς, and many other passages from different authors. 11. σκευήν, *a cloak* or wrapper sufficient to cover the whole body, as is implied in περιθέμενος. The word is often used of robes or costumes for the stage.

Διφθέρα is a *dress of skins*, worn by rustics, and hence peculiarly fit for a disguise. 18. Σχῆμα is also referred to the dress by Stallbaum, but it is better to take it in the more general sense of gait, or *personal appearance*, as the Latin *habitus* also is often used. Page 100

E. 16. ἴσως, ἂν μή, κ.τ.λ., *perhaps not, if you do not offend any one; but if otherwise*, i. e., if you do offend any one, *you will hear*, etc. 18. ὑπερχόμενος δὴ βιώσει, κ.τ.λ., *so you will pass your life in fawning upon everybody and being their humble servant—doing what, but feasting in Thessaly, having gone abroad for an entertainment, forsooth, into Thessaly.* The irony, which runs through the whole, is made more pungent by the contemptuous repetition of *Thessaly.* 22. ποῦ ἡμῖν ἔσονται? *what will become of them*—where shall we find them? G. 184, 3, N. 6; H. A. 770.

A. 22. Ἀλλὰ δή = *at enim, at inquies.* Stallb. 24. τί 54
δέ; *why, pray?* A question of surprise. 26. ἀπολαύσωσιν is, of course, ironical, as it often is taken in a bad sense. ἢ τοῦτο μὲν οὔ, *or not this indeed*, sc. ποιήσεις, i. e., you will not take your sons to Thessaly. αὐτοῦ, *here*, in Athens. 27. θρέψονται καὶ παιδεύσονται, fut. mid. in the sense of fut. pass. G. 199, 3, N. 4; H. A. 496.

B. 10. οὔτε γὰρ ἐνθάδε . . . οὔτε ἐκεῖσε, *neither here* in Page 101
this life . . . *nor when you come thither*, into another world. These two clauses beginning with οὔτε are correlative to each other, while those beginning with οὐδέ are only emphatic additions to the former.

D. 25. οἱ κορυβαντιῶντες, those who celebrate the rites of the Corybantes in the worship of Cybele in Phrygia. As these rites were accompanied with noisy music and wild dancing, the Corybantes were an expressive figure of persons so inspired and possessed with certain ideas or feelings, as to be incapable of seeing or hearing anything else. In the case of Socrates, it is the voice of the Laws, in other words, the voice of God, that so rings in his ear and possesses his soul. The passage is one of singular beauty. The Laws stand before him personified, embodied, clothed with more than human authority. They reason with him. They expostulate with him on the folly and wickedness of the course which his friends are pressing upon him. They draw nearer and nearer to him, and speak in more earnest and commanding tones, till at length he can see and hear nothing else, and puts an end to the fruitless arguments and entreaties of his friends in those words of humble yet sublime piety: It is the voice of God—let us obey.

THE END.

CPSIA information can be obtained
at www.ICGtesting.com
Printed in the USA
LVHW081607131120
671649LV00004B/89

9 781377 595962